URBAN MIGRANTS
IN RURAL JAPAN

URBAN MIGRANTS IN RURAL JAPAN

Between Agency and Anomie in a Post-growth Society

SUSANNE KLIEN

SUNY
PRESS

Cover photo of Okinoshima Island, Shimane Prefecture (taken by the author).

Published by State University of New York Press, Albany

For information, contact State University of New York Press, Albany, NY
www.sunypress.edu

Library of Congress Cataloging-in-Publication Data

Names: Klien, Susanne, 1972– author.
Title: Urban migrants in rural Japan : between agency and anomie in a
    post-growth society / Susanne Klien.
Description: Albany : State University of New York Press, [2020] | Includes
    bibliographical references and index.
Identifiers: LCCN 2019016744 | ISBN 9781438478050 (hardcover : alk. paper) |
    ISBN 9781438478067 (pbk. : alk. paper) | ISBN 9781438478074 (ebook)
Subjects: LCSH: Urban-rural migration—Japan. | Rural-urban relations—Japan. |
    Amenity migration—Japan. | Lifestyles—Japan. | Japan—Social conditions—
    21st century.
Classification: LCC HT381 .K55 2020 | DDC 307.2/60952—dc23
LC record available at https://lccn.loc.gov/2019016744

10 9 8 7 6 5 4 3 2 1

This book is dedicated with love to my mum,
who has been an incredible fighter all her life.

Contents

Illustrations

All photos were taken by the author, except figure 3.2.

Acknowledgments

A book is a lengthy project that in many ways resembles one's own life: moments of intense positive emotion and excitement intercepted by resignation and even depression about the direction of the project. Ethnographic research involves close contacts with a multiplicity of people, which in itself contributes to the fluidity of the research process. These encounters often evolve in ways that are difficult to predict in all their details. Regardless of the diverse circumstances that led me to each interviewee, I am deeply grateful for the time they gave me despite their tight schedules. Without their cooperation, this book could not have been written.

The number of people to whom I am indebted is too large to name each individually, but I would like to express my deep gratitude to David H. Slater at Sophia University, from whom I received invaluable feedback on various occasions. I would also like to thank my inspirational colleagues at Hokkaido University for the constructive atmosphere, especially Paul Hansen, Emma E. Cook, and Stephanie Assmann. I also appreciate incisive comments by Barbara R. Ambros of University of North Carolina at Chapel Hill, Sachiko Horiguchi of Temple University Japan, Makoto Osawa, Flavia Fulco of Tohoku University, and Jun Nagatomo of Kwansei Gakuin University. I also thank (in no particular order) John W. Traphagan at University of Texas at Austin, Florian Coulmas at Duisburg-Essen University, Fumitoshi Kato, Keio University and Johannes Wilhelm, Kumamoto University, Ofra Goldstein-Gidoni at Tel Aviv University, and Wolfram Manzenreiter of Vienna University for their constructive advice and support at various stages of the project. Great thanks are due to Zoe B. Woodward for her professional proofreading of parts of the manuscript for this book. I thank Christopher Ahn, senior acquisitions editor at SUNY Press, for his continuing support, and the copyediting staff at the press for their meticulous reading of the manuscript. I would also like to express my gratitude to the reviewers for their constructive comments.

I am grateful for funding from the Japan Society for the Promotion of Science (JSPS) for the three-year Grant-in-Aid Research Project 16K03212, "Moratorium Migration in Contemporary Post-Growth Japan: Lifestyle Volunteers between Insecurity and Fulfillment" (FY 2016–FY 2018).

It is impossible to name everyone who helped me, including all the representatives of local governments across Japan who kindly offered their support in getting to know the field(s). The number of individuals to whom I am indebted is exceedingly high, but all mistakes are mine.

Introduction

This book explores what values, dreams, and aspirations urbanites between twenty and forty-five years of age maintain who choose to relocate to rural areas in Japan. I present empirical data obtained from multisited fieldwork across Japan, examining how individuals position themselves in their new surroundings and engage with their environments in their pursuit of a personally more meaningful private and professional life.

I start with a simple proposition: being on the move has become a "way of life" (Urry 2002: 265) for many younger individuals in Japan, and the simultaneity of sedentary and mobile elements (Ralph and Staeheli 2011: 581) shapes people's lives. The situation in Ishinomaki, Miyagi Prefecture, a town that was devastated by the Great East Japan Earthquake, is commensurate with these claims: coworking spaces equipped with broadband wireless internet open to everyone, designer-style collective housing, former disaster volunteers turned entrepreneurs, temporary part-time workers, corporate refugees, multiple dwellers dividing their time between Tokyo and Ishinomaki, and short-term visitors who are still employed conventionally side by side in the "Reconstruction Bar" (Fukkō Bar). The emergence of shared office space, collective housing, and urban-style deli takeout in Kamiyama, Tokushima Prefecture, has also recently caught the attention of media. In addition, "ijū [rural relocation] concierges," that is, staff employed by local governments whose task is to provide advice to individuals interested in moving to a rural town, have recently appeared across Japan.

In other words, rather than nostalgia-evoking rice paddy fields, the rural tends to be represented through more fuzzy images these days. In popular lifestyle magazines, articles about organic farming seem to have been replaced with information about sleek IT venture entrepreneurs in rural areas who make use of the best of both worlds. Some rural towns such as Kamiyama in Tokushima Prefecture have also tried to sell themselves as perfect working environments for IT employees. Last but not least, the rural has increasingly been constituted in association with subjective well-being and happiness. References to "marginal villages" (Ōno 2008), that is, remote villages that are not sustainable any more due to more than half of the residents being over sixty-five years of age, have begun to be replaced by terms like "communities of hope" (chapter 3), "creative depopulation" (Ōminami in Matsunaga 2015), or "happy depopulated area" (*kōfuku na kasochi*; Sashide 2016: 116).

Many interviewees kept moving to other places over the course of my fieldwork. Against the background of the increased complexity of modern living (McIntyre 2006: 14), Japan is clearly changing in terms of lifestyles and values. "Ongoing semi-permanent moves of varying duration," as Duncan, Cohen, and Thulemark define "lifestyle mobilities" (2013: 4), have become ubiquitous. Yet, narratives reveal that in their renegotiation of work-life balance, individuals are rearranging their every-day lives between persistent conventional understandings of work ethic, life courses, and sense of obligation and their personal aspirations to live more self-determined, diverse, and sustainable lives that make sense to them. Migrants find themselves between creating a "new rural" and being caught up in conventional views of the countryside as "second-class," trying business ideas before moving into Tokyo. A female migrant aged forty shared her parents' concern about a return to her home prefecture after attending university and working in the capital for twenty years, asking her what had gone wrong in her career in Tokyo. Many lifestyle migrants are very clear about their reasons for leaving urban lifestyles behind and have ideas of what they would like to do in the future, but they seem to struggle for ways to implement these ideas. Hence, while rural areas hold hope and constitute experimental grounds for many, I have also encountered numerous individuals who talked about their quest for something meaningful and were not certain they would find a pur-pose in life. I argue that the flip side of hope and aspiration is risk and insecurity; mobility embodies both freedom and challenge, creativity and precariousness, with the lines between these poles being fuzzy more often than not. Many interviewees spoke about the sense of fulfillment they derive from creating their own work in accordance with circumstances they deem appropriate and having control of their own time. However, many also mention the challenges and pressures that come with "freedom."

This condition of being caught between hope and constraint, aspiration and resignation, these poles of the "ethics of probability" and "possibility," as Arjun Appadurai calls it when he describes contemporary migration (2013: 295), is a recurring feature in settlers' narratives. Appadurai argues that the ethics of probability is salient "in the modern regimes of diagnosis, counting and accounting," while the ethics of possibility is intricately related to hope, aspiration, and perspective as it "expands the field of the imagination."

My argument is that in the case of Japan, the line between these apparently dichotomous poles is not as clean-cut as Appadurai suggested. Governmental actors in Japan increasingly like to refer to the paradigm of possibility with regard to rural areas. On the one hand, at the "macro" level, local governments' initiatives are often the result of the pressure to show that they are taking measures to fight depopulation, regardless of most locals being aware that these measures will not make a great difference in the long term. This also ties in with Bridget Love's cogent argument that recent initiatives by diverse actors to revive localities in remote rural areas are nothing but attempts to "convert legacies of marginalization into celebrations of cultural diversity as a way of shifting responsibility for the future of the deplete countryside onto its inhabitants" (2013: 112).

Against this background of increasing despair over the impossibility of turning around the ticking demographic time bomb of aging, depopulation, and lack of offspring in rural areas and sustained attempts at decentralization, programs such as the Ministry of Internal Affairs and Communication's volunteers for cooperation in community revitalization (*chiiki okoshi kyōryokutai*) have resulted in a palpable rise in urban youth residing in rural areas. According to the Ministry of Internal Affairs and Communications, in 2009, the initial year of the system, 89 volunteers were dispatched across Japan; in 2016, this number has increased to 3,978 (http://www.soumu.go.jp/main_sosiki/jichi_gyousei/c-gyousei/02gyo-sei08_03000066.html). As a result of this influx, a partial shift in perspective and thinking has occurred with regard to what rural areas have to offer. Recently, Ishiba Shigeru, Japan's minister in charge of regional revitalization (*chihō sōsei tantō daijin*), since September 2014 argued in the 2015 winter issue of the magazine *Turns* that previously the conventional idea was to move to Tokyo from rural areas to fulfill one's dream and then move back to one's original home after retirement. Now, the idea that has recently been gaining ground is for people to move to rural areas to fulfill their dreams. Furthermore, Minister Ishiba, himself originally from Tottori Prefecture, the least populated prefecture in a remote part of Western Japan facing the Japanese Sea, explains that the individuals who will change rural areas will change Japan, arguing that in Japan's history, change of the governmental regime always originated in rural areas, referring to the Meiji Reform as an example (*Turns* 2015: 10). The minister predicts that twenty-first-century Japan will be shaped by the regions; Ishiba's statement clearly shows the shifting position of rural areas in Japan's governmental discourse and the high priority it ascribes to the paradigm of possibility, quite in contrast to Appadurai's polarized structure of government as probability and civil sector as possibility. Simultaneously, Ishiba's position could also be interpreted as in accordance with the neoliberal stance of elegantly handing over responsibility for the viability of remote hamlets to local actors (and those who identify themselves with them).

This brings us to the lingering sense of precariousness due to neoliberal working conditions that have been on the increase in Japan and globally. Lifelong employment is only available for a quarter of university graduates, as opposed to more than half in 1991 (Chiavacci and Hommerich 2017: 9). The Lehman Brothers stock collapse showed that lifelong employment does not mean secure employment for life. Numerous migrant narratives are characterized by a sense of "just getting by" financially, being too busy holding several jobs at once so that individuals have no time to reflect on their lives and what they actually aspire to. Almost every interviewee mentioned their quest for "happiness," "a sense of satisfaction," and "self-realization" at some point in interviews and during participant observation, yet many seemed at a loss how to find it or implement it and many did not seem to have a clue what they are actually looking for.

Chapter 1 provides an outline of recent discourses of the role rural areas can and should play in the world and, specifically, in Japan. Starting out with more theoretical reflections on the variety of meanings attributed to "the rural" as a "category of thought" (Mormont 1990: 40), this chapter is concerned with disentangling the production and reproduction of the "rural" as an idea, both generally and in the case of Japan. Recent terms such as "radical rural spatiality" (Halfacree 2007), "creative depopulation" (Ōminami in Matsunaga 2015), downshifting, and "small-scale happiness" (Furuichi 2011) and an increasing interest in flexible modes of working and living, such as, for example, Bauman-esque notions of "living in a manner that involves living for oneself"

(Nishimura 2009) and "a lifestyle that does not opt for employment" (Mori 2011) will be examined. Such discourses show the ongoing shift from a negative perception of rural areas as backwaters of civilization to fields of experimentation and diverse lifestyles. This chapter critically discusses the shift in the Japanese discourse from the countryside as a "repository of nostalgia-laden cultural heritage" (Schnell 2005) to more diverse perceptions of rural areas, with urban-rural linkages as the key to recent attempts to pursue more sustainable lifestyles. While the demographic statistics suggest that it is impossible to stop the trend of depopulation as such, some "hamlets at their limits" (*genkai shūraku*, a term coined by sociologist Ōno Akira in the 1990s) have made efforts to buck the trend by introducing measures to attract highly qualified individuals. This chapter aims to outline the heterogeneity of societal representations of the countryside in Japan beyond the threefold narrative on the rural as "pre-modernity," "productivist," and "rural renaissance" (da Silva et al. 2016: 79), introducing a fourth narrative in the Japanese discourse, that is, rurality as experimental ground for pioneers. Narratives will also show, however, that the true heterogeneity of rural regions (Marsden 1999: 505) and the dispositional heterogeneity of our thinking (Bell 2007: 410) have redefined "the rural" as rurality is perceived as "a problem, a resource, a region of growth and a victim" all at once (Nilsson and Lundgren 2015: 88–91, cited in Kuhmonen, Kuhmonen, and Luoto 2016: 89).

Also building on insights from the theory of lifestyle migration and lifestyle mobilities as well, chapter 2 will analyze the forms and modes of urban-to-rural migration in contemporary Japan, highlighting the perspectives of female migrants in post-growth Japan. Interviews and participant observation with a range of female settlers in their twenties, thirties, and forties illustrate the ongoing negotiations of women trying to assert change yet finding themselves exposed to systemic constraints. The individuals portrayed also show that these self-initiated migrants do not necessarily make a commitment to rural lifestyle by moving to the countryside. Instead, they tend to maintain urban modes of working and living despite their aspiration to a better quality of life. This diversification of approaches to life in the countryside adds to the potential of rural living and its appeal to a wide variety of individuals, not only in conventional terms of the countryside providing relaxation but also as a place for innovative ways to solve persistent societal issues. This chapter provides empirical proof that in contrast to previous studies of lifestyle migration (Nagatomo 2014; Sato 2001) that presented individuals pursuing transnational trajectories in order to slow down and opt out of the work life, this generation of lifestyle migrants is struggling to combine professional careers, family, leisure, and self-realization.

Chapter 3 depicts the increasing shift from a focus on economic growth and material affluence to more emphasis on subjective well-being, work-life balance, and social capital. This is evident in the emergence of coworking spaces, TED-like events, shared houses, and similar facilities geared toward a more relaxed lifestyle and the exchange of information and networking among like-minded peers. I contend that over the past few years, urbanites in their twenties and thirties have taken numerous initiatives across Japan by turning to barter, sharing, and networking that point to a distinct move toward post-growth Japan. Yet, the empirical data discussed in this chapter shows that contemporary youth and middle-aged migrants approach life in the countryside as a natural extension and evolution of their previous lives rather than as a radical break in the sense of the conventional idea of relocation to the rural idyll. At the same time, ideas such as self-development, self-growth beyond material wealth, and pursuit of an individualized lifestyle in Giddens's sense of a "project of the self" (1991) are clearly evident in personal narratives, individual spatial practices, as well as migrants' representations of the rural.

Chapter 4, entitled "Between Agency and Anomie, Possibility and Probability: Lifestyle Migrants and the Neoliberal Moment," examines the emphasis of Japanese migrant youth on the here and now against the background of an increasingly insecure job market. Korpela argues that lifestyle migration "suits the neoliberal agenda" (2014: 229). Drawing on Beck's notion of "living your own life" (2003) and viewing lifestyle mobility as a "fluid and dynamic process" (Duncan, Cohen, and Thulemark 2013), my argument is that in their pursuit of "small-scale happiness" and self-realization, individuals live in the moment in order to grapple strategically with insecurity and risk. This chapter provides empirical evidence both for migrants' agency, that is, efforts toward greater self-determination, and systemic constraints. In the vein of Nikolas Rose's contention that "the human is neither an actor essentially possessed of agency, nor a possessive product or puppet of cultural forces; agency is produced in the course of practices under a whole variety of more or less onerous, explicit, punitive, or seductive, disciplinary or passional constraints and relations of force" (1998: 189) and Rob Stones's theory of the conceptual separation of structures and agency with the assumption of an analytical dualism but an ontological duality (2005: 189), I examine how individuals are caught between their aspiration to live a more self-determined life and the pressures of inadvertently reproducing systemic values such as following a relatively rigid life course and the challenges of making a livelihood in rural areas with limited job prospects. Case studies from Hokkaido, Shimane, and Niigata prefectures indicate that resistance to societal mainstream values often coalesces into co-optation of conventional thinking and modes of working.

Chapter 5, entitled "Convergence of Work and Leisure: Blessing or Plight?," critically depicts the increasing convergence of work and leisure in the lives of migrants (Klien 2016) and assesses both positive and negative implications of work-life balance of individuals who identify with their work to the extent of total engagement/immersion. Drawing on previous research about the destabilization of the binary divide between work and leisure by Duncan, Cohen, and Thulemark (2013), I investigate the search of mobile youth for more self-determination and, ultimately, control over their lives, but I show how they often end up becoming immersed in work as the lines between work and leisure blur in their quest for the eventual achievement of a better quality of life.

Chapter 6, entitled "Liminal Belonging and Moratorium Migration: Lifestyle Migrants between Limbo and Purpose of Life," introduces case studies from Shimane (Ama Town), Tokushima (Kamiyama Town), and Niigata prefectures (Iketani hamlet) with the aim of examining how settlers relate to the communities to which they have relocated. Specifically, the notions of liminal belonging and moratorium migration will be discussed. This section highlights the complex, shifting position of settlers within the communities, as well as their relations with other (nonlocal) settlers.

Chapter 7 examines the experiences of social entrepreneurs in former disaster zones, for example, tsunami-stricken Miyagi Prefecture (Ishinomaki and Oshika Peninsula) and Tokushima Prefecture, who are making efforts to combine a contribution to the community by creating jobs for locals with making a livelihood and experimenting with novel modes of working and living. Cases presented include revitalization projects that entail the collaboration of local and nonlocal stakeholders such as Ishinomaki Laboratory, the Ocica and Hamagurido project, and others.

Despite the focus of contemporary youth on downsizing and introversion, they aspire to making a social contribution that has a wider impact beyond their immediate environment, as also argued by Furuichi (2015: 96). One section of this chapter examines the coexistence of individualism and collectivism in mobile youth that is salient in individual narratives and practices. Another section deals with mobility and marginality, that is, how mobile entrepreneurs conceptualize their subjectivities both theoretically and practically with regard to the community to which they have relocated, which tends to take the "sedentary lifestyle" for granted. This chapter yields insights into the transformative effects of these activities on the individuals involved, on the communities they have relocated to, and on Japan altogether. This chapter explores the inherent paradoxes of post-growth Japan as up and coming social entrepreneurs aspire to having more control of their time and lives yet struggle to achieve professional success. Despite the outstanding importance notions like "purpose in life," "quality of life," and "happiness" seem to carry for interviewees as discursive concepts, many entrepreneurs are ultimately so immersed in their work that little time is left in their tight schedules for reflection and leisure.

The conclusion, entitled "Deconstructing Japan's Rural-Urban Divide," ties together various threads that run through this monograph. It sums up the findings of the book by wrapping up the diverse cases of urban migrants in the countryside and teasing out characteristics in their trajectories. Discussion of the empirical data presented illustrates that the reality of contemporary Japan cannot be envisaged as an urban-rural divide anymore. The discussion in this conclusion thus confirms that Gkartzios's notion of "urban-rural continuum" (2013: 160) also applies to Japan. Here, the ethnographic cases of migrants presented in this monograph are placed in the wider context of demographic trends and interpreted as a phenomenon that embodies a gradual but comprehensive value and paradigm shift in contemporary Japanese society.

Drops in the Ocean or the Beginning of Formative Change?

If we contextualize these urbanite migrants in Japan's countryside in the wider demographic picture, they may be considered as drops in the ocean given the overall trend of depopulation and aging that rural regions inevitably face across Japan. So why do these few individuals matter? These migrants may be negligible in quantitative terms, yet their decision to leave urban areas shows that Japan has come of age from its postwar model of lifestyle employment geared toward fulfilling the dream of eventually purchasing their own houses in suburbs of urban areas. Contemporary youth have not only started to move from urban areas, but they have also abandoned conventional unified lifestyles in cramped apartments with grueling daily work routines in favor of lifestyles that entail facets of shared economy and challenge the neoliberal emphasis on material gain and achievement: they do so by opting for cohousing and coworking spaces in remote villages.

As Gordon Mathews points out, Japan is still replete with a number of inflexible structural features that seem likely to create unhappiness in a significant number of its members, but change is nevertheless happening as "Japanese society as a whole seems notably more individualistic and accepting of individual difference than 30 and 40 years ago" (2017: 230–231). In a similar vein, the vignettes of my interviewees illustrate that, for them, migration is a "project of the self," to borrow Anthony Giddens's term, that is, mobility and their choice of lifestyle profoundly affects and shapes their sense of self (1991). The lifestyle migrants examined here embody features of the "new rural development paradigm" as opposed to the "modernization paradigm" since rural areas have emerged to be associated with endogenous development, bottom-up innovation, social capital (instead of financial capital), sustainable development, small-scale niche industries, and local embeddedness (Woods 2011: 140).

Deconstructing Rural Japan

This book is about mobility primarily based on lifestyle concerns in contemporary Japan, but the narratives, experiences, and trajectories of migrants depicted throughout the volume are relevant beyond Japan for the following reasons.

First, activities of the individuals who have relocated from urban to rural areas show that the widespread professional networks of individuals connect them to places well beyond the bounded place to which they have relocated. Many lead lifestyles that entail commuting between two places, one rural and one urban. The majority of interviewees engage in lifestyles that entail the consumption of goods that are not available at their chosen site of living but ordered through the internet. Many maintain social contacts through visits or social media that result in frequent exchange with partners in areas other than the one they have relocated to. Hence, one of the aims of this book is to rethink rurality as a theoretical concept on the basis of abundant empirical data and examine the position of rural areas in general.

Second, the modes of living and working that migrants' everyday lives contain suggest "post-growth" values of relevance to other countries that will eventually face the same fate of depopulation, aging, and economic stagnation that are typically salient in postindustrial societies. Features of the sharing economy—networks of similarly minded peers forming ersatz families; downsizing; small-scale happiness; a coexistence of societal engagement; and withdrawal, agency, and subjection—are recurring themes in all post-growth societies and thus make the empirical data presented here pertinent beyond Japan. Another reason why I argue that these migrants matter in the larger societal context of Japan and beyond is the aspect of creative depopulation. Ōminami Shinya, founder of the NPO Green Valley in Kamiyama Town, Tokushima Prefecture, has coined the term "creative depopulation." Kamiyama has become famous for its revitalization policy of attracting a small (160 individuals in 2016) but growing number of visionary migrants from diverse areas including IT, design, architecture, fine arts, food revitalization, and so on, with the idea being that though depopulation is inevitable, as a town, residents can try to cope with depopulation while still maintaining the attractiveness of Kamiyama as a vibrant place. Compact towns, close-knit networks of locals and other migrants, and face-to-face chats all offer professional opportunities apart from emotional benefits, especially for young entrepreneurs.

Third, the complexity of human experiences categorized as "lifestyle migration" and mobility depicted throughout this book suggests that there is no type; rather, the diversity and fuzziness of narratives and practices indicate that like any other postindustrial society Japan is a "complex society" with a distributive culture (Barth 1989)—one more reason that makes the findings relevant beyond the context of Japan. Distributive takes on culture perceive culture "as complex knowledge systems unevenly appropriated in social and political time and space" (Shore 1996: 209). Many interviewees had spent considerable time studying, living, or working abroad or in other locations in Japan. This raises the question concerning what is specifically "Japanese" about them. I would like to claim that the emergence of an increasingly transnational and translocal generation of Japanese individuals as documented in this book requires us to rethink the relevance of local and national categorizations as bounded entities, as is often the case in previous research. The limitations of approaching Japan as a monolithic entity have recently been impressively highlighted by Guarné and Hansen (2018). Similarly, rather than focusing on the aspect of culture or nation, I am more interested in the relevance of the societal phenomena described in this monograph for other post-growth societies that will face similar issues in the near future. The distinctly translocal and transnational lifestyles of the individuals depicted in this book also raises the question of a "sense of belonging" (*ibasho*).

In conventional discourse, a sense of belonging, and the concept of "home" used to be wedded to a clearly bounded physical place. However, settlers' trajectories, everyday lives, and narratives suggest that many seem more comfortable with the idea of a home that they can put into a pocket and move on, that is, a mobile sense of belonging, a mindset that resembles Lise Gundersen's statement that "home is where you are; home is the moment you are in" (2008: 27). For many, work continues to be the most important factor shaping their decision of where to move. Networks are extremely important as individuals in postproductivist Japan are increasingly concerned with a sense of *waku waku*, that is, a positive sense of excitement, inspiration, and drive that comes with engaging in work perceived as personally meaningful and societally important. Many interviewees observe that their decision to relocate resulted from existing professional networks.

Fourth, the findings presented in this book draw on extensive fieldwork in Shimane, Tokushima, Niigata, Iwate, and Miyagi prefectures and Hokkaido conducted between 2009 and 2017. Fieldwork consisted of participant observation at multiple sites across Japan and included attending a variety of events targeted at lifestyle migrants such as information events in Tokyo about life in certain regions, migration turns in the regions, group interviews and individual interviews with migrants, as well as hanging out with migrants in diverse settings. I also interviewed individuals who had decided to return to their original urban environment after realizing that rural living did not match their expectations.

Data for this study derive from semi-structured interviews with 118 respondents who had either migrated from urban areas to rural areas or were dividing their time between the rural and urban areas. Thirty-five of the interviewees were female, eighty-three were male. No special attempt was made to consider gender balance; rather, the result reflects the overall dominance of males in lifestyle migrants. Conducted between 2009 and 2017, these interviews lasted between one and four hours. In most cases, I sent the questions I hoped to discuss to my interviewees in advance; in some cases, however, the focus of the interview shifted to different directions. I interviewed migrants in their homes, places of work, in public places such as local government buildings, restaurants, cafés, outdoors, and via Skype. In a few cases, I conducted group interviews or interviews with couples. With twenty-four collaborators I conducted multiple interviews at different sites.

Follow-up fieldwork in regions like Shimane also made the changing position of rural areas within Japan evident by the fact that when I went there for the first time, back in 2008, most of my interviewees were early-career radical dropouts from elite companies with highly individualist visions that few could relate to, especially in the local community. In 2017, increasingly, successful midcareer salarymen choose to relocate to rural areas to engage in professional activities relating to *machizukuri* (placemaking, revitalization) in cooperation with local municipalities, something that did not happen previously. I have also interviewed male corporate employees working in IT with no interest in rural lifestyles who found themselves living in the countryside as they were initially dispatched by their urban companies to work there for a limited period but then ended up liking it so much that they extended rural life. In other words, living in the countryside has gained more recognition as a valid career option, and hence, communities of migrants have also emerged, with both merits and demerits for the migrants themselves. This growing professional interest in rural areas is also reflected in the increasing numbers of inquiries that the Tokyo-based Furusato Kaiki Shien Center (literally, Center for Supporting a Return to One's Home Region), a nonprofit organization that provides advice on life in rural areas, has received since 2008 from individuals in their thirties and forties. Back in 2008, only 12 percent of inquiries were from individuals in their thirties, while now they account for 28.7 percent. Back in 2008, 14.4 percent were people in their forties; now they account for 22.6 percent. In other words, rural areas seem to hold increasing appeal for relatively young and midcareer professionals (Yoneda 2017: 27).

Nine years ago when I started my ethnographic research for this project, I mostly interviewed individuals in their late twenties or early thirties who aspired to diverse versions of "chilled-out" life, better work-life balance, and sustainable lifestyles; now, increasingly, my interview partners are highly driven entrepreneurs with an interest in collaborating with local communities catering to an urban market or drawing on and appropriating rural elements to fit into their global lifestyles and networks. But I have also interviewed a broad spectrum of individuals concerned with healthy eating and sustainable lifestyles in general and entrepreneurs bringing a leisure-oriented mindset with a highly focused sense of business together. In addition to migrants per se, I have met with numerous representatives of local government responsible for in-migration policies, members of NGOs, and local citizens to discuss their views of in-migrants in their communities.

In retrospect, I feel that my own background as a European living in northern Japan made it easy for me to achieve rapport with my research subjects for this long-term project. On the one hand, I got the impression that my own migrant status facilitated interviews (in comparison to other research projects I had engaged in simultaneously). I also suspect that in line with Hertog's observation, being a non-Japanese researcher helped informants to open up about intimate issues (Hertog 2009: 17). Given the fact that many of my interviewees had experience living or working abroad, in some cases especially with female lifestyle migrants, it seemed natural to start the interview in an eerily familiar way as if the interviewee and I had met before. This applies particularly to discussing issues such as gender and work, where I expressed my heartfelt empathy during our conversation, which helped to promote an atmosphere of casual rapport and amicability.

Mobility and Methodology

Latour has compellingly argued that "movements and displacements are first, forms and sites come second" (2005: 300). Not only does mobility play a crucial role in the lives of my interviewees, but as a researcher undertaking this project, movement has also impacted the research methodology in sometimes unforeseeable ways. In addition to "real" fieldwork in the field, I engaged in "virtual" fieldwork through social media. For example, members of a collective house featured in chapter 3 asked me to join and contribute to an Advent calendar—an internet forum in which on each day between December 1 and 25, someone related to the collective would contribute an essay. This was a great way of learning more about and engaging with other members of the collective house whom I had not met when I was there last year beyond the means of conventional fieldwork. And, of course, social media such as Facebook and Instagram do have some benefits since they afford extended insights into interviewees' everyday lives and activities after leaving the (spatial) field. As mentioned earlier, I also conducted some interviews on Skype.

Many scholars in the field of lifestyle migration and mobility have elaborated their interpretations of mobility by inscribing them with ontological meanings for settlers as it allows them to pursue professional options that were not available to them in their previous places of living. Yet, what remains a lacuna in my opinion is mobility as a means to play for time, hedge their bets, mobility as a period of grace—a moratorium so to speak. I draw on psychoanalyst Okonogi Keigo's term *moratorium ningen* (literally, moratorium being; Okonogi 1978) from the 1970s, which incorporated Erik Erikson's "identity diffusion syndrome," denoting individuals who arbitrarily chose to evade their obligations and responsibilities to society.

In a similar vein, many settlers portrayed throughout this ethnography have degrees from top universities and possess valuable working experience yet are at a loss as to how to proceed with their lives in the sense of a committed societal engagement beyond mere work for monetary incentives. Rural living comes as a viable option for them to rethink their work and lives and gain time to carve out niches that allow them to find what they want. These settlers have embarked on their quest, yet many seem unsure what they are actually looking for. Angela McRobbie has previously described forms of a "mobility, which does not quite know where it is going" (2016: 90). Numerous settlers described throughout this volume may have a larger vision but seem uncertain how to translate it into a reality that relates directly to their everyday lives. We have tended to take it for granted that mobility is movement imbued with meaning (Cresswell 2001, 2006) and that movement is a means for individuals seeking to render their lives more meaningful. What if it were not? What if settlers were "haunted" and externally shaped by the ubiquitous discourse about the quest for subjective well-being and happiness yet did not partake in this quest at a deeper emotional level? I hope that the findings presented in the following chapters illustrate that multisited ethnography with its immersive methodology is appropriate for capturing these moments of moratorium and exemption.

Moratorium migration fuses the previously contradictory elements of "lifestyle" and "precariat" into a fuzzy gray zone where work, lifestyle, leisure, self-realization, and precariousness all blend into one.

Finally, and indeed related to the latter post-growth fuzziness, the inherent focus on the moment and lack of medium- and long-term planning is another striking feature evident in many migrant narratives. The overwhelming majority of migrants' trajectories are characterized by postconsumption lifestyles, the eminent focus of individuals on living (and working) in the moment that I have analyzed in previous research (Klien 2017) and that could be categorized as a feature conventionally ascribed to neoliberalist emphasis on ephemerality (Harvey 2005) and precariousness—the other side of freedom, flexibility, and creative dynamism. Bloch has referred to this mix of aspiration and despair as the "ontology of Not Yet Being" (1986: 11). Harvey talks of "spaces of hope" (2000) yet also elaborates on the "romanticism of endlessly open projects" (2000: 174). Similarly, Berlant has coined the intriguing term "cruel optimism" (2011) when she explored individuals' fantasies about realizing "the good life" in the neoliberal context of individual responsibility and achievement. It is this gray zone where aspiration and resignation coexist rather uneasily in which individuals attempt to create something new and find themselves entrapped in existing systemic constraints that this book examines ethnographically.

The coexistence of contradictory features in one and the same fragmented experience of a single individual may ultimately be what is the essential trait of post-growth Japan and what is bound to emerge in other postindustrial societies in the near future. Perhaps the remark by a female lifestyle migrant aged thirty originally from Chiba Prefecture who now lives on Itoshima Island illustrates the concurrence of disparate themes in a nutshell: "Personally, I think that if we manage to acquire skills to live without relying on capitalism, establish a community we can rely on and find ways of earning cash living in this way, we can solve most of the issues that we are faced with today" (Isa 2017: 122).

As argued by Rosenberger drawing on Foucault, the resistance shown by migrants to values favored by postwar mainstream life and their ensuing attempts to live according to their own values is never completely outside of the generally accepted truths and power dynamics of the times but is always present in a society (Rosenberger 2014: 107; Foucault 1980b). Such nascent confluence of resistance to and appropriation of mainstream societal values, possibility and probability, aspiration and subjection, societal engagement and withdrawal, regeneration and stagnation is key to the fuzzy experiences of mobile subjects grappling to negotiate their lives in shifting contemporary Japan. Self-monitoring patterns of behavior like posting on social media about one's professional activities as a freelancer in rural Japan go hand in hand with emotional withdrawal; vision and precariousness coexist uneasily. On the one hand, urbanites in rural areas express high satisfaction with their daily lives; yet, the other side of the coin is that they are living in permanent limbo, with many on the cusp of finding their purpose in life without actually having a precise idea of what it could be. Evidently, being in flux can also be perceived positively as having potential for self-growth and productive development. In this sense, migratory moves need to be approached more as ongoing processes rather than given points and fixed decisions, as has previously been argued by Cohen, Duncan, and Thulemark (2013).

The moments of stalling, withdrawal, disenchantment and dislocation, uneasy limbo and vibrant spirit of challenge when being torn between diverging directions that moratorium migrants experience are the focus of this ethnographic study and, I would claim, the essence of post-growth Japan.

Chapter One

Lifestyle Migration and Mobility

Negotiating Urban Lifestyles in Rural Communities

Rural to urban migration is common with increasingly more individuals relocating from the countryside to Tokyo and other urban areas; however, Japan has recently seen a small but steady increase in urbanites aged between twenty and forty-five who make a conscious choice to move to rural settings (Klien in Assmann 2016). This trend was accelerated by the Great East Japan Earthquake in March 2011 but had gathered momentum well before the disaster.

Changes in Urban Perceptions of the Countryside

Television documentaries and print media have been reporting on the increasing attraction of the countryside for the young urban generation. Publications focusing on urban to rural relocation have begun to emerge, such as *Turns* (established in 2012) or *Sotokoto* (literally, things outside, established in 1999). These magazines showcase a slower pace of life, ecological concerns, the creation of personalized lifestyles coupling ideal employment and quality of life, saving tips, and social entrepreneurship. Their target audience is twofold: those considering relocation and those who have already taken the leap into rural areas.

Sotokoto's February 2016 issue was published under the title *Finding a New Home* (*Atarashii ijū no katachi*, literally, forms of new migration) and featured articles about migrants throughout Japan, from Miyagi Prefecture in the northeast to Miyazaki Prefecture in the southwest. Even mainstream publications, such as *Pen*, that are targeted at male corporate employees regularly publish issues about moving to rural areas; from this we can reasonably conclude that mobility has become more acceptable as a lifestyle choice.

Ordinarily, *Pen* leads its feature articles with topics such as design, architecture, or male grooming. An example that highlights this changed perception of rural living would be the April 2016 *Pen* issue entitled *Let's Move House: People Who Made Their Ideal Lifestyles into Practical Reality* (*Ijū shiyou: Risō no kurashi wo te ni ireta hitobito no jireishū*). Some time ago, a change in the perception of the countryside began to take hold, with a gradually perception as a more "trendy" yet stereotypically "rural" place due to the sudden popularity of female lifestyle migrants (*ijū joshi*); however, urbanites who prefer rural settings have been found to pursue a broad variety of livelihoods that are not necessarily typical "rural" professional activities.

In many cases introduced in this monograph, newcomers conceded that "the countryside" and "country lifestyle" was not the key incentive for the move; instead, for the majority, the countryside seemed the perfect setting for self-growth, challenge, and furthering their career goals. Improving their quality of life was one element, but it was not their main goal.

Broadly categorized, individuals who have relocated to rural areas are referred to as "lifestyle migrants," that is, individuals who relocate for noneconomic reasons with the aim of leading a more meaningful life and consequently view migration as "a route to a better and more fulfilling way of life, especially in contrast to the one left behind" (Benson and O'Reilly 2009b: 1). Benson and O'Reilly define lifestyle migration as "the spatial mobility of relatively affluent individuals of all ages, moving either part-time or full-time to places that are meaningful because, for various reasons, they offer potential of a better quality of life" (Benson and O'Reilly 2009b: 2). Diversifying lifestyles (*raifusutairu no tayōka*), self-realization (*jiko jitsugen*), "living for oneself" (*jibunrashiku ikiru*), a better work-life balance (*wāku raifu baransu*), and a greater emphasis on quality of life have emerged as the main incentives for relocation. Other factors include the decreasing attractiveness of lifelong employment to some individuals against the background of lack of self-determination in conventional large-scale Japanese corporations. Many of my interviewees indicated that given the choice between leading a life where decision-making is left to the top-tier management in large-scale companies and a life where they can make their own decisions in a small-scale company, they would opt for the latter, even if this choice entails a reduced salary. Other migrants have opted out of regular work altogether, devising their own ways of earning a livelihood through a combination of sharing economy and freelance work—usually a lifestyle that involves close giving and taking with the immediate environment combined with an engagement that crosses physical boundaries through work and leisure (e.g., through social media and various forms of communication through the internet). Benson and O'Reilly's concept of lifestyle migration has gained significant traction, but some scholars have pointed out that the inherent weakness of the framework's effectiveness is due to its excessive comprehensiveness: "Lifestyle migration is a flexible conceptual framework that covers heterogeneous groups of individuals all seeking to improve their quality of life through international geographic mobility" (Bantman-Masum 2011).

Similar to Benson and O'Reilly's definition of lifestyle migration, the concept of "lifestyle mobilities" is described by geographer Norman McIntyre as the "movement of people, capital, information and objects associated with the process of voluntary relocation to places that are perceived as providing an enhanced, or at least, different lifestyle" (McIntyre 2009: 230). To illustrate this change that occurs in migrants after their move, a female migrant in her mid-thirties who relocated to a remote island observes that in her leisure time, she has started to spend time outdoors in ways that she did not in Tokyo, picking wild flowers and plants to spruce up her home or preparing her own breakfast cereal mixes because breakfast cereal is not available in this remote location. She remarks that as a result of her short commuting time to work and the lack of entertainment and shops, she has considerably more time at her disposal in comparison with her previous life in Tokyo—a change in her routine that made her somewhat anxious at first. She says that in retrospect she "unconsciously ended up buying clothes and other products" when living in Tokyo (interview on 16 September 2016). Now she enjoys quiet days on the remote island, going to bed much earlier and having more time to sleep due to the brief commuting time. She states that she is satisfied with her present work-life balance and also uses less money since her relocation while enjoying a richer lifestyle (*yutaka na kurashi*). In other words, in her case corporeal mobility has resulted in a lifestyle change that coincided with a shift in values brought about by her partner's decision to move to a rural area.

Fieldwork since 2010 in Niigata, Shimane, Miyagi, and Iwate prefectures and Hokkaido has shown gender-specific behavior patterns in migrants: Generally, female migrants tend to make greater efforts to engage directly with their local environment and nature in their leisure time as in the aforementioned case from Shimane Prefecture. Male migrants typically focus more on work, with many so engrossed in their professional activities that they end up neglecting leisure and social relations. For example, one of my male hosts during fieldwork, a migrant in his late twenties who is originally from Osaka but worked in Tokyo for three years in corporate employment before relocation to a remote island for work reasons, observes that without the specific vacancy notice, he would not have chosen to relocate as he is not particularly attracted to rural areas. In other words, the attractiveness of the work (not in financial terms, but in terms of self-determination and growth potential) was the main incentive for him to move. On reflection, he chuckles to himself, only a week after he started working on the island and formally changing his address, his manager ordered him back to Tokyo for one month because part of the activities that he was in charge of needed to be planned and negotiated in the capital. This example demonstrates that the conventional notion of relocation as a final, fixed, and distinct point in time is more imaginary than real and that mobility as such is contingent and permanent in many cases. Even when migrants make a conscious decision to relocate, they keep on moving out from their new home and coming back to it again after their initial relocation, both for work and leisure—a feature of the lives of the relocated that will be addressed in a section in chapter 3 in which I discuss the notion of lifestyle mobility. The example of this settler from Osaka also shows that lifestyle migration or mobility does not necessarily go hand in hand with counterurbanization, as has been claimed by Berry (1976) or Mitchell (2004). I advocate the view that the migratory moves of individuals need to be interpreted not as given points or fixed decisions but rather as processes that may include the option of second homes, repeated departures, and do not exclude the possibility of further moves in the future. In other words, motility, that is, the potential of mobility (Bonss and Kesselring 2004), is a salient feature in many narratives and individual trajectories: the majority of migrants encountered during fieldwork across Japan talked about their high satisfaction with their lifestyles after relocation; yet, they were not sure where they will find themselves in five years. Indeed, when I revisited field sites in Shimane Prefecture six years after my first visit, half of the migrants I had interviewed had moved on somewhere else (either back to their hometowns or to a third place).

"Mobility Turn" in the Social Sciences

The "mobility turn" in the social sciences has resulted in mobility practices and migratory trends being increasingly investigated by scholars from a wide range of disciplines, including anthropology, human geography, psychology, sociology, as well as political science. Sheller and Urry refer to a "new mobilities paradigm" (2006). Mobility is presented as an "all-inclusive category" (Croucher 2015: 168), which generally is ascribed positive nuances (Glick Schiller and Salazar 2013) against the background of Appadurai's global "flows" (1996) and Bauman's "liquid modernity" (2007). Many narratives make Giddens's "reflexive project of the self" evident (1991:81), with lifestyles being defined as a set of practices that "give material form to a particular narrative of self-identity" (Giddens 1991: 81). As for the case of Japan, extended-stay tourism (Ono 2009), retiree migration to other countries, sociocultural refugee tourism to other countries (*sotokomori*) (Yamashita 2009), Japanese lifestyle migration to Australia (Nagatomo 2007a, 2007b, 2015) and the relocation of individuals in the creative scene to New York (Fujita 2009; Kanzaki Sooudi 2014) have attracted ample attention. Lunsing (2006) has conducted ethnographic research into individuals who decide to resign their posts and go freelance. However, in retrospect, urban-to-rural moves by the young, many of whom are "corporate refugees" (Benson and O'Reilly 2009b: 1) and invest in lifestyles of choice in their quest for a better way of life, have been largely neglected to date, with more attention having gone to "retirement migration," as Gaspar also observes (Gaspar in Torkington, David, and Sardinha 2015: 14). Exceptions are Rosenberger's ethnography of individuals engaging in organic agriculture as an alternative lifestyle (2014, 2017); Osawa's research (2014) on new farmers (*shinki shūnō*), that is, urbanites with no family history of farming who migrate to rural areas with the purpose of engaging in agriculture; and my own (2016, 2017) research on disaster volunteers who decide to remain in Tohoku to engage in alternative lifestyles.

Individuals seek a "less conventional, less hurried lifestyle" in a different, often romanticized environment based on the classic image of the "rural idyll," although some have to accept that it eludes them

(O'Reilly 2014: 218, 234). In fact, numerous interviewees mentioned the gap between the life of anticipated rural tranquility and the lived reality of a higher workload than in their urban setting—the only difference being that postrelocation, the distinction between work and leisure was fluid. In many cases, these work and leisure activities were voluntary posts or work for the community, again, something that related to their work in various ways. Numerous interviewees described their lifestyles after relocating as a "work-life mix," whereas they had a clear-cut divide between work and leisure in their previous careers in urban areas; some narratives suggested that individuals' original ambitions to break out of corporate constraints in fact had been brought to naught as a result of their dedication to their projects and the fact that work and interest coincided. For example, an interviewee in his early thirties whom I had interviewed six years ago discussed his joyful sea fishing trips and his agricultural work; he had opted out of an elite corporate trajectory and relocated to a remote island to set up his own company that provided services in the field of regional revitalization. Six years later, the company that had been housed in a ramshackle building next to the local municipal agency had moved to a picturesque historic building, the workforce had grown by more than half, and our interviewee admitted that he hardly had any leisure time because he and his company have more work offered than they can accept. When I ask him about his work-life balance, he replies that now is the time to focus on work and deliver—if he took a rest now, he would lose everything he had achieved so far. Ultimately, his present reality is that he commutes between his home and office apart from his frequent business trips mostly to Tokyo and he can hardly recall the last day he took off. Outings to the seashore are not on the agenda of what I now refer to as a "lifestyle workaholic"; he mentions that his only form of recreation is meditation and soaking in a hot bath in the morning.

Another male interviewee is in his early forties and looks back on a successful career in human resources in a well-known elite company in Tokyo. Originally from a small town in Kyushu, he remembers that he thoroughly enjoyed his previous job as it entailed trips across Japan. Yet now he is situated on a remote island with his family; when I ask about his motivation for accepting the offer of managing a local cramming school (*juku*) with an aim to improve the educational success rate of island children, he responds that it was a combination of gut feeling, a sense of contributing something to society, and the challenge of starting from scratch. He clearly sees his mission as contributing something positive to Japanese society by turning this cramming school into a success story for the island. Rather than harboring romanticist notions of a slow life in the countryside, he sees his life on the island as part of his career trajectory—it is evident that he is not planning to stay forever, but that he intends to do his utmost to turn the project into a success.

This vignette of the manager illustrates the major shift that has become evident in Japanese society: the viability of changing jobs, linking "experience" and "challenge" to one's personal contribution to societal innovation while working on one's career, even if this involves decisions that seem unconventional. Generally, the factor of "personal challenge" or "happiness" has featured increasingly in considerations of work, as testified by a recent edition of the journal *Neko Mook* on the issue *Work Style Book: Working in a Happy Manner* (*shiawase na hatarakikata*). The quest for *waku waku* (positive energy and drive) is high on the agenda. Six years ago, initial fieldwork on the Oki Islands brought only a few encounters with pioneer migrants in their late twenties; they were perceived as highly talented but eccentric "dropouts," even if they had elite backgrounds. Now, corporate warriors from Tokyo in their forties have relocated to the island after more than ten years in classic urban careers. These migrants often mention personal connections as the first stepping-stone to their place of relocation; some respondents had friends, acquaintances, or former working colleagues who already lived at the new location. Conversely, others lacked personal connections but mentioned media coverage as having caught their interest so that they decided to pay an initial commitment-free visit. However, on arrival, these potential migrants were greeted by local government representatives as if they had already decided to settle. Some of the long-term pioneer settlers hinted at their disappointment in migration altogether, since with increasing societal acceptance of migration, more and more migrants decide to move to a given place since some of their acquaintances or older peers had gone first; in the view of senior settlers, this mainstream turn had resulted in the decreased creativity of newcomers. In short, they suggested that it has become "hip" to relocate to rural areas and that individuals are not as motivated by genuinely personal incentives as they were five or ten years ago. Younger migrants who have settled more recently, in turn, perceive their senior peers as "distanced" (interview on 23 November 2016). In other words, areas with a high influx of urbanites offer new settlers the chance to engage in social relations with other migrants; yet, within this migrant community, different groups have emerged that tolerate each other but do not necessarily befriend one another.

Lifestyle Mobilities

The interviewees introduced in this monograph could also be categorized as participants in "lifestyle mobility" (Cohen, Duncan, and Thulemark 2013), defined as "on-going semi-permanent moves of varying duration" that constitute a more flexible conceptual lens for analyzing mobility since the boundaries between travel, leisure, and migration are blurred and their narratives make collapsing work and leisure divides evident. Contrary to Benson and O'Reilly's definition that implies a clear-cut divide, Cohen, Duncan, and Thulemark suggest a more fluid category.

Japan is a highly centralized country with the majority of the representative government institutions and companies centered in Tokyo and Osaka. Recently, some efforts have admittedly been made to relocate some government institutions to other areas to prevent administrative damage potentially resulting from a major earthquake in the Tokyo area. However, a fair number of the nation's elite universities are still located in Tokyo, and the mindset that one needs to go to Tokyo to have a real career is still deeply ingrained. So why would young aspiring individuals make the move down the career ladder, away from corporate safety, urban convenience, and around-the-clock entertainment?

Motives for relocation include self-realization, self-fulfillment, food safety (in the wake of the Great East Japan Earthquake and Tsunami), concerns about physical and mental health due to consistent overwork in corporate jobs, aspirations for a better work-life balance, time to think about what one really wants to do with one's life, time to establish a start-up enterprise, realizing one's long-held dream of opening a café or shop, and more generally taking on a challenge and personal development.

One example would be an editor and writer from Tokyo who relocated to Okinawa with his wife. Before, both of them were so caught up in their daily work routines that they hardly spent time together. Only once their relocation was complete did she conceive their first child, and consequently they successfully led a balanced family leisure life together. About their former life in Tokyo, he observes, "During the week I was busy with my job as an editor, on weekends there were career events and more work so employment occupied 95% of my time and I felt a sense of unease about my lifestyle" (*Pen* 2016: 72). The family lives in the *gaijin jūtaku*, literally, foreign accommodation, which was constructed in the postwar period until Okinawa's return to Japan for staff working at the US military base. He observes that the unique architecture of the foreign accommodation gives the place an exotic feel, which he really likes.

Similarly, a family from Tokyo with four children decided to move to Higashikawa Town in rural Hokkaido due to the father's high workload at an institution for disabled children, resulting in his having no time to spend with his own children. The parents of that family made the decision to relocate when they came across the Higashikawa Town homepage; there they read that measures were actively implemented to promote child-rearing and family life. Furthermore, the parents report that water purity was a major incentive for their move. With hindsight, they report that spending more time playing together and spending their leisure time outdoors has positively reinforced the harmony between individual family members (*Pen* 2016: 80).

A Drop in the Ocean or the Beginning of a Major Societal Shift?

Sociologist Jun Nagatomo has also noted the combined elements of structural change in Japanese society with shifting priorities in individual lifestyles (2016: 6). While overall figures for urban to rural settlers appear small compared to the general trend of moving from the countryside to the city, the recent increase of both "U-turners" (those who return to their hometowns after a period in urban areas) and "I-turners" (individuals who move to provincial areas in which they have no connections) has been used skillfully by some municipal agencies across Japan to attract more in-migrants.

This emerging shift in perception of the Japanese countryside as a stagnant backwater that serves as the last resort for individuals who have not managed to make it in Tokyo (*miyakoochi*) to an experimental ground for aspiring individuals, as well as a site of resistance, is the subject of this chapter. Many of the narratives introduced in this chapter resemble those of lifestyles migrants who move overseas to pursue a more meaningful and personally satisfying life (Fujita 2009; Ono 2009; Kanzaki Sooudi 2014; Sato 2001; Nagatomo 2014; Favell 2015; Aoyama 2015b) with a clear focus on nonmaterial values. In fact, the first known lifestyle migrants emerged in the early 1990s. It was a time after the economic bubble burst, when Japanese women in their twenties chose to relocate to Hong Kong, Singapore, or other countries in Asia (Maemura, Kato, and Fujihara 2015: 134). Thang, MacLachlan, and Goda (2006) conducted ethnographic research into Japanese working women in Singapore, arguing that these women had relocated with an aim to pursue a lifestyle of personal fulfillment unattainable in Japan. Nagatomo analyzed Japanese lifestyle migrants in Australia (2007b) and found the key motivation for most migrants was their desire to break out of the constraints of corporate employment.

Around two decades ago, a trend for individuals to relocate across Japan began to take hold; for example, Okinawa has attracted urbanite lifestyle migrants in their twenties and thirties. Despite being a prefecture in Japan, Okinawa has been labeled "Asia that can be accessed without a passport" (Ota 2000). This suggests that despite its location within geographical Japan, Okinawa has exotic allure that rivals foreign destinations. This trend suggests that relocation to rural areas is not considered a "rural idyll" any longer, in the sense that it is not motivated by nostalgia or a quest for nature; rather, the focus has shifted to a rural landscape that also provides the challenge of a ground for experiment with a new lifestyle. The underlying message is that the low living cost, available space, and social capital offer creative individuals an environment to try out their ideas in the form of projects, business start-ups, and other experimental forms.

Tokushima local government has published a pamphlet aimed at potential newcomers entitled "How About Living in Tokushima?" (*Tokushima de sundeminde*). The leaflet focuses on support of migrants and their integration into the close-knit but open community. It features locals from various hamlets across Tokushima Prefecture, their personal stories told in local dialects with reports on how these original residents of Tokushima have supported recent migrants to the area. On the back of the pamphlet we find the following message: "Tokushima—here we are on to a positive vibe that can be felt with one's heart" (*rikutsu ja nai yosa ga koko ni aru*). Despite the idyllic images in this and other pamphlets targeted at potential migrants, projections of a less hurried, stress-free lifestyle, stronger community relations, and peace and quiet do not necessarily prove to be true for many migrants; in fact, some admit to working more than in their urban careers as they feel more committed to their self-chosen projects. All in all, the diverse array of lifestyle migrants introduced in this chapter and volume do not seem to view their personal relocation as moves of counterurbanization, in the sense of their rejection of urban lifestyles. As it is, many continue to indulge in elements of urban life even after their relocation, collaborating with urban business partners, returning to cities for both work and pleasure, traveling to other urban areas, even working and living in two different locations, one urban and one rural.

Post-Growth Focus on Individual Priorities and Societal Innovation

Migrants' narratives suggest that Japan has made a distinct departure from the postwar mantra of economic growth, coping, and endurance inherent in collective *gambarism* (Sai 1995: 53) and the sacrifice of individual interests for the good of large-scale entities toward activities that combine personal growth, social innovation, contribution, and challenge. In discussions with lifestyle migrants I encountered in the field about their reasons for leaving previous jobs, the majority pointed to their inability to envisage change or personal growth under circumstances of no change as a factor. Instead of interpreting change as inherently risky, migrants across the board take the stance that maintenance of the status quo entails a greater personal hazard, no matter whether they are in their twenties, thirties, or forties. Lack of self-determination resulting from hierarchism still prevalent in Japanese corporations was another oft-cited factor inspiring their decision to move.

Migrants depicted in this study share features with an organic farmer Rosenberger introduces in her research who expresses his satisfaction about not being exposed to the stress of a salaryman and being able to decide for himself (Rosenberger 2017: 11). The migrants portrayed in this volume also express their gratitude for freedom from direct authority and are willing to accept a lower income for more self-determination and greater control of their lives. A distinct emphasis on individual interests and lifestyle priorities is evident in migrants' narratives—what is more, individuals are not shy about saying that they are committed to pursuing those interests. These individuals grew up in Japan's lost decade(s) (Funabashi and Kushner 2015) with growing unemployment and decreasing prospects to obtain lifelong employment, and they have witnessed their parents' sacrifices; for many members of this post-growth generation, the continuing pressure to sacrifice leisure for a job that is increasingly less secure does not make sense. These men and women feel entitled to a different approach to life and consciously opt for a different path with added emphasis on personal well-being, also taking issues affecting the wider society into consideration in their decision-making process.

This dual interest is intricately related to this contemporary genera- tion's increasing reliance on open structures known to them as "networks." "Networks" are relevant on two levels: they help individuals cope with the labor market's structural instability, and they result from the pervasiveness of the internet, with groupings emerging from social media and other platforms. One positive feature of these "networks" is that individuals do not necessarily need to be in the same physical place to exchange opinions on a given theme; on the flip side, a negative legacy is the burden on individuals who are expected (or put pressure on themselves) to be available and online around the clock.

Fieldwork in 2012 led me to the northeastern part of Japan, Tohoku and the city of Ishinomaki. The area was severely affected by the Great East Japan Earthquake of March 2011. There, I met and interviewed a twenty-four-year-old male graduate from the prestigious Tokyo Uni- versity. He moved to Ishinomaki to start a social business project with like-minded peers from Tokyo.

What is striking about this graduate is that he did not choose to join the conventional trajectory of corporate employment, even for a limited time, but opted for freelance social entrepreneurship right from the beginning. However, one year later, he had dropped out of the proj- ect in order to pursue a fully funded master's degree at an Ivy League university on the US East Coast, and two years later he had joined corporate employment as a full-time employee. His statement from 2012 contradicts his factual trajectory that eventually turned "mainstream."

Many of my interlocutors live in shared houses, often with peers that work on the same projects; many work in coworking spaces—the line between paid and unpaid work is fuzzy, it is often unclear who the regular project staff are, who is an intern, and who is just a visitor. For example, when I conducted fieldwork in 2012 in Ishinomaki, Miyagi Prefecture, after the Great East Japan Earthquake, I regularly used the office space of the grassroots movement Ishinomaki 2.0 because the space provided high-speed internet free of charge and I could meet various local and nonlocal stakeholders there and engage in participant observation. Anyone visiting Ishinomaki is welcome to visit the space, use the internet, have some coffee, or browse books displayed on the shelves near the entrance of the office. I also helped with painting walls and clearing out trash from abandoned spaces with group members, so I could have been an intern as well—in fact, the line was fluid and nobody asked too many questions about my status. In fact, many of the group members earn their money with other jobs, with some having their work base in Tokyo while coming to Ishinomaki regularly to pursue their projects. For example, one of the founding members, originally from Tohoku, has worked for the giant advertising company Dentsu for many years and states that his engagement in Ishinomaki 2.0 gives him great satisfaction because he can see the immediate results of his work. Dentsu made headlines in 2016 when one of its young female employees committed suicide as a result of excessive work pressure. In 2012, he came to Ishinomaki for four days on average per month but otherwise lived in Tokyo as a corporate employee in the fast-paced global advertising agency.

For many neorurals, there is no clear line between what is work, what is networking, and what is leisure because the projects they are involved in largely correspond to their personal interests, beliefs, and values and are carried out together with peers they like to relate to in their free time as well. Intensive daily socializing—that is, working in the shared office, sharing lunch with collective orders of lunch boxes, group meetings, eating and drinking together during network events, sharing accommodation—means that many migrants have less privacy than one would expect, and the fact that many are neither in any partnerships nor have family does not come as a surprise. The network, project group, and so on, takes on the role of the family as individuals spend a large part of their time with other network members. "Identity is formed on the move," as Chambers observes (1994: 25)—lifestyle migrants adapt to their changing circumstances by permanently rearranging and reinventing themselves—as part of a network or group.

Negotiating Urban Lifestyles in Rural Communities: Three Case Studies

"Reinventing myself through moving."

I meet Nana through the introduction of a friend, so we both visit Nana's flat. Thirty-eight and from Saitama Prefecture originally, she spent her childhood and youth in various places, including Yokohama and Shizuoka due to her father's corporate moves. She lives in a spacious two-floor flat with wooden flooring that is full of stuff. It is obvious that Nana is a collector, but also that she likes archiving and keeping order. When I visit her flat a second time, Nana—called "Sensei" by everyone—is teaching two local guys in their twenties how to cook Western food: today's menu is spaghetti carbonara. The "cooking apprentices" tell me with gleaming eyes what treasures are hidden away in Nana's cabinets. Nana laughs, opening one of the many drawers that are all neatly labeled with stickers, and presents me with a pen that she got from some drug company as a PR gift. She works as a pharmacist and enjoys her work but also puts great priority on leisure—she enjoys surfing, diving, yoga, and a variety of outdoor activities, but she also has a great interest in fine food. She moved to Oki in October 2015 but had lived there once before for three and half years. She initially wanted to live in Okinawa for a while but then ended up living in Saigo on the main Oki Island. She takes care of people, but also observes that she tends to get caught up in social relations that become difficult to handle, especially with men. She says with a shrug that she is not made for marriage (*kekkon ha jibun amari muiteinai*). Having her own professional career and enjoying various financial benefits that come with living in a remote area, she leads a materially comfortable life. She is a regular customer of the internet shopping website Amazon and other internet services since the range of products and entertainment on the island is limited. She says that when her long-awaited cheese or red wine arrives, her weekend finally starts. The wide selection of gourmet food ingredients is neatly placed in small containers and drawers in the kitchen, which looks somewhat like a scientific laboratory. She also enjoys receiving her DIY-entertainment sets that she has ordered from a Japanese clothing company. Nana could be seen as the ultimate contemporary lifestyle migrant who brings together the best of urban and rural lifestyles because she enjoys outdoor pleasures on the island, relates to the locals, and maintains her "urban" emphasis on indoor material pleasures such as her liking for choice food. Her flat looks just like the flat of a thirty-something hip urbanite somewhere in Tokyo with the only difference that it is more spacious. Instead of the more usual sofa in her living room, she keeps camping furniture from a high-end outdoor brand. Nana also uses her frequent short-term trips to Tokyo and other urban areas to enjoy culinary delicacies not available on the island. She sighs with a smile that she has been trying to cut down on her purchases, yet the conversation makes clear that she derives great pleasure from her regular Amazon orders and other catalog purchases.

When I ask her about her long-term plans, she laughs, saying that she does not have any but will probably return to Yokohama at some point. She points out that her upbringing with a salaryman father who frequently had to relocate (and so the entire family had to as well) probably made mobility seem a normal feature of life, and for her, moving is a means of starting again, reinventing herself when she has encountered something difficult.

In fact, only a few months after our initial encounter she announces on social media that she is moving to Izumo, mainland Shimane Prefecture. Nana may be a representative of an emerging generation of cosmopolitan women with fast-paced careers who have high demands on their lifestyles and prefer to focus on work and leisure rather than dedicate themselves to family and the domesticated image of *ryōsai kenbo* (good wife, wise mother) that so often comes as an uncontested demand on women when starting a family in Japan. Sustained mobility and the idea of mobility as an everyday practice (Edensor 2007) appear to be a way out for individuals from dead-end emotional trappings and difficult social relations at work and in the private sphere, and they often constitute a high-end lifestyle choice significantly shaped by options afforded by class and education. While Bell and Ward (2000) have argued that identities are based less on class now and individuals can pick their identities from a "cultural supermarket" (Mathews 1998), Nana's case suggests that lifestyle migration and mobility are often an option concurring with relatively high education and income and could hence be interpreted as an indulgence of those of an affluent middle class aspiring to cosmopolitan lifestyles. Furthermore, as she mentions growing up in a *tenkinzoku* family (characterized by frequent moves due to her father's professional transfers), her childhood clearly has been shaped by routine travel practices from early on. Besides the functional aspect of relocation affording emotional freedom to individuals, mobility does not primarily constitute a means to a better life (Benson and O'Reilly 2009b) but a way of life per se. Sustained indulgence in material consumption coexists with practices of social engagement with locals, yet individuals avoid emotional commitments at a deeper level as a result of previous negative experiences. As can be ascertained from Nana's daily routine, practices shaped by urban living coincide with outdoor experiences, and thus Nana's trajectory of sustained mobility can be taken as an embodiment of a high-end Post-Fordist lifestyle focused on career and recreation; self-induced and self-controlled mobility is used as a strategic resource to afford individuals the freedom to "be subjects and agents in their own right" (O'Regan 2013: 36) and can hence be considered a mechanism of achieving self-determination against social constraints. However, beyond such emancipatory incentives, itinerant lifestyles constitute a way of seeking out new experiences for highly capable individuals with a distinct set of professional skills. In the past, "lifestyle migration" or "mobility" were mostly associated with the image of "lifestyle travellers" (Erskine and Anderson 2016: 130), that is, individuals who travel for the sake of experience in lieu of pursuing work—a mode of extended backpacking as it were. Migrants like Nana, however, manage to link their professional careers with the mobility they require for maintaining emotionally sustainable lives and are thus essentially different from classic lifestyle travelers who are primarily committed to traveling.

Emergence and Disappearance of New Entrepreneurial Projects

Sachiko, thirty-one and originally from Shizuoka, worked as a web designer in Tokyo and Fukuoka and spent much of her teens and twenties traveling to Canada, the United States, Australia, and Asia. She spent one year on a working holiday visa in Australia. Her previous work in web design was strenuous with long hours in her office every day. Prolonged lack of sleep combined with the permanent pressure of looming deadlines and overwork took a heavy toll on her physical and mental health. Hence, she decided to relocate, having a long-nurtured dream of living on an island. Rather than push herself beyond her capabilities, Sachiko discusses her ideal life—the dream she wants to live—that is a reasonable combination of employment and living (*seikatsu to umaku ryōritsu shinagara shigoto*) and enjoying life, being free, and living in peaceful coexistence with nature. Sachiko moved to Oki in 2013 and worked and lived in a hotel at first; during that time, she realized that most of the tourists were senior citizens despite Oki's many attractions for younger people as well.

In retrospect, she observes that through her experience of working in the web industry, and being already in her late twenties, she was aware that she could not afford to be unsuccessful anymore (*mou shippai shicha ikenai*). One year ago she opened a guesthouse in an idyllic hamlet, twenty minutes' drive north of the main port, with prefectural funds and funds obtained through crowdfunding. The house is 120 years old, so it took eight months to get it into shape by restoring the bathroom and kitchen. Sachiko's plan was not only to have foreign guests visit, but also to use the guesthouse as an event space and place to meet and exchange ideas for various people, local and nonlocal. In August 2015, there were as many as one hundred reservations for the guesthouse, so Sachiko recruited temporary staff from Hyogo Prefecture since she could not manage the guesthouse by herself. Locals were surprised that so many visitors appeared out of nowhere. Because a stay in the guesthouse also offered the option of additional tours, for example, sea kayak or fishing tours, this experiential tourism package appealed to urban visitors, and Sachiko's previous work in web design evidently helped her spread the word about the guesthouse on the web. Until then, Oki Island only had conventional business hotels or Japanese-style *ryokans*. Sachiko's guesthouse filled a niche and was appreciated by local government as well as residents.

Yet, when I hear about Sachiko during my fieldwork in September 2016, the guesthouse is "temporarily" closed. It turns out that Sachiko is in Matsue where she is giving birth to her first child. She has married a local government employee there and nobody knows what will happen to the guesthouse, including herself perhaps. When I ask her about her long-term plans, she says that she does not really have any. Representatives of the local government in the main port on Oki seem frustrated about the project after having invested substantial money into restoration of the guesthouse. I cannot help but detect a sense of resentment among my local informants about Sachiko, who left for personal reasons despite locals having trusted and supported her in many ways.

This vignette is typical not only of the story of Sachiko, but it also highlights the great potential as well as uncertainty inherent in entrepreneurship, relations between locals and nonlocals, and the outstanding potential of internet sources both for funding and disseminating information. On the website of the guesthouse, her blog from November 11, 2016, reads as follows:

> These days the media have taken up the issue of death by overwork. Since I previously worked in the web industry, I also was faced with the idea that one needs to do overwork as a service and work on weekends was normal. But working every day, this mode of work seems normal and the right

thing to do. And the fact that I could not put up with it in the long term made me feel like a loser [. . .]. As someone who used to believe in working as hard as you can to get a career I decided to change my life completely and I am really happy about having done it. I think it is correct to prioritize a life that one personally aspires to. Leaving stress and negative experiences behind is OK. I also put my environment into a bind when I left my former job, but nevertheless I think it was a good choice. What is real wealth, what is a fulfilling life? Everyone has a different opinion on these issues, so I would like to express my hope that more people will come forth who think carefully about what they really want in life and change accordingly. (http://oki-tsukudaya.com/20161111-2/, accessed 13 November 2016)

Sachiko's story shows that the pressure to succeed does continue well beyond relocation, and the sense of competition, self-presentation, and streamlined trajectory is enormous due to the permanent connection of migrants through virtual media.

Architect with a Social Conscience or Just Another Salaryman?

Originally from Gunma Prefecture but having studied architecture in Yokohama, Koichi is in his early thirties and has worked since the Great East Japan Earthquake in March 2011 in Ishinomaki as part of his job assignment in one of Japan's up-and-coming architect offices based in Yokohama that aim to pursue architecture with a social twist, that is, with a focus on *machizukuri* (town-making, revitalization). He tells me that there are limitations inherent in traditional architecture and its effect on the built environment. In our conversation, Koichi emphasizes that he and his office partners prioritize the social context behind buildings. Koichi says that he is aware of Ishinomaki's attractions as a small-scale local harbor town in Miyagi Prefecture, but he has been so busy with work that he hardly has time to explore the town; for him, factual reality is now that work has become equivalent to living. Usually, he has Tuesdays off, but he has been so overwhelmed with work that he sleeps in a little longer, then commutes to his shared office even on his free day. From the point of view of an observer, it is often unclear to what extent his activities are actually work related. For example, a recent barbecue was work-related even though it took place on the weekend. In other words, his life in Ishinomaki is no different from his life when working in Yokohama or other urban locations.

In the case of Koichi, there is a further factor: he keeps a small room in Yokohama where he stores his belongings, and he to which he regularly returns—so he leads a life between two places, which is time- and money-consuming. In Ishinomaki, he shares a house with three other office staff only a few minutes on bicycle from his work. He does not have family, nor is he in a relationship. He enjoys his professional life and seems well-liked among locals, yet he lacks the time to benefit from his life within the town in his own leisure time. Koichi seems so engrossed in his professional work and daily routine that he has no time to reflect on his long-term aspirations, although he mentions a desire to work overseas for a while and do something for the benefit of society there. Just like his fellow corporate workers in Yokohama and Tokyo, he lives on convenience-store food hastily consumed in the office.

The irony for Koichi is that despite the declared mission of his architectural firm, namely, the implementation of "town-making with an aim of creating a better place and higher life quality for its residents," Koichi's own life as a member of the architectural firm's staff seems no different from the exhausting, repetitive, stressful work mode faced by average salarymen elsewhere. This factual salaryman reality defies the stylish office space containing furniture by Herman Miller. Working past personal limits in a stylish environment does not change the fact that Koichi's is still an unsustainable mode of work, no matter how much hope Koichi and his fellow creative types polemicize about future change for the better.

Wrapping Up: The *Waku Waku* Factor in Post-Growth Neoliberal Japan

Thinking about these three biographies of "lifestyle migrants," there do not seem to be too many common features between Nana, the pharmacist career woman from Saitama Prefecture; Sachiko, the aspiring female entrepreneur from Yokohama; and Koichi, the socially committed, overworked architect from Gunma Prefecture. Yet, all of these trajectories share a focus on the here and now (Klien 2017). Individuals in post-growth Japan tend to seek temporary "small-scale happiness," to borrow Furuichi Noritoshi's expression in *Happy Youth in a Desperate Country* (2011). None of the migrants introduced here have medium- or long-term plans and live as they deem appropriate (or don't, as in the case of Koichi). While none of them suffer financial hardship with two of them having a regular income, they all have excellent social skills that have facilitated their adaptation in their new environments. Yet, none of them seem committed to one job, institution, or even place in the long term. On the one hand, they seem successful in their respective careers since they have managed to carve out a niche combining work and leisure (although not so much in the case of Koichi); yet, they also seem to hedge doubts whether they can pull through their projects, achieve work-life balance, arrive at a stage when they envisage themselves as permanent residents. This may be one of the essential features of post-growth youth in Japan. Mobility is a practice that is ingrained in their everyday lives to an extent that they are not even aware of, it is part of their daily routines. As Cresswell and Merriman put it, "Mobile, embodied practices are central to how we experience the world, from practices of writing and sensing, to walking and driving" (2011: 5). And this lack of stability may not be necessarily an Achilles heel as long as lifestyle migrants manage to turn their sense of liminality into something productive.

In fact, this may be an appropriate time to recall Liisa Malkki's trope of "sedentarist metaphysics," that is, the preconceived and unquestioned assumption that the sedentary lifestyle is the only way of life (1992). The emergence of biographies such as the ones outlined here are testimonies of the increasing diversification of life courses in Japanese society and the inherent reflexivity of individuals who question (to varying extents) what they are after in their lives. None of the interviewees introduced earlier seem to work for the sake of pure financial gain, although some enjoy the material benefits of their work. Yet, their narratives suggest that they seek something beyond the material that relates to the benefit of others: Nana likes to take care of others, yet she seeks regular retreat; Sachiko's entrepreneurial project is closely related to visitors as well as locals; Koichi's work also is intricately entwined with the local population. They all seem to be seeking positive drive—the *waku waku* factor I mentioned earlier, something new, something that keeps one going that also implies the potential for change. Takeru, a thirty-three-year-old social entrepreneur with a degree in economics from Tokyo University, has been on the move since the Great East Japan Earthquake in 2011, with projects in Tokyo,

Miyagi, and Shimane prefectures: he set up a social entrepreneurship project with local women on a remote peninsula in Miyagi Prefecture to create jobs for female residents in the disaster zone; another project has seen the establishment of a small restaurant that also creates jobs for local women. The young entrepreneur remarks that in retrospect, he was someone that did not have a passion/clear goal (*kore wo yaritai to iu tema no nai ningen deshita*) until the disaster. In 2012, he derives great satisfaction and a sense of achievement from the fact that he conceives and manages his project together with peers: "Numerous times I have experienced that possible eggs of ideas just remain ideas when I stay by myself but turn into something when I share this with someone; this is why I like to be the 'second person.' Respecting the people around me, I like to be the second person who turns 0 into 1. This mode of working fits me personally and I feel *waku waku* (inspired and happy)" (*Sotokoto* 2016: 88). When I meet him again in 2017, he has dropped out of the social entrepreneurship project, moved back to Tokyo, and earns his money as a well-paid freelancer in venture consulting.

Migrants' denial of sedentariness may be interpreted as the rejection of stagnation and the opting for change, challenge, and growth in a world that dismissed risk and emphasized security and status quo—urbanites who held prestigious jobs in editing but now work in the fishing industry: a trajectory many would shake their heads over. Yet the editor used to eat convenience food in a predetermined time frame during lunch break while now, as an employee of the fisheries association, he has the luxury of having access to rare and fresh fish and vegetables. Participant observation and the interview I conducted with this respondent made evident that the *waku waku* factor is a strong pull after his relocation. In fact, he observed that even during his initial visit to the island, he was not at all determined to move, having already bought property in Tokyo. Yet, after his first visit, he could not get the images of the island out of his mind. When he noticed a vacancy for his ideal job in the fisheries association, he applied and was accepted. The majority of narratives introduced here and encountered during fieldwork contained negative presentations of life before migration, with the move being perceived as a "new start" in the sense of "re-negotiation of the work-life balance, quality of life, and freedom from prior constraints" (Benson and O'Reilly 2009a: 609). Many represent their relocation as the result of an acute sense of crisis about their high-pressured previous work and the need to achieve change by taking control over their lives, which had been regulated to a large degree by their previous employers. Yet, after their relocation, many of my respondents continue to face professional and personal difficulties, feelings of liminality and insecurity; nevertheless, most say that they are altogether satisfied and do not regret the move.

The trajectories discussed in this section suggest that rather than being a form of mobile escapism, lifestyle migrants in post-growth Japan tend to balance the quest for a personally gratifying lifestyle with the strategic pursuit of their professional careers in unconventional ways; hence, migrants only partly fall into the category of utopian lifestyle migrants (ULMs) as defined by H. M. Zunino (Zunino, Hidalgo, and Zebryte 2014: 96–107), that is, mobile individuals who aim to invent, create, and reproduce "styles of life" that escape the conventional norms framing late capitalist societies. In the case of Japan, individuals dismiss the paradigm of economic growth and material affluence, yet few of them drop out of the capitalist society altogether—their activities could perhaps be more adequately described as a balancing act between the pursuit of their values while finding a niche approach to make a livelihood, in some cases deftly selling this as a career move and others as a societal contribution.

In this chapter and throughout this monograph, I argue that rather than the black-and-white clear-cut departure of ULMs, migrants' trajectories and narratives from sites across post-growth Japan are gray and fuzzy. For example, a lifestyle migrant in his early thirties from Tokyo, who had lived in Kyoto before the Great East Japan Earthquake occurred in March 2011, moved to Ishinomaki in Miyagi Prefecture in spring 2011 to help as a disaster volunteer initially but then remained there. He eventually started his own shop. Despite his close relations with a wide community, both local and nonlocal, he laughs when I ask him what he likes about the place, chuckling that it is the mixture of arbitrariness (*iikagensa*) and a relaxed pace of life that characterizes small towns like this. This remark suggests that even if migrants live in a place for several years, they continue to perceive it with a sense of distance and objectivity, that is, with nonlocal eyes. I argue that just like a sense of liminality, this paradoxical condition does not have to be negative but should be interpreted as having great potential of bringing in a novel and constructive perspective to local communities for change in the medium and long term.

Search and Assemblage

Narratives also suggest that rather than an act, "lifestyle migration is thus a search, a project," with an open-ended destination that is intricately related with individual priorities, visions, and drives (Benson and O'Reilly 2009a: 610) that are not necessarily consistent throughout the migratory process. As has become evident in the vignettes discussed in this chapter, some migrants started out with a slow-paced lifestyle after their relocation to find themselves becoming increasingly busy to the extent that they eventually work more than in their previous urban lifestyles due to their high identification with their self-created work. Some have thus shifted from a slow-paced lifestyle associated with the "rural idyll" to a more "urban" routine that consists to a large degree with work, just like in the city prior to the move. Some are playing with the idea of going freelance in the countryside but find themselves trapped in safe though constraining municipal employment that is different from the work they engaged in previously—still far from the dream they initially had prior to their relocation. Put differently, individual lifestyles constitute "assemblages," as defined by Elliott and Urry, in a Deleuzian manner, that is, "relational complexes that continually oscillate in their fusing of properties or identities of the component elements of systems, and thus can be cast as an emergent actualization moving through space-time and concretized in historically specific processes" (2010: 14). In a similar vein, narratives introduced throughout this monograph show the coexistence of a diversity of time and space modalities and identities that very much confirms the strong presence of assemblage in migrants' lived experiences.

The view of the migratory process as a search is based on a poststructuralist interpretation of identity; rather than the view that individuals are born with a more or less permanent sense of identity and self, I refer to the notion of "doing identity" (rather than merely "being") (Widdicombe 1998), that is, individuals actively positioning themselves and shaping their identity in accordance with their respective needs, which evidently implies a high degree of individual agency and, as a result, change. This view essentially draws on Bauman's description of identity as "bio-degradable plastic" continually under reconstruction and redefinition (1996: 18) and Elliott and Urry's concept of "portable personhood" (2010: 3), with mobility serving as a strategic means of pursuing these malleable selves. Nevertheless, as this section has revealed, elements of agency and constraint, hope and moratorium, intention and serendipity, contentment and despair can be gleaned from the trajectories of individualized mobility discussed earlier; migrants simultaneously shape their lives and are being shaped by their circumstances.

Chapter Two

The Countryside between Aging, Lack of Perspectives, and Creative Depopulation through the Lens of Female Settlers

This chapter examines changing roles of rural areas through the lens of female settlers who have relocated to rural areas across Japan. Starting out with further theoretical reflections on the variety of meanings attributed to "the rural" as a "category of thought" (Mormont 1990: 40), this chapter is concerned with disentangling the production and reproduction of the "rural" as an idea in individual narratives and focus on the aspect of gender, that is, "culturally-mediated expectations and roles associated with masculinity and femininity" (Lips 2014: 2). Evidently, most settlers have never heard of recent terms such as "radical rural spatiality" (Halfacree 2007), "creative depopulation" (Ōminami in Matsunaga 2015), downshifting, "small-scale happiness" (Furuichi 2011); yet an increasing interest in flexible modes of working and living such as, for example, Baumanesque notions of "living in a manner that involves living for oneself" (Nishimura 2009) and "a lifestyle that does not opt for employment" (Mori 2011) are salient in many vignettes.

The emergence of such terminology shows the ongoing shift from a negative perception of rural areas as backwaters of civilization to fields of experimentation and pioneering grounds for diverse lifestyles. This section critically discusses the shift in the Japanese discourse from the countryside as a "repository of Japan's distinctive cultural heritage" (Schnell 2005: 212) to more diverse perceptions of rural areas, with urban-rural linkages as the key to recent attempts to pursue more sustainable lifestyles. While the demographic statistics suggest that it is impossible to stop the trend of depopulation as such, some "hamlets at the margin" (*genkai shūraku*, coined by sociologist Ōno Akira in the 1990s) have made efforts to buck the trend by introducing measures to attract highly qualified individuals.

This chapter aims to outline the heterogeneity of societal representations of the countryside in Japan beyond the threefold narrative on the rural as "pre-modernity," "productivist," and "rural renaissance" (da Silva et al. 2016: 79), introducing a fourth narrative in the Japanese discourse, that is, rurality as experimental ground for pioneers. Narratives will also show, however, that the true heterogeneity of rural regions (Marsden 1999: 505) and the dispositional heterogeneity of our thinking (Bell 2007: 410) have mixed up "the rural" since rurality is perceived as "a problem, a resource, a region of growth and a victim" all at once (Nilsson and Lundgren 2015: 88–91, cited in Kuhmonen, Kuhmonen, and Luoto 2016: 89). The second part of this chapter discusses aspects of gender as they emerge from the narratives of female migrants.

The coexistence of these diverse associations of the countryside is particularly evident in the narratives of female lifestyle migrants. In their twenties and thirties, many migrants possess degrees from top universities in the Tokyo area and some have experience living and working abroad. Some have moved to rural areas because they married locals; others have come by chance and have chosen to pursue their own careers. Yet others find themselves in their late thirties, doing odd jobs to make ends meet, with no relationship and no time to reflect on what they actually want from life. Female trajectories and narratives highlight the continuing challenges women face in Japan in bringing together career and family, quite a contrast to Prime Minister Abe's declaration that he intends to create a society in which "all women can shine" and his government's announcement of a series of measures to support career women.

Furthermore, the narratives of some young female lifestyle migrants show the ingrained structures of female roles as supportive of their husbands rather than initiating their own enterprises. I interviewed female neophytes who were in the process of establishing their own businesses, but those were in the absolute minority and often had a background of living abroad or attending a university associated with international education. In this chapter I discuss five cases of women mostly from Tokyo to show the diverse and changing functions of rural areas in individual careers and lives. I finish with a dissection of how these cases can be interpreted in terms of gender roles.

Making Moves on Local Fishermen

Twenty-five years old, Eri attended a well-known private university in Tokyo to study sociology. Wearing handmade earrings and with a husky voice, Eri had an optimism about making a difference in the world that seemed unbridled. Her university provided funds to take a year off during her studies to support communities in remote rural areas. In her second year of study, she thus took the opportunity to live on the Karakuwa Peninsula in Tohoku for the whole year, engaging in activities to support the stagnating fishing industry. Until then, Eri had spent all of her life in the Japanese capital and remembers feeling jealous when her peers at school talked about going to see their grandparents somewhere in the countryside in the summer holidays since all her relatives were based in Tokyo, so she never had a change to visit the countryside.

Since the Karakuwa Peninsula is a remote area that hardly has visitors from outside, Eri indicates that it was challenging at first to get accepted by the locals; however, after a while, residents became incredibly warm and supportive. She hardly used any of her university funding since she did a homestay with a local family, eating out was not an option on the peninsula, and locals were constantly concerned whether she ate enough. Eri eventually returned to Tokyo to continue her studies. However, she felt that she wanted to go back to the peninsula as soon as possible. First of all, due to her one year off (and later graduation), she had the chance to observe her university peers find jobs in Tokyo that seemed unfulfilling. This is why after her graduation, instead of seeking a conventional job in a company (as her parents and many others advised her to do), she decided to come back to Karakuwa Peninsula and engage in some work that helped to support the local community, rather than doing some work in Tokyo where she would not see the effect of her work on others.

Another reason why she felt the urge to start working in Tohoku right away after her graduation was the fact that the restoration progress was ongoing after the 2011 Great East Japan Earthquake and she got the impression that the timing was right for making a change locally. She started working in a nongovernmental organization founded by a peer from West Japan that seeks to contribute to regional revitalization.

The organization has recently established a homepage for potentially interested migrants seeking to relocate to the area, with information on available housing, jobs, and the like. Eri has been fascinated with the local fishing industry and organizes tours for nonlocals to experience fishing firsthand, encounter the lifestyle of fishermen, and hear about their issues. She laughs, saying that she has been saying for three years now that she would like to get married to a local fisherman. Rather than working in fishing herself, however, she argues that she is interested in "providing support for people taking on challenges" (interview on 4 August 2017). One could argue that supporting others provides great satisfaction in itself, but one could also interpret this as an ingrained pattern of behavior in women, whose societal role in traditional Japan has been to step back, keep in the background, and make sure everything goes smoothly in the domestic arena, in other words, assume the role of *ryōsai kenbō* (good wife, wise mother).

She observes with a chuckle that she loves the company of *jiichan baachan* (an endearment for elderly people in Japanese) since they have experienced so much in their long lives and possess valuable knowledge of local traditions. Eri regularly posts images of her senior local friends on Instagram, explaining briefly about their daily activities on the peninsula.

Although she also has nonlocal friends, she indicates that about 90 percent of her friends are local senior citizens. Eri says she is 100 percent satisfied with her life on the peninsula, and as she feels her work is fulfilling and every day brings new surprises and opportunities to learn and grow as a person and professional, she does not have any complaints about rural life. She adds that the demographic decline in rural areas has resulted in many issues that need to be addressed urgently and she feels that she is making a difference through her work. She also indicates that she thinks that she has improved her social skills because she needs to communicate with fishermen, convincing them to cooperate with her for various activities. Asked what her special skill is, she laughs saying, "making moves on local fishermen" (*ryōshi san wo kudoku skill ka na*) (interview on 4 August 2017).

When living in Tokyo, she spent more money on buying clothes since she grew up in an environment of material affluence; now she hardly buys commodities and rarely feels the urge for things, which means it is much easier to save money. Before, she was eating out a lot and did not care very much about what she was eating; now most of the vegetables she eats are from friends and neighbors. Eri points out that entertainment is quite different in rural areas, with more outdoor activities. She hardly watches television anymore since her relocation and says that she hardly has free time because she engages in many activities, for example, regular *taiko* drumming practice for a local festival and social events related to this. She talks about the pleasure she derives from "seeking new things" rather than the mind-set urbanites often have about the countryside "not offering anything."

Presently, she lives in collective housing with two other lifestyle migrants, one of whom she also works with in Kesennuma. At the back of the house there is a small field for growing vegetables. At night, they can hear the sounds of squeaking frogs, and they also have a view of the sea. Elements of the sharing economy pervade her daily life as each cohabitant leaves leftovers from cooked meals in the fridge for others who may need them. They rarely eat together since they are all busy at work, with other meetings, and they spend little time in the house. Ultimately, Eri's long-term aim is to contribute to a different perception of the countryside as a place of opportunity and challenge. She hopes to bring about change both in locals as well as urbanites and thus contribute to a more evenly balanced demographic distribution between urban and rural areas. Eri says that she and her peers aspire to turn the Karakuwa Peninsula into a successful model for tackling the depopulation issue by making it a viable region, although she concedes that she is not sure whether she can achieve this during her lifetime (interview on 4 August 2017). According to Eri, many local youth leave Kesennuma and environs after graduating from high school to pursue university education or attend vocational school. They tend to remain there and continue working. Eri hopes to contribute to a gradual change of local youth, who often take it for granted that their home region does not offer opportunities for work, by bringing together local companies seeking employees and local youth (who have moved elsewhere).

As a Tokyoite, she says that Tokyo is not necessarily the wonderful place rural residents tend to think it is. Furthermore, she gets the impression that, these days, people at the vanguard actually move to rural areas. She aims to share the fascination and fulfillment of engaging in some work that can only be done here. Eri shares her sense of satisfaction that, recently, she brought local high school students and nonlocal settlers together for a discussion about the positive points of the region. Despite her great satisfaction with her job and life right now, Eri says that local residents often ask her how long she plans to stay. "Isn't that a kind of heavy question? I don't have a fiancé here or something so I usually say that I am probably going to be around for two to three years, but I really don't know" (interview on 4 August 2017). As Eri's work contract is also for a duration of three years, her response that some may perceive as uncommitted, others as pragmatic, makes sense. It also represents the mentality of many nonlocal settlers who are seeking professional and personal fulfillment, yet also face precarity and lack of a long-term prospect in professional terms. Nevertheless, she explains that her sense of satisfaction about making a small societal contribution through her work and dealing with new challenges every day outweighs her sense of insecurity about her future. "I feel a sense of satisfaction, and I can keep on learning as every day brings new tasks. I am not sure whether one can say that, but I feel that dealing with issues such as depopulation and aging is very instructive." Even on weekends, she hardly has a free moment as there are all kinds of events taking place. Yet, she argues that she is 100 percent satisfied with her life and work at present and does not regret having relocated to a rural area rather than seeking a corporate job in Tokyo. Eri's narrative gives us pivotal insights into the routine and values of aspiring youth in post-growth Japan who seek out ways of carving their own career paths that make sense to them personally. Eri presents her life in exceedingly positive terms, yet one could also perceive her present state of sharing a house with cohabitants she hardly meets, not being in a relationship but aspiring to marry a local fisherman, and having a limited contract as being very close to what Bloch referred to the "ontology of Not Yet Being" (1986: 11). Finally, Eri's vignette and her statements also suggest that regardless of university education, young women in contemporary Japan continue to endorse prescriptive gender roles by co-opting into the androcentric societal system even if they aspire to pursuing independent career objectives.

"I am not yet sure what I can do here.
Right now, I am just supporting my husband
at his work, but I hope that I can eventually
express myself through this."

Originally from Hitachi City in Ibaragi Prefecture, Keiko moved to Ishinomaki after marrying a local last year. She had previously worked there as a volunteer after the Great East Japan Earthquake and had enjoyed living in Ishinomaki so much that she had in fact hoped to come back. She remembers that when she came to Ishinomaki for the first time, she felt that it was easy to blend in as many aspects of this port town resembled Hitachi City, where she had grown up. I met her for the first time during work, in fact, her husband has a small outdoor stall in downtown Ishinomaki where I have dinner with friends. Keiko is taking the orders and asks me for help as an interpreter when an African guy arrives with no Japanese-language skills. She may look just like any other friendly waitress at first sight, but in fact she has a degree in sociology from a top university in Tokyo. Keiko thought for a long time that she would pursue a corporate career just like her father who works in a big company. However, the Great East Japan Earthquake in March 2011 occurred when she was in her third year at university, the time when students usually start their job search. After careful consideration, she decided not to engage in job-hunting activities in her third year at university as she was certain she would have regrets if she started working right after graduation from university. Instead, she took a year off and worked as a volunteer in Tohoku. Eventually, she started working for a Tokyo-based company in the field of revitalization (*machizukuri*) for one year; the project she was in charge of focused on children's education.

Looking back, she laughs that working in a bank would certainly be more financially stable, but she is sure that she would not have been happy in that kind of job because she does not like the idea of following instructions in a large organization from morning to evening. Whereas her present work at her husband's food stall is physically demanding and the pay is low, their dream is to reopen the boardinghouse of her husband's family that was destroyed in the tsunami in 2011. Keiko hopes to make use of her educational skills by establishing a boardinghouse that offers a facility for children so that young parents can take some time off. Many hotels in Japan do not accept families with babies and infants, and so far, there have not been any with special services for parents. Despite having this interesting idea, she argues that she does not have a grand vision and rather thinks that it is important "to laugh and enjoy living" (interview on 9 August 2017). She argues that during her time as a disaster volunteer in Tohoku, she acquired this positive mind-set in any circumstance—even if one faces challenges in one's environment.

As for her present work, she says that her previous work experience was in revitalization and education; the common element between her previous and present work is the close relation with people, which she enjoys. However, right now, her position is mostly about supporting her husband; she describes herself as "riding on the back of her husband" and indicates that she cannot see yet quite how she can use her previous skills in her new environment. While she is making utmost efforts to support her husband and describes her sense of fulfillment when she sees how some regular customers leave with happy faces after eating at their stall, she indicates that personally she feels that something creative is missing in the work (interview on 9 August 2017). She also adds that she does not feel intellectually challenged in her daily job as a waitress.

Keiko is only in her late twenties, comes from an urban background, and has an elite education and working experience in Tokyo. The way she makes fun of her husband's way of inviting her before they started a relationship to go looking for mountain vegetables rather than inviting her for dinner (as would be the norm) indicates her urban expectations and illustrates that she is clearly a member of "translocal elites," adapting Sassen's "transnational elites" (2007).

Nevertheless, her narrative suggests that female attitudes toward professional careers may have changed less compared to postwar Japan than we tend to assume. True, Keiko grew up in a household with a mother who was a full-time housewife and a father who was a corporate warrior in the classic sense. But she also has work experience in Tokyo and plenty of other experiences as a long-term volunteer in Tohoku. Placing herself and her ambitions back, trying to find ways of using her professional skills at her husband's workplace, may be admirable values and virtues, but they also mean that valuable human skills are not put to full use. Keiko's narrative confirms ingrained structures of female behavioral patterns that ultimately reproduce gender hierarchies and put female professional careers on hold for an unspecified period of time.

"This may look like an awful environment at first sight, but I can live quite happily even here!"

Aya and I are sitting on a wooden terrace surrounded by containers and makeshift furniture, with a washing machine outside (see figure 2.1). At first sight, this may be a landscape that few would associate with rural Japan. When I say that the coffee we are drinking tastes fantastic, Aya smiles, joking that she appreciates high-quality coffee, quite different from what first-time visitors may think about her (interview on 2 August 2017).

In her late thirties, I have known Aya for seven years, since her days as a disaster volunteer in Ishinomaki. Bubbly, outgoing, and brimming with curiosity, entrepreneurial spirit, and the drive to make a difference, she is originally from Shikoku in central Japan but attended a top university in Tokyo. After working in a well-known advertising company for over ten years, she decided to go freelance. When the Great East Japan Earthquake occurred, she went to Tohoku as early as in late March to see with her own eyes how she could help. Aya continued to commute regularly on weekends to Tohoku while working as a freelancer in Tokyo. Initially, she had planned to be in Tohoku only for a few days, but when she saw the extent of the disaster, she felt that she needed to go regularly to extend her support to the area. In retrospect, she estimates that she moved between Tokyo and Ishinomaki more than one hundred times in one year. At one point, she was leading a lifestyle based from residences in Tokyo, Sendai, and Ishinomaki. She says that she used up all of her savings of 150 million JPY from her well-paid work in the advertising industry in the process.

Figure 2.1. View of containers and washing machine, Ishinomaki, Miyagi Prefecture.

It may strike some readers as surprising that someone like Aya, who could have remained in her well-paid job in an elite company and lead a comfortable, if predictable and stressful, urban life, has chosen to live a lifestyle that some would perceive as insecure, precarious, and fluid. After all, the reality is that Aya is presently living in a container that she bought secondhand from China, although she adds that this is just a temporary solution because she has taken a loan and is in the crucial phase of getting her business on track. Until recently, she was living in collective housing. Legally speaking, living in a container is not permitted, but with a staff of five for her small business, she points out that she does not have another choice. Somewhat hesitantly, she shows me the space where she presently sleeps—hot, full of clutter, with low ceilings. She jokes that these are conditions worse than the ones faced by some victims in the wake of the triple disaster in 2011.

Despite these living conditions, Aya seems to enjoy the challenge of mastering DIY techniques she was not familiar with previously. Creating a space with a limited budget, taking on the challenge of making things, is what she has recently been enthusiastic about. Despite her sense of shame about her present living condition, Aya exudes a sense of vibrant energy, a quest for adventure, and vitality that comes with starting something new.

She laughs, saying that until now, she has hardly used a public bus for transport, but now, she occasionally uses it because she does not have a driver's license and the site is not in central Ishinomaki, but in Watanoha, an area that was badly struck by the tsunami due to its closeness to the sea. Yet, talking to Aya, her enthusiasm and drive to make a difference in society is evident. She describes her present project of providing a site for a participatory restaurant, that is, a place where customers do not only consume prepared food but also participate actively in preparing the food. However, the details and logistics are still a work-in-progress, as is the material site. She also discusses the different ideas her project staff (all of them locals) hold about what good food should taste like. In order to solve these existing differences, Aya aims to provide food with individuals having the option to adapt the taste in accordance with their preferences, hence the idea of the participatory restaurant.

Before, Aya had run a restaurant on the first floor of the municipal office in downtown Ishinomaki catering to disaster volunteers for four years; at the time, the staff was divided into locals and other (former) disaster volunteers. Some of her present staff are single mothers, so Aya has a keen interest in turning the project into a success and making them earn their own livelihoods. While Aya says that the project is not a social entrepreneur project, her support of single mothers through her business strongly indicates that there are distinct aspects of societal contribution. What she hopes to provide to her staff in this small-scale enterprise is the chance to live a viable life while earning a decent salary. She thinks that as long as one is healthy, earning money is not a big challenge, but what is difficult is establishing a working environment that is worthwhile where employees are not exploited in the process (interview on 2 August 2017).

At some point in the interview, she mentions somewhat defensively that she has chosen to live a relaxed lifestyle (*nobi nobi*) after quitting her fast-paced job in Tokyo and has missed the chance to get married. Her longtime boyfriend in Tokyo eventually confronted her with the choice of either choosing him (and their relationship) and coming back to Tokyo or remaining in Ishinomaki. Needless to say, she chose the latter and they split up recently. In other words, in Aya's case, her strong interest in supporting single mothers and other local residents in making a viable livelihood has gone side by side with a neglect of her private life. This is also the reason why she hopes to lead a lifestyle based between Ishinomaki and Tokyo because she feels she cannot find an appropriate partner in Ishinomaki. Aya's story highlights the enormous struggle individuals face in bringing together professional fulfillment, local integration, and private happiness. Ultimately, as Aya's living circumstances and her neglected private life illustrate, her own well-being tends to come last on her long list of priorities. Whereas she talks about her aspiration to dedicate more time and energy to her own well-being and private life, the reality is that it will take several years for her emerging business to take off and stabilize, during which it seems difficult for her to get to Tokyo and find a partner. Aya's case highlights the challenges female entrepreneurs face and their liminal position both in the local community as well as back in Tokyo. Despite all the issues, Aya does not seem to have regrets for having chosen the life she has; rather, she seems so busy in making it all happen that she hardly has time to step back and reflect on her life. She seems to thoroughly enjoy the challenges she has set for herself: mastering new skills required for this enterprise such as DIY skills, communicating with a new genre of people, mostly craftsmen at the construction site.

But she concedes that after having worked in a well-known company for more than ten years, she prefers to work in a less stressful way and have more time to herself. Ironically, her present mode of working and living may be even more exhausting than her job in a "traditional company": the mental stress of establishing one's own business and making it run successfully, the financial burden and risk involved in this, the huge toll on one's private life and health. Yet, many individuals who share Aya's drive and entrepreneurial spirit talk about the vigor and energy they derive despite all the stress involved. Aya observes that a few years ago, this kind of entrepreneurial spirit was not as prevalent as it is now. She ultimately wants to live a free life while helping others to achieve this kind of free life themselves, even if this takes time and effort. What drives her is the experience of bringing together the interests of diverse actors and creating something beneficial for everyone involved; Aya indicates that there is something about Ishinomaki that makes this kind of rare experience with heterogeneous actors doing something together for mutual benefit possible. In sum, Aya's chaotic-creative container space can be interpreted as a "space of hope" (Harvey 2000); she talks about her aspirations of making a success of her business yet also broaches her precarious financial (and emotional) situation. Her trajectory contains "the romanticism of endlessly open projects" that go on and on (Harvey 2000: 174), with all the devastating implications this condition has for her private life.

"The five hours when my son is in kindergarten is my fighting time at work."

Born in Tokyo in 1979, Rika belongs to a generation of polyglot Japanese who have spent the formative years of their childhood abroad and for whom switching from one culture and language to another seems nothing special. Having been born in Detroit and attending primary school and the first half of high school in the United States, Rika studied in Tokyo and worked in France for one year. Rika effortlessly switches from Japanese into English during our interview, talking about her transnational life feeling so natural to her, "Like you and me, it's natural for us to move around, we don't really think about crossing borders, it's just in our blood I guess" (interview on 4 August 2017). Rika writes in both English and Japanese on social media and presents herself as feeling "American" in a recent entry when she describes her feelings when returning for a visit to the United States. Rika worked for one year in France after dropping out from an elite university in Tokyo. Her comprehensive global living and working experience makes her a member of the emerging generation of Japanese with an external view of Japan. This is evident from the harsh criticism she directs at the way Japanese women put themselves down in order to support their husbands: "Women in Kesennuma are very strong and they are really good at concealing their own nails and doing their best to make their husbands earn the money." Rika explicitly states that in contrast to local women, she herself aims to set up a business that helps local women to get the training necessary for "bringing home their own bacon" rather than just earning an additional income (interview on 4 August 2017). Her business philosophy seems to combine American pragmatism and fighting spirit with an urban sense of business that aims for global rather than local success. She observes that presently she disseminates information about her business only on Facebook, mostly in English. This is why she has received no attention from local media but has been featured by NHK World (the national television program in English). She intends to start internet sales in the near future.

Like Keiko, she married a local; her marriage formed the basis for her need to create some livelihood for herself because the opportunities for work are limited in Kesennuma. However, unlike Keiko, Rika describes her strong incentive to start her own business rather than supporting her husband; she talks about the importance she attaches to "bringing home her own bacon" rather than earning an additional income as a part-timer, as is so often the case with Japanese mothers (interview on 4 August 2017). It is evident throughout our conversation that Rika's mentality is more American than Japanese. She does not beat around the bush with her critique of the inherent exploitation of women in everyday life in the rural town she has moved to. She also criticizes the local government, who keeps women from reentering the workforce after giving birth because the kindergarten fee for infants in their younger years (before age four) is much higher. Evidently, this policy works as a strong incentive for women to stay in the house and look after their children rather than return to work. Rika explains that her urban upbringing has made her take for granted having a variety of choices, something that seems not available to women in rural Kesennuma. "I know I am asking for much [wagamama], but I would like to have choices," she laughs (interview on 4 August 2017).

She points out that her husband spent eight years in Tokyo studying and fully supports her entrepreneurial efforts by doing half of the domestic work, quite rare in Japanese households. "I think I am quite blessed here," she smiles happily. Another positive aspect she describes is the fact that back in Tokyo, she used to deal mostly with people who shared her values, regardless of work or leisure. In Kesennuma, she has encountered a wide variety of people of diverse backgrounds and income levels, something that has considerably broadened her perspective and social skills. "Whether I can be successful in this rural town depends on whether I can receive support from its residents, so it's all about how one relates to locals that counts. Back in Tokyo it was more about accessing the right information to know how you can solve a problem" (interview on 4 August 2018).

Rika is in the midst of setting up an indigo textile business, although she does not have any background in indigo dying. The idea is to train local women who have limited time in a craft that secures a reliable income for them so that they can be more independent from their husbands. Implicitly, Rika's enterprise aims to break up the traditional family structure centered on the male breadwinner with all its social implications, such as the dominance of men in public life and the supplementary role of women that shores up male dominance. She is presently trying to organize funds for this project and for restoring a more than one-hundred-year-old house in central Kesennuma where she has opened her office. The customers she is targeting in the project are located in the United States and urban Japan because the prices of hand-dyed indigo textiles are high—out of reach for most residents in her rural vicinity. Rika's narrative provides valuable insights into emerging entrepreneurs with a powerful transnational background. Through their upbringing and high professional mobility, these highly skilled individuals access "global cultural capital" (Kim 2011) that affords them independence from institutional constraints at the national level.

Life at the Limits

With curly long hair hidden beneath a beret and a pale complexion, Maki is in her late thirties and originally from a midsized town in Hokkaido. She came to Ishinomaki as a disaster volunteer soon after the Great East Japan Earthquake and has remained in Tohoku ever since. When I interviewed her in August 2013, she was uncertain how long she would stay, saying that it all depended on whether she would meet someone appropriate. She commented that she is not the kind of person who can work independently; rather, she is happy following instructions from someone else. Initially, after graduating from high school, she intended to work in a local shrine as a shrine maiden but dropped out because she felt that it was not the kind of job she had envisaged, and she faced difficult social relations at work. After that, she engaged in various forms of work across Japan, mostly in the resort hotel industry as reception staff. In retrospect, this seems ironic as she herself observes that she does not feel comfortable dealing with people. Yet she still works as a waitress in various bars and restaurants in Ishinomaki. "I already feel the limits of my physical capabilities. I feel that this place here is not the place for me to settle down and I have to go on fighting every day without ever getting a rest. So I really need to go somewhere else to relax but I am too busy for that. Before I was fine sleeping only three hours, now I need six hours at least. I was assuming that I could go on with this kind of life forever, but it seems difficult with my increasing age" (interview on 9 August 2017). On the one hand, Maki repeatedly states that she does not feel that Ishinomaki is a place for long-term residence for her; but then, when we met three years ago, she was saying the same thing and still lives there. At the same time, she remarks that, perhaps, Ishinomaki is the best place for her after all while saying that she hopes to find a place that really offers her a sense of belonging. I ask her whether she considers herself an *ijūsha*, that is, a migrant from some other place. She nods, saying that she is definitely not seen as a local and would not remain in Ishinomaki if it were not for her work.

Just like three years ago, Maki works in a textile design shop owned by a fellow former disaster volunteer from Tokyo six days a week. She makes objects that will later be sold in the shop in accordance with the instructions of the shop owner. Recently, she has also started supervising a new staff member in order to pass on her own knowledge in case she becomes sick or has to leave (interview on 9 August 2017). In addition, she works in a restaurant owned by another former disaster volunteer from Tokyo three times a week in the evening, as well as working in another bar. In other words, she is juggling three different jobs during the day and at night to make ends meet. It is not surprising that she feels permanently exhausted and looks older than her age. Maki adds that her neighbors and acquaintances are concerned about her physical and mental well-being. She sighs that nothing has changed compared to the last time we met; she is doing nothing but work and has no time for anything else. She mentions that as an exception, last Sunday she took a day off and enjoyed seeing art works on display at the Reborn Art Festival around Ishinomaki with a friend. She adds that she does not remember when she last took a day off because she feels the pressure to keep on working to pay her bills. She has never taken an extended holiday in her entire life.

Yet she comments, "I really need to make sure I get some time for myself as I need to think about my future. There are some things I would like to do, such as get the license as a cook, but at present I am too tired to do this. Doing the work I do right now is fine, but I cannot do it forever as I get older and my physical capabilities decrease" (interview on 9 August 2017). Maki's narrative highlights the precarious conditions of some individuals who have chosen to relocate to rural areas: low pay in jobs that offer few opportunities for professional development, hardly any free time apart from work, and limited social relations due to the heavy focus on work. Maki indicates that she has never met locals who engage in various jobs at the same time, only new settlers. This remark emphasizes the considerable precariousness settlers are exposed to on the labor market, especially individuals with no expert skills. Furthermore, Maki's remarks about her need to acquire more specialist knowledge highlight the fact that women are particularly vulnerable on the labor market with increasing age: positions for waitresses and generally in the service industry are usually for females in their teens, twenties, and thirties, seldom for older women. This is also why she feels that she needs to acquire additional skills. Furthermore, Maki argues that she does not have a partner, is not married at present, and does not expect to get married in the future, although she would like to if there is a chance. Her status as single in a country that prescribes marriage as a precondition to be acknowledged as a full-fledged and respectable member of society implies a vulnerability beyond her economic precariousness.

Her case also illustrates her ongoing search for belonging inherent in many narratives of settlers and the lack of planning with regard to her life course. She shakes her head, saying that she has become spoiled experiencing life and work at various places across Japan. Maki feels the need for change, yet she does not seem able to get out of her routine because she is too busy making ends meet and has no time for reflection and rest. She concedes that part of the issue is that she finds it difficult to decline any work offers. She lives only thirty seconds walk from the restaurant where she works and all her other places of work are within walking distance, something that is convenient but also means that mentally it is difficult to get a rest from work. Her present flat came with a refrigerator and washing machine and the rent is only 30,000 JPY, very cheap for central Ishinomaki. She adds nonchalantly that if the flat had not come with the fridge and washing machine, she would have had to live without these utilities because she does not have the money or time to buy them.

As for her eating habits, she says that she used to eat more home-made food. Now, she is too busy to cook for herself and lives on leftovers she gets after work at the restaurant, food she receives from friends and neighbors, or snacks she buys from shops nearby. She explains that since she needs to keep working without taking a rest, she is permanently tired and often suffers from stomach problems, especially when it is hot and humid. Maki's narrative is evidently multilayered, as are most other narratives. On the one hand, her trajectory could be perceived as emancipatory in the sense that she implemented her choice to move away from her native Hokkaido, giving up a job that she did not feel comfortable about. On the other hand, Maki's narrative seems to be full of what Berlant refers to as "cruel optimism" (2011), that is, individuals' fantasies about realizing "the good life" in the neoliberal context of individual responsibility and achievement. In other words, hope that seems to be on the horizon, yet ever unreachable, coexists with lingering precariousness and self-exhaustion. As for gender, like other interlocutors introduced in this chapter, Maki also describes herself as someone who is made to support and take instructions from someone else. She also indicated that she seeks a partner, yet she still lives as single. Economic precarity concurs with emotional fragility in a society that tends to prescribe marriage and family as an ontological legitimation for women.

Furthermore, Maki's case suggests that physical mobility can go hand in hand with emotional stasis. Movement has been generally perceived as something positive and dynamic to the point of being "fetishized" (Baker 2016: 155), although the weakening of social structures has been observed (Bauman 2000). Yet, little attention usually goes to the inherent sense of exhaustion, the lack of direction, and the gap between aspirations to freedom and harsh reality while being on the move.

In sum, Maki may be seen as the quintessential neoliberal subject who has been permanently on the move in emotional terms as she has felt the need to find a sense of belonging, yet she has not seemed to find it. Nor does she seem to know what she is actually looking for. Maki's story is perhaps more a story about what she does not want: she makes it clear that she does not intend to move back to Hokkaido because there is no work for her there, and she seems positive that she cannot find a sense of belonging there, having only thin emotional ties with her family. Maki's narrative is characterized by a sense of resignation, permanent exhaustion both physically and mentally, and the lingering hope that, someday, things will improve. Yet, she seems too busy to make the changes necessary to achieve this improvement. In some way, Maki could be taken to stand for youth in post-growth Japan—having experienced various places and forms of work yet finding it difficult to pinpoint what they want in life, they opt for small jobs that keep them going financially but do not offer any long-term prospects. Many of these individuals do not have the time or interest to engage socially, start relationships, or get married. In some way, individuals like Maki seem to be opting out from society in small steps: cutting down on their material interests due to their financial issues, having limited social relationships because of their focus on work, which is mostly low-paid. In other words, they find themselves in a vicious cycle that keeps them from making any changes to their deeply unsatisfying situation of living and working.

In this chapter I have discussed five cases of female migrants from diverse social backgrounds in their twenties and thirties. Two of them, Keiko and Rika, have moved because they married a local; Eri talks about her wish to get married to a local fisherman. Aya and Maki, both in their late thirties, are not in relationships and seem very much absorbed in their work. What do these narratives tell us about the changing role of rural areas in Japan? First of all, for the two women who moved to the countryside for reasons of marriage, the rural constitutes an opportunity for entrepreneurship. Evidently, Keiko is not planning to start anything by herself, but she has worked in Tohoku before her marriage and has made a conscious decision not to opt for corporate employment in Tokyo. The same holds true for Eri, who could have returned to her hometown Tokyo and joined the corporate sector. Rika and Aya are both in their late thirties and have experience in corporate employment. Both refer to their confidence in making money since they know "how the market works" (interviews on 2 and 4 August 2017, respectively). Both women "use" the rural as an experimental ground to create their own businesses. Aya has a global vision and does not target local customers; Rika works closely with the local community, which can be assumed to result from her many years of living in the place where she is setting up her business now. However, Rika also talks about her dream of living a lifestyle based in two locations at some point so that she can spend time in Tokyo as well to dedicate more time to her private life.

Maki adds yet another angle: in her case, the rural could be seen as a temporary workplace, a place that "she has ended up at" (*nagareta*; interview on 9 August 2017). Maki has neither the knowledge nor the funding to set up an enterprise, but for her, the rural seems a place of moratorium. This sense of temporariness, fluidity, and substitution also features in other narratives, both female and male. For example, Rika remembers with a smile that she intended to stay for two days as a disaster volunteer and ended up staying for six years—a sense of serendipity that is echoed in many other narratives.

The tendency of individuals regardless of their age to opt for careers outside of the (urban) corporate sector suggests the decreasing attractiveness of conventional corporate work. Many individuals describe the sense of satisfaction they derive from engaging in work that allows for more self-determination and closer contact with the people they work for. Eri contrasts her own sense of fulfillment about engaging in work that aims to contribute to the solution of societal issues such as depopulation and aging in rural areas with the work experience of her former senior peers at university, the majority of whom seemed unsatisfied with their work in companies. Keiko's narrative closely resembles Eri's as she explains her reasons for deciding to work for an NGO rather than corporate work like her father. Interestingly, Aya depicts the ambivalent reactions to her move to a rural town in Tohoku on social media, implying that many of her former urbanite acquaintances are wondering why she would choose an unknown rural town. But then, she continues, she herself shared exactly this mind-set some ten years ago when she was working in the fast-paced advertising world in Tokyo. Now, she concedes with a chuckle that she is more interested in making a positive contribution through work at a small scale rather than working her life away in a company (*gatsu gatsu hataraku*). And she constantly seeks new challenges and the freedom to make her own decisions as an entrepreneur.

Eri, more than ten years younger than Aya, argues that in contemporary Japan, rural areas seem to attract those at the vanguard, individuals who wish to make a difference, contribute to society, and engage with locals face to face. It goes without saying that these cases constitute just a very small sample, but they indicate the continuing change of perception with regard to rural areas and their role in Japan from stagnant backwaters to experimental grounds for aspiring entrepreneurs.

Many new settlers discuss some issues they experienced when trying to blend into the local community, yet all of them describe merits of their rural life and emphasize how they have grown emotionally and how their perspectives have expanded as a result of being exposed to a broader spectrum of people in their everyday lives since their relocation. We could interpret these remarks about growing social skills as an emerging function of the rural as a "social ground," that is, a place that provides unfamiliar and inspiring perspectives to individuals who have grown weary of a faceless society that is regulated by the flow of money and social obligations. Eri talks enthusiastically about her friendship with local senior citizens; Keiko mentions her gratitude to loyal customers mostly in their fifties and sixties who come to her and her husband's stall even on rainy days. Aya's driving passion seems to start an entrepreneurial project that helps single mothers live a more viable life. Aya also speaks about how easy it is to meet locals while drinking. Since she has lived in Tohoku for six years, for her, the focus is more on how to carve out time for herself as she has a wide network of (local) acquaintances. Most narratives make the thorough engagement of female settlers with local residents evident and illustrate their respective growth as a result of this exposure. Eri mentions how her communication skills have evolved as a result of the need to persuade fishermen of the validity of her project in order to ensure their cooperation. Rika describes the need for her business project to obtain the support of locals as a precondition for success even if her target group in terms of customers is nonlocal. In Maki's case, she does mention the concern of her neighbors and acquaintances about her self-exploitative mode of working, yet overall she seems too busy in her work to engage thoroughly with local residents.

As diverse as these cases of female settlers may be, they suggest that, more often than not, women in their twenties, thirties, and forties tend to act in ways that imply an internalization of patriarchal norms and endorsement of traditional gender roles. Education does not seem to make too much of a difference here. Eri, a university graduate, talks about "making moves on local fishermen" and imagines herself in a supportive role for the future that reminds us of the "backstage self" Rosenberger depicted in her ethnography of Japanese women and the search for self in changing Japan (2001: chapter 3). Maki, a high school graduate, also wishes for a partner and describes her ideal of being in a supportive role. Keiko, a university graduate, envisages herself in a supportive role for her local husband even if she finds it intellectually unfulfilling now. The only interlocutors who act as independent female entrepreneurs are Aya and Rika, both with educational backgrounds in an international university or overseas. Nevertheless, even the narratives of these two emancipated pioneer entrepreneurs show that they are well aware of the necessity to obtain support from the local community; in other words, agency always comes with structural limits in order to be viable. These cases indicate that rather than systemic constraints of a patriarchal system constituting the main issue, for better or worse, women often co-opt ingrained patriarchal norms to pursue their aims—a strategy that is commensurate with the propagation of patriarchal values by educated women in the Edo period with the ultimate aim of resisting male domination for reasons of morality (Ambros 2015: 103). In a clearly androcentric society, contemporary women from a wide variety of backgrounds continue to navigate around patriarchal constraints, balancing their aspirations to pursue independent careers with pervasive roles of women as gentle shadows in the background and taking care of their families (if they have them) in the process. The narratives discussed in this chapter also illustrate the continuing relevance of "virtue" and external perception as a parameter in female behavior (Rosenberger 2001: 1–2). After all, interlocutors implicitly or explicitly mentioned the need to be likeable and obtain support from their in-laws, the local community, and most importantly, their husbands (if they are married). However, this sustained urge to be likeable may also be seen as a reflection of Post-Fordist forms of gender, with women being particularly vulnerable to acting as "active, but docile" subjects (McRobbie 2016: 87).

Regardless of the broad spectrum of female settlers introduced in this chapter, all of them share a distinct focus on the here and now. They all seem highly committed to the work on projects they are in charge of; however, none of them posit that they will stay in the area all of their lives, with some observing that they may move on to another place if their project does not work out, or if they get married, or if they have the opportunity to engage in a lifestyle based in two locations. Incidentally, two of the unmarried women argue that remaining in the area will depend on their meeting a partner. Whereas many female narratives indicate that the inherent co-optation of androcentric norms continues, the preceding cases also make evident the distinct departure from conventional notions of trajectories rooted in one and the same place that seemed to dominate postwar Japan. The experiences of the five women introduced in this chapter indicate that despite numerous references to ingrained ways of gender roles, change is happening on a small but gradual scale. Rosenberger posits in her ethnographic study of young organic farmers in rural Japan that these entrepreneurs try to "make selves that are alternative to the neoliberal narrative, yet act as entrepreneurial subjects that risk bringing their versions of morality to the market, via delicious, organic food sold to self-creating consumers" (2017: 14). In a similar vein, the vignettes depicted provide ethnographic evidence of the complex ways in which agency and risk are intricately intertwined, how mobility creates new opportunities for aspiring and driven women but at the same time also reproduces systemic constraints of class, education, and gender.

Last but not least, all five vignettes confirm Latour's statement that "movements and displacements are first, forms and sites come second." (Latour 2005: 300). In a similar vein, Urry has shown that "mobilities rather than societies should be at the heart of a reconstituted sociology [. . .]) (Urry 2000: 210). Regardless of whether settlers engage in trans-local or transnational mobility, their lives and career paths are clearly characterized by ongoing movement between various sites as well as transformational ontological processes resulting from their engagement with vernacular actors as well as stakeholders beyond the local and national levels. Given this emergence of translocal and transnational assemblages (Deleuze and Guattari 1987), the narratives introduced in this chapter point to a need to rethink the meaning of local and national sites. Hence, rather than providing insights into specifically "Japanese" societal phenomena, I propose that these narratives shed light on crucial processes occurring in a post-growth society (that happens to be Japan) that will be highly relevant to other societies globally as they are bound to face similar issues in the near future.

Chapter Three

Post-Growth Forms of Living and Working

Countryside as Experimental Ground and Social Imaginary

From "Communities on the Edge" to "Communities of Hope"

Media representations usually focus on Tokyo as the bustling cosmopolitan capital of Japan rather than agrarian images (Schnell 2005); yet if we take a train from Tokyo for two or three hours in any direction, chances are high that we arrive in a rural area with a rapidly dwindling population. In fact, Japan has been examined as a worthwhile case of "a pioneer shrinking society" as the United Nations forecasts a 26 percent shrinkage for Japan's population by 2085 (Matanle 2014). It is common knowledge that rural areas will be especially hard hit, with population drops of 30 percent or more and continuing concentration of the population in Tokyo and other urban conglomerations. A brief look at the statistical facts and figures confirm the bleak prospect: according to an estimate by the National Institute of Population and Social Security Research (Kokuritsu Shakai Hoshō Jinkō Mondai Kenkyūjo), the population in Aomori Prefecture will see an 11.9 percent decrease by 2020 (as compared to 2005); Iwate a 10.9 percent decrease, Akita a 14.8 percent decrease, and Yamagata a 10.9 percent decrease; Shimane Prefecture an 11.6 percent decrease, Yamaguchi an 11.6 percent decrease, and Wakayama Prefecture a 13.3 percent decrease; whereas Tokyo will see a 4.2 percent decrease and

Kanagawa Prefecture a 2.3 percent decrease (Kakei 2011: 37), so there is a distinct trend toward depopulation of rural areas versus a continued influx into urban conglomerations.

Hence it comes as no surprise that the first image associated with rural areas is the same across Japan: a predominance of elderly citizens, a society that heavily relies on cars due to the lack of public transport, infrastructure that reminds us of suburbia rather than the rural idyll with the typical combination of pachinko gambling parlors, shopping malls with adjacent parking lots, gasoline stands, convenience stores, discount clothing stores, DIY centers, family restaurants, and other facilities of mass consumption that are easily accessible by car. Chances are also high that we will encounter a considerable number of abandoned houses (*akiya*) and a few hunched-over ladies with straw hats tending the few rice fields that are still being maintained, closed elementary schools due to the lack of children, as well as a number of closed shops ("shuttered stores") along the main shopping street. The decline and eventual collapse of rural communities is referred to as *genkai shūraku* (communities on the edge), a term coined by sociologist Ōno Akira to describe municipalities with more than half of the population being over sixty-five years old (2008). Depopulated areas have typically been perceived and depicted as bleak places with no future that have been forgotten by the rest of the nation (Knight 2003: 269). A similar polarized perception and representation of rural regions with their dense social relations versus urban areas with social relations mostly centered on business is evident in numerous academic sources (e.g., Tsuji's chapter on social relations in Yamada and Kobayashi 2015: 163–177). In contrast to this polarized view of distinct entities, geographer Doreen Massey has previously observed that places "may be imagined as particular articulations of social relations, including local relations 'within' the place and those among connections which stretch beyond it" (1999: 22).

When I meet Kana, who is in her early thirties, in June 2016 in Tokamachi, Niigata Prefecture, however, she points out that her experience of living in a hamlet that by mere statistics would doubtlessly be categorized as a *genkai shūraku* was actually that it more resembled a "community of hope" (*kibō shūraku*) rather than a community on the edge. This may have been partly due to the fact that the hamlet of Iketani deep in the mountains has already attracted several young I-turners and the senior residents seem more open and outgoing than average citizens in remote villages. The young farmer observes that, in retrospect, the senior residents turned out to be quite different from her initial expectations. She managed to learn key agricultural skills from them and narrates that the citizens in their seventies and eighties were much more energetic, fit, and optimistic than their counterparts in urban areas. Kana, who finished her agricultural studies at a university in Tokyo, has married a local and decided to settle in the area after living in the Iketani hamlet for some two years. She has established her own company that sells agricultural produce and products. This episode about the gap between expected image and reality illustrates how much rural areas continue to be fraught with images of the past rather than being perceived as relational tropes in the vein of Massey (1999).

Numerous migrants shared their impressions with me during interviews that life in the countryside turned out to be much easier than expected, less provincial, with locals less closed and senior citizens much more vibrant, outgoing, and brimming with energy than their peers in the city; yet some, especially migrants who had a longer history of residence, also mentioned limits of integration despite all their efforts of participating in local traditional performing arts and other communal activities and conceded that they felt most at ease sharing their thoughts with other nonlocal residents. Nevertheless, in the majority of migrant narratives, postrelocation life in the countryside was implied to be a major improvement of individuals' mental and physical well-being and was hence depicted as an overly positive experience, despite issues such as the lack of restaurants, cafés, bookstores, and clothes shops geared toward the younger generation being mentioned by some interviewees. However, they also added that they felt it was not a big issue as they did their shopping when they returned to their hometowns or other urban areas on business trips or other occasions. Many remarked that they felt better and more focused because they spent less time and money on material goods and realized that many of the things they had amassed when living in the city were in fact not really necessary.

Another "community of hope," to borrow Kana's expression, can be found in Ama Town, Shimane Prefecture. For a remote island that used to have about 7,000 residents after World War II with just 2,361 residents left now, 38.8 percent of which are older than sixty-five years old, the prognosis looks bleak (San'in Keizai Kei'ei Kenkyūjo 2015: 108). Yet, the island has seen more than 483 in-migrants between twenty and forty years of age over the last twelve years who either work in the Ama Tourism Association, the municipal agency, or start-up enterprises.

The majority of migrants have decided to relocate to the island through recruitment of project members by the town office or by local businesses and possess distinct professional skills and a university degree (Nagatomo 2016: 6). Yu, a former company employee in his late thirties who worked as an editor for a well-known publishing house in Tokyo, chose to relocate after eight and a half years in the publishing business since he could not see a long-term future there for himself. He now works in the local fisheries association and observes that when he goes back to Tokyo once a year to see his relatives, "everyone's eyes seem dead, just like before" (interview on 21 September 2016). He has lived in Ama Town for six years now and seems highly satisfied. This is not surprising given the fact that his typical day in Tokyo consisted of sixteen hours of work plus close to four hours commuting on densely packed trains. This only left some four hours for sleep and literally no time for leisure. In Ama, he sleeps eight hours on average, works from 7:30 a.m. to 5:30 p.m. and has plenty of time to spend with his family. He lives in a comfortably big house with an adjacent garden to grow herbs and vegetables some fifteen minutes by car from his workplace. He remembers that back in Tokyo he used to "buy time with money"; for example, around 1:00 or 2:00 a.m., after finishing work, he took a taxi home just to get a bit more sleep, regardless of how much it cost, since his salary was high but he did not have any time to spend it because he was so busy at work. Now he regularly posts images of the fresh fish he caught and the mackerel sandwiches he makes outdoors with a friend on social media—creative and delicious engagement with natural resources at its best. When he shows me his house with its adjacent spacious garden, I am impressed by the great variety of fresh herbs he has cultivated. When we are invited for dinner, he proudly garnishes the delicious meals with his Japanese ginger (*myōga*) buds that we harvested ourselves some steps from the kitchen a few minutes earlier. Yu's conversion from an elite corporate warrior in Tokyo who was buying time with money to an employee of the fisheries association may strike some readers as incomprehensible. Why would someone with a comfortable income and lifelong employment contract in a prospering industry like publishing give up his job, sell his flat in Tokyo, and opt for manual work on a remote and depopulated island?

Yu's story can be seen as the story of the end of attractiveness of lifelong employment and all the social constraints and obligations that employees trade for the "safety" of such jobs. Yu recounts that he felt that his job eventually did not entail as much potential for development and growth as he had expected. The work mainly consisted of executing instructions and orders and it entailed work-related social dinners, which meant that he could not spend time with his family or was forced to eat twice for the sake of following social obligation; generally, he spent twenty hours per day on average on work or commuting, so he felt that there was an overall lack of life quality as he did not have any time for leisure or family. Furthermore, work meant prescribed hours to take lunch as well as a lack of freedom to decide what to eat. Lunchtime coincided with peak lunch times of other companies and so choices for eating out were limited to "what was fast"—Yu speaks of "getting something to eat just to take in calories" (*shokuji wo sumaseru*) rather than enjoying food for its own sake. Even during his time as a corporate employee, Yu devised strategies of resistance by, for example, bringing his own rice ball so that he did not have to eat lunches he did not find appetizing. After more than eight years in central Tokyo, Yu decided to prioritize agency, self-determination, and the potential for self-development and growth rather than material concerns and safety. According to numerous interviewees, lifelong employment is in fact not safe because decisions are made by top management, and the average corporate worker does not have the chance to shape these decisions. Migrants pointed out that in their view, taking no risk, that is, remaining in the large-scale company, constitutes the bigger hazard. Yu observed that he never had second thoughts about his decision to relocate, although he shared his concern with me about education and providing his children with a global perspective. In fact, he narrated that he is planning to spend some time in Europe with his family once his children become a bit older. A deep sense of engagement with the local community through his work coincides with an inherent translocal understanding that was shaped by Yu's own history of spending time in the United States when he was in high school. Being on the move does not seem to add an element of insecurity; rather, mobility carries nuances of challenge, promise, and hope in most of my interviewees' narratives. Yu's and Kana's story can be characterized as the narratives of individuals in search of meaningful lifestyles and personal happiness.

Yet, in these trajectories of well-educated, motivated young people in contemporary Japan who impact wider society through their lifestyle choices, their engagement in innovative projects can be interpreted as a profound change of values in Japanese society as well as a radically new approach to rural areas—from beacons of the past to experimental grounds of the future. In fact, representatives of local government who work in the departments concerned with promoting in-migration confirm this novel approach to the role of rural areas. They observe that unless newcomers maintain their values and create innovation, they will be a burden on the local residents and therefore not be a plus to the community. They describe ideal settlers as individuals who have a strong sense of adventure that aims to create their own employment (Honda 2015: 272).

Dropping Out: Or, Rural Moves as a Career Move?

Whereas rural-urban migration is common with ever more individuals relocating to Tokyo and other urban areas, Japan has recently seen a small but steady increase in urbanites aged between twenty and forty-five, like Kana and Yu who make a conscious choice to move to rural settings (Klien in Assmann 2016). These individuals are referred to as "lifestyle migrants," that is, individuals who relocate for noneconomic reasons, aim to render their lives more meaningful, and see migration as "a route to a better and more fulfilling way of life, especially in contrast to the one left behind" (Benson and O'Reilly 2009b: 1). Throughout history, key incentives for migration were of political, economic, and religious natures. Furthermore, "retirement migration," that is, relocation after the end of professional careers, has also been prevalent. Previous research has analyzed the search for oneself (Kato 2009), cultural migration (Fujita 2009; Favell 2015), migration as the pursuit of an ideal lifestyle (Nagatomo 2007b), and retirement migration (Ono 2009, 2014). Representative researchers of lifestyle migration like Michaela Benson and Karen O'Reilly tended to focus on clean-cut breaks of migrants from their previous lives, thus presenting the relocation itself as a distinct moment of change in individuals' quest for authenticity in their lifestyles (Benson 2011). Lifestyle migrants used terms such as "making a fresh start," "getting out of the trap," and "a new beginning" when talking about their relocation (Benson and O'Reilly 2009a: 609).

More recently, scholars have approached migration as intricately related with travel and leisure. The informants introduced in this chapter could also be categorized as participating in "lifestyle mobility" (Duncan, Cohen, and Thulemark 2013), defined as "on-going semi-permanent moves of varying duration" that constitute a more flexible conceptual lens for analyzing mobility, since the boundaries between travel, leisure, and migration are blurred and their narratives make collapsing work and leisure divides evident. Narratives presented throughout this volume illustrate the fact that relocation is a permanent process for many migrants whose trajectories tend to be fusions of urban and rural, past and present, dropping out and blending in, food choices, introspection and sociality, visionary and neoliberalism. Hence, rather than seeking an "authentic lifestyle," interviewees introduced here can be considered embodiments of the paradoxes of contemporary post-growth Japan, where postwar values of consumption and pursuit of growth have been discarded without a replacement for these values. Ultimately, many trajectories of migrants could be interpreted as being examples of the search for novel values in a post-growth Japan characterized by emotional bleakness, uncertainty, and material precariousness (Allison 2013).

Japan is a highly centralized country with all the representative government institutions and companies centered in Tokyo and Osaka. Recently, some efforts have admittedly been made to relocate some institutions to other areas to prevent the damage resulting from a possible major earthquake in the Tokyo area. However, a fair amount of the nation's elite universities are still located in Tokyo, and the mind-set that one needs to go to Tokyo to have a real career is still deeply ingrained. So why would young aspiring individuals make the move down the career ladder, away from corporate safety, urban convenience. and around-the-clock entertainment?

Motives for relocation include self-realization, self-fulfillment, food safety (in the wake of the Great East Japan Earthquake and Tsunami), concerns about physical and mental health due to consistent overwork in corporate jobs, aspirations to a better work-life balance, time to think about what one really wants to do with one's life, time to establish a start-up enterprise, and, more generally, taking on a challenge and self-development. This shift in perception from the Japanese countryside as a stagnant backwater that serves as the last resort for individuals who have not managed to make it in Tokyo (*miyakoochi*) to an experimental ground for aspiring individuals as well as a site of resistance is the theme of this chapter. Many of the narratives introduced in this chapter in fact resemble those of lifestyles migrants who move abroad to pursue a more meaningful and satisfying life (Fujita 2009; Ono 2009; Kanzaki Sooudi 2014). Some recent narratives in Japan interestingly combine both postwar pessimistic views of the countryside as a place of losers and lack of ideas with the emerging perspective of rural areas as grounds for elite visionaries, such as Yamada who refers to a "new rurality" (*atarashii chihō*; 2016: 4).

This increase in interest in rural areas and resulting influx of urbanite youth to Japan's "periphery" has inevitably led to a coexistence of urban and rural lifestyles in remote hamlets. For example, stylish coworking spaces that could be found just as well in Shibuya have surfaced in Kamiyama Town, Tokushima Prefecture, or in Ishinomaki, Miyagi Prefecture. When I come back to Ama Town in the autumn of 2016 for a follow-up of my fieldwork six years after my first visit, I find an Italian restaurant with excellent espresso that is frequented by neophyte customers who could be found in central Tokyo—and chances are that some of the guests are indeed Tokyoites. Furthermore, when I visited the picturesque island for the first time in 2010, there were a few individuals with elite backgrounds—"pioneers" who had dropped out to set up their own organizations; such individuals were seen as *kawarimono*, eccentrics, at that time. Now, due to the work of these pioneers, the island has seen a steadily increasing influx of migrants who have decided to relocate not only for quality of life reasons but also for career reasons. For example, I run into a hardworking manager type in his early forties—let's call him Tomo—in my favorite local restaurant when I am meeting other migrants for lunch. Having worked for a well-known human resources company in Tokyo for two decades and being on the move across Japan for work, Tomo thoroughly enjoyed his job when an acquaintance asked him to give a lecture in Ama. In retrospect, he had no intention of moving to the island, but when he was offered the job of managing a newly established municipal cram school with the aim of raising the local education level, he remembers it was just a gut thing: he could not resist that challenge despite the fact that his salary would go down almost by half. The reason is that he feels he needs to make a contribution to a "better Japan." Rather than having a work-life balance, Tomo jokes that his work is equivalent with his life. Six years ago, people like Tomo would probably have dismissed the job offer without second thought. Now, stories of migration within Japan from urban to rural areas for job reasons are in the media; Tokyo and other cities have regular "I-turn fairs" where individuals who ponder a move can get more detailed information about a range of places across Japan and consult with professional staff familiar with local employment, life, and culture. Students have plenty of opportunities to do internships in rural areas, with a number moving into permanent jobs there.

All these changes taken together suggest a shift in the way rural areas are perceived by youth in contemporary Japan, from places of the past to places to learn from or "communities of hope," to borrow Kana's expression. Migrants who have lived in rural areas for more than a decade on the other hand lament that lifestyle migration has gone "mainstream" and that the number of new settlers who have an original vision has been on the decrease. Generally, contemporary Japanese society has seen "increasingly diversified and fluidised life course models in the middle class" (Nagatomo 2016: 5), with a higher job turnover rate for youth and greater numbers of individuals who leave Japan for a working holiday or just take a private gap year or period, as examples in the following section will show. The Japanese literature distinguishes between "U-turn" (return to hometowns) and "I-turn" (moves to rural areas other than one's hometown) (Nagatomo 2016: 6); most of the migrants discussed in this monograph are "I-turners," that is, individuals who have relocated to areas in which they have no family roots.

Of Social Introverts and Start-Up Entrepreneurs

Case 1: Haru, Forty-Five, Niigata Prefecture

Living the life of a social introvert (*sōsharu inkyo seikatsu*)

Driving through a steeply mountainous area some ten minutes by car from downtown Tokamachi, the place I am looking for turns out to be a wooden house located directly on the road to a mountain village I have been to before many times for a previous research project. The hamlet where the house is located only consists of a few households. There is no visible sign that this is the shared house I am looking for but when I stop my car in front of the house, a girl looks out from the window on the second floor and waves her hand. I still find it hard to believe that individuals in their twenties and thirties would choose this location to open a share house. What is even more surprising is that on the second floor of the share house, one of the tenants has opened a temporary clothes shop; next to it there is a small space that contains a self-made bar where residents and visitors occasionally enjoy drinks and engage in interaction. Everyone is welcome to visit—the house is totally open and the operator of the house himself points out that, at first sight, it may be impossible to tell who is a resident, who is a supporter, and who is a visitor.

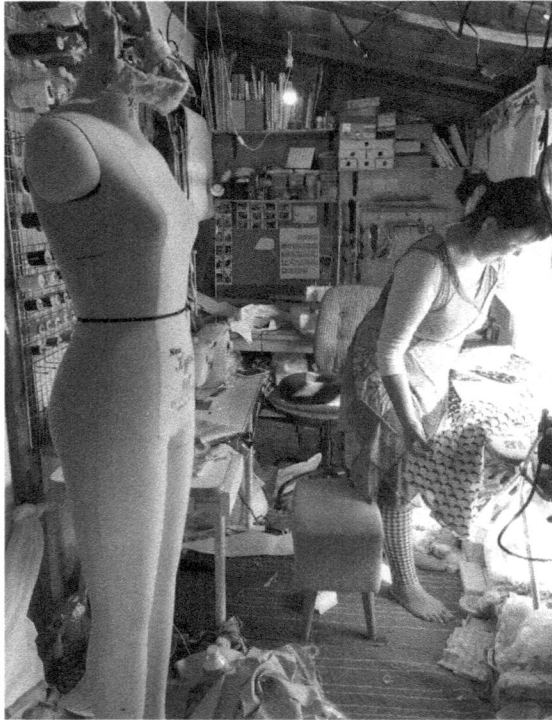

Figure 3.1. On the second floor of the share house, Tokamachi, Niigata Prefecture.

When I visit the collective house for the first time in June 2016, its founder, Haru, is not there as he is giving a lecture in the Tokyo area, which he does on many weekends. After having worked in IT for seventeen years as a company employee in Tokyo, he decided to quit work at the age of forty, "starting from zero," as he puts it. He observes that in retrospect, with increasing age he was insecure whether he could continue to put up with all the stress and overwork both mentally and physically. After traveling without a plan for three years across Japan, checking out various collective housing, he opened his own, reproducing all the good things he had seen. He narrates that his share house is an "accumulation of values" (*kachikan no katamari*) with the most important rule being that there are no rules, as he puts it, but his understanding is that residents should focus on what they are really passionate about rather than thinking about others (*jibun hon'i*). He himself does nothing but what he enjoys (*suki na koto shika yatteinai*), spending only 10 percent of his time on work, that is, blogging on social media about the share house. As a *shakaijin* and company employee in Tokyo, he only averaged three to four hours of sleep; now he sleeps some nine hours and has time to do what he wants, that is, watch anime and check new IT technologies. During his corporate career he ate food from convenience stores every day; now he mostly eats fresh vegetables from the neighborhood; so altogether his life is much healthier, although he continues to live an indoor life despite having relocated to the countryside. As people come to and go from his share house, he can meet all kinds of people without having to leave his home (*koko ni iru dake de ironna hito ni aeru*). Hence his network evolves almost naturally. Haru makes a living from the rent paid by his ten coresidents (which is cheap by Tokyo standards), some of whom pursue regular work, others being freeter (i.e., individuals who do not work full time, excluding students and housewives) or preparing new projects. Sixty percent of residents are male and forty percent are female, although 60 percent of short-term visitors and guests are female.

He observes that his main aim is to have a good time until he dies (*jibun ga shinu made tanoshiku suru*) as he believes that the much-touted value of endurance (*gaman*) in Japanese culture is not good for one's health and well-being. He does not really have a long-term plan because he believes that 90 percent of life consists of serendipity and having no plan is so much more fun. He does not own a car and asks other people to give him a ride when he needs one; he does not consume much apart from food and tobacco. He observes that since his relocation, the cash in his wallet hardly decreases since he has little opportunity to actually spend his money in places such as convenience stores, and he needs a car to get there. Since he does not have a family, collective housing or "open living" (*sumibiraku*), as he puts it, constitutes his personal way of risk management, facilitating a reasonable way of living, solving the issue of snow removal during the long winters, ensuring healthy food, and preventing a lonely death as well as day-to-day loneliness. He points out that rather than a contribution to rural revitalization, his main motivation is self-centered, even if the side effect may be positive for rural society.

Figure 3.2. Outside the share house, Tokamachi, Niigata Prefecture. Photo by Nishimura Machiko.

Coresidents include a female in her early thirties who graduated from the top university in West Japan, is back from several years as a development worker in Africa and the Pacific, and plans to start her own project in Okinawa. Tired from her interesting but grueling work schedule, she says she is "taking a rest" this year, hinting at physical and mental exhaustion. Numerous female lifestyle migrants I encounter during my extended fieldwork mention that they have a history of "broken bodies" and that they hope to slow down their pace of working and living in the future. Another resident is in his mid-twenties, from Shizuoka Prefecture, and has established his own company with a friend with a branch in Tokamachi and one in Shizuoka. Highly satisfied with his life in a share house, he comments that he intends to stay until he gets married, observing that taking his own apartment seems like a waste of resources, he enjoys meeting unfamiliar faces at home, and he enjoys being caught in conversations that cannot be anticipated. He says that he has lived in share houses since being a student in the Tokyo area. A single mother with her two-year-old daughter also resided in the share house between September 2015 and April 2016, along with a youth in his mid-twenties, who described himself as a NEET (not in employment, education, or training) who worked for one year in India after his graduation from university, as well as an architecture student from Niigata University who regularly stays at the share house as part of his graduation thesis project. The number of visitors to Haru's share house, which Haru describes as "the house where people can spend a life having fun until they die," has exceeded five thousand since its opening in spring 2015, with attention growing as a result of articles in journals such as *Sotokoto*. According to Haru, on busy days, more than fifty persons visit. The share house attracts not only residents but also short-term visitors who stay for a few hours or days or just visit occasionally for weekends. The share house has also become the research topic of university students and researchers (including myself). Former residents like to come back and maintain the connection in other ways as well, by, for example, having visits from present residents in the places they have moved on to. The clothes designer mentioned earlier in fact moved back to Tokyo in autumn 2016 and writes that she does not "feel the geographical distance" between Niigata and Tokyo, since she comes back to the share house and former roommates see her in Tokyo. She also says that despite her rather short residence in Tokamachi, she receives seasonal vegetables in her apartment in Tokyo from local friends and explains with pride that when she held a clothes workshop in Tokyo recently, her Tokamachi friends asked her to do the same in Tokamachi.

The fluid, ever changing community of the share house illustrates that share houses exceed place and geographical location when (former) residents share their daily experiences through social media. For example, the owner of the collective housing project set up a virtual "Advent Calendar" where various individuals related to the share house either through a living or visiting experience were asked to contribute their thoughts on various days. I was also part of the project, which afforded me valuable insights into a wide range of individual experiences. My participation in the virtual calendar also redefined conventional understandings of fieldwork as limited to physical presence in a site to "extended fieldwork" as existing contacts are expanded through social media, meeting acquaintances, and making new contacts. In other words, not only did I describe my experience of visiting the share house and engaging in conversation with its residents as well as interviewing some members on Skype after my initial visits, but I used my contribution to outline my research project and invite informants to come forth if they felt comfortable about cooperating in the project.

Some of the residents engage in daily work, for example, in their own companies, and recently, the share house has attracted individuals interested in start-ups. Haru has been increasingly in the public limelight as he was chosen for the third place of the MVP Award—a contest for ideas that change society. Furthermore, the director and guild master is also the representative of the Niigata version of the Startup Weekend Niigata, which attracts entrepreneurs of all kinds to the rural hamlet and promotes entrepreneurial thinking among residents and visitors of the share house.

Case 2: Masa, Ama Town, Shimane Prefecture

"Work-life balance? I think I have more of a work-life mix at present."

Thirty-nine years old and originally from Yanaka, Tokyo, Masa relocated with his wife to Ama Town in April 2016 for lifestyle reasons. He studied robot engineering but eventually realized that this was not really what he was enthusiastic about and decided to study graphic design at the mature age of twenty-six. He and his wife worked at one of the representative marketing companies in Tokyo for eight years. Having visited Ama numerous times since one of his high school friends had already relocated there, he liked it so much that he and his wife moved to the island last year. Masa says that after eight years in the same company, he asked himself whether he wanted to continue working there or go freelance. He decided to relocate as freelancing seemed more interesting. When I ask him about the risk that comes with such a large-scale professional and lifestyle change, he laughs, saying that he was confident that he and his wife could make a living and that doing what they want was more important to them (interview on 17 September 2016).

In retrospect, he remembers that when he came to visit for the first time, he was surprised that there were so many events going on in the countryside, with so many interesting people to talk to. He observes that Ama Town is an ideal place for a start-up as there are only a few residents, rental space is cheap, and there is an amicable network of similarly minded I-turners. He has rented a spacious house close to Hishiura ferry port overlooking the sea, which he also uses as an office. He likes the fact that he can manage his time by himself and his present lifestyle is more a "work-life mix" rather than a work-life balance as work activities and leisure are intricately entangled. Back in Tokyo, he used to work long hours on weekdays but enjoyed leisure on weekends. Now he works depending on clients' requirements, regardless of weekdays or weekends. He regularly uses the local library to do research related to his work. He says that quite contrary to his expectations most of his present projects are orders from local clients since there are only a few other designers living on the island, and he receives most of his work from local clients who have heard about him from other locals with whom he worked before. When we talk about his future plans, he mentions opening a guesthouse with an adjacent coworking space in the near future and is also thinking about relating his projects on the island to activities in Tokyo in the medium and long term—a statement that brings us back to Massey's aforementioned interpretation of rurality as a notion that transcends geographical boundaries through its sociality (1999).

Despite the fact that he and his wife live in a more environmentally friendly manner since their move, thinking about the garbage that results from their consumption, and his wife mentions that rather than clothes, her interest has recently shifted to agricultural devices and knives for preparing various fish they caught, their lifestyle is certainly urban—asked about where he goes for good coffee, he replies quickly that he has brought his own coffee machine. The fact that the second part of the interview takes place in an Italian restaurant close to Hishiura port that offers authentic Italian espresso and pasta shows the shift of Ama to a hybrid place with both urban and rural aspects due to the influx of urbanite migrants. Masa mentions that there is no place to eat good ramen on the entire island, something he took for granted when living in Japan's capital.

Masa's story is clearly different from previous narratives by lifestyle migration researchers who presented individuals as aspiring to a rustic lifestyle that adopts local ways. Masa obviously enjoys the landscape and nature of the island, yet his lifestyle choice was primarily motivated by career incentives; after all, the island seemed like a place where he could pursue his career while having a better quality of life than in Tokyo. Masa belongs to an emerging generation of creatives in post-growth Japan who manage to draw on their vast network of professional contacts and friends while seeking out a niche in which to earn a living and simultaneously enjoy themselves, with an inherently unclear line between work and leisure. The fuzziness between what constitutes work and what is free time especially with freelancers in the creative milieu has also been touched upon by Keiko Matsunaga in her discussion of Kamiyama Town in Tokushima Prefecture, a small town with a population of approximately six thousand residents that counted twenty-one thousand residents in 1955 and that has seen an influx of IT-based young entrepreneurs (2015: 38).

Similar to Masa, rather than aspiring to life in the countryside as such, Haru has strategically chosen rural relocation as his personal way of crisis management in an emotionally and materially precarious Japan. His decision to relocate thus carries undertones of a self-realization project reflected in the work of Beck (1994) and Giddens (1991), personal management of risk, and the quest for challenge and professional growth while optimizing work-life balance.

Case 3: Rina, Ishinomaki City, Miyagi Prefecture

> It's actually fun having two workplaces and places of residence. And in today's economically unstable world there is no absolute security. Having two places of residence and several jobs also means a reduction of risk. This lifestyle helps me maintain my motivation and has a positive effect on me mentally speaking.
>
> —Rina (interview on 3 August 2014)

Leading a lifestyle working as an architect based in Tokyo with weekends spent in Ishinomaki, thirty-six-year-old Rina is originally from Tokyo but has been in and out of Ishinomaki since working as a volunteer after the Great East Japan Earthquake that hit the northeastern provinces, including Miyagi Prefecture, in March 2011. Rina has restored an abandoned house in central Ishinomaki and opened a restaurant to support volunteers arriving from Tokyo on the night bus in the early morning hours. The restored wooden house exudes a distinctly sophisticated urban ambiance, with furniture that one would expect in a stylish café somewhere in an urban area rather than in some back street in a depopulated town in Tohoku. Rina lives on the second floor of the café. She has local and nonlocal staff working in the café when she is not there, nonlocals being mostly former volunteer peers. The café also serves as a venue for various events related to the revitalization of the city, such as dating events aimed at helping individuals who wish to start a family. This is intended to serve the larger goals of rural revitalization and increasing the population of Ishinomaki City as such. In the initial stage of her time in Ishinomaki, Rina used to stay with a friendly elderly couple but did not have any privacy. She seems very content with her present accommodation on the second floor of her own café, which is only a few minutes by foot from JR Ishinomaki Station. Some may argue that opening the café in April 2013 has not made a decisive impact on Ishinomaki's demographic reality of aging and depopulation, which is commensurate with the situation faced by other towns in rural areas across Japan. However, the opening of the café makes a huge symbolic and atmospheric difference in a neighborhood where numerous shops have closed and abandoned spaces predominate.

The preceding comment by Rina highlights the strategic aspect behind relocation in her case, as well: in an age of nagging recession and increasingly precarious working conditions, especially in the creative industry, Rina considers her relocation to a small-scale town in north-eastern rural Japan a conscious way of limiting her risks while leaving her the leeway to try something new. The café is her first self-managed project. She observes that she earns her money from her work in Tokyo, and the café is more of a volunteer contribution and does not provide an additional income at present—although she managed to obtain funding from municipal and prefectural sources to restore the dilapidated house. The café also provides local food such as venison on special occasions. The project received the "Good Design Award" in 2013 for its reinterpretation of local traditional food from a nonlocal vantage point. It combines local revitalization, creation of employment, promotion of community resources, and involvement of existing local industries.

However, Rina's initial aim of achieving more leisure time seems more distant than ever: commuting between two places and maintaining social lives in both Tokyo and Ishinomaki is time-consuming. She indicates that her numerous activities make her feel permanently overworked and is seeking ways to spend more time in Ishinomaki. According to Rina, her move from a small room with an elderly couple to her own café may be the first step:

> I feel that the restaurant can be seen as a first step toward finding my roots in Ishinomaki. Before, I felt more like coming home to Tokyo when I went back but now, it's not so clear anymore. I have friends in both places, I feel at home in both Tokyo and Ishinomaki. [. . .] Leisure? I don't really

have it now, but thinking about it, I have more of it in Ishinomaki. In Tokyo, I just work, also because I usually spend my weekdays in Tokyo and the weekend in Ishinomaki and also take part in local *matsuri* [festival] here in Ishinomaki. (Interview on 3 August 2014)

Like other migrants, Rina implies that she is embedded more strongly in the local community in Ishinomaki compared to her hometown. This may also be due to her initial experience of Ishinomaki as a disaster volunteer, which provided her with a dense network of contacts in the town, both locals and nonlocals.

When I ask Rina about her future plans, she replies that she is not the type of person who makes long-term plans but feels more comfortable adapting to the respective needs of changing circumstances—an attitude she may have taken on as a volunteer in the wake of the disaster. This lack of medium- and long-term planning is a prominent feature in many migrant narratives and could be interpreted as a way for individuals to hedge their bets in an increasingly insecure postindustrial society (Klien 2017: 176).

Diverse Migrants with Hybrid Lifestyles and Complex Rurality

Wrapping up this chapter, the empirical data presented here indicate a salient shift of the countryside in Japan from a stagnant backwater associated with nostalgia and lost values to an experimental ground for creative individuals who seek new challenges, are concerned about their subjective well-being, and look for ways of finding niches to sustain their livelihoods in remote hamlets. A major incentive for individuals to relinquish their secure lifestyles is the desire to lead "a life of their own," that is, to lead lives over which they can have control (Beck 2003: 272) against a background of a growing "ethic of individual self-fulfillment and achievement" (Beck 2003: 273) and the wish to depart from standardized life courses and pursue personalized trajectories (Klien 2016: 168).

Although they both were corporate employees in Tokyo in their previous professional careers and have obtained abundant professional experience, Haru and Masa differ in their professional backgrounds, origins, aims, values, and everyday lives. Yet both have made the decision to relocate despite having the (theoretical) option of a lifelong corporate job in an urban area, and both report a considerably higher satisfaction with their work-life balance now compared to their previous lifestyles. Both work at home and strongly rely on networks of similarly minded peers and the local community to sustain their lifestyles. Both continue to maintain partly urban lifestyles despite having relocated to remote rural areas and engage in activities that exceed their place of residence. Many of the newcomers I have met during fieldwork over the years expressed high-levels of satisfaction with their life since relocation yet also indicated concern about the lack of urban convenience; gourmet options such as high-end, freshly roasted coffee; or the complete lack of ramen shops or shops with fashionable clothes for younger generations on remote islands. Others commented that the laid-back comfort and lack of ambition prevalent in small local towns and in the countryside is just what they needed. Rina seems to prefer the laid-back and tight-knit sense of community in Ishinomaki and embodies the rural-urban continuum through her lifestyle with work based in Tokyo and activities of community contribution based in Ishinomaki. Masa's aspiration to connect his activities on the remote island to his previous work in Tokyo also carries Masseyan undertones of a geographically fluid interpretation of rurality (1999).

I have only presented three cases in this chapter, but there is a wide range of migrants between twenty and forty-five who choose to move to rural areas, as amply documented throughout this book. The increasing interest in rural living is also attested by the fact that numerous events across cities in Japan have been organized by municipal and prefectural organizations that present certain regions to individuals who are considering a move. Such fairs usually come with booths that provide information on work and life in the countryside with the aim of increasing the number of residents.

During my recent fieldwork in Ama Town, I was an observer at an information tour for individuals and families from Tokyo who were considering a move and visited the town with the aim of obtaining firsthand information on life and work. The two-day tour included a presentation by a municipal government employee who presented comprehensive information on Ama Town, visits to major sights, discussion with I-turners about the experience of living in Ama, as well as a barbecue including delicious local seafood. Topics during the discussion with individuals who have relocated to the island several years ago included issues of integration into the local community, communication styles, local prices as compared to prices in Tokyo, issues of finding employment, and accommodation and other practical themes. A couple with an infant expressed their surprise at the low rents compared to Tokyo, where they lived at the time.

In addition, structural measures taken by the Japanese government to provide incentives to individuals to move from urban to rural areas have also played a considerable role, programs like the Chiiki okoshi kyōryokutai (Regional Revitalization Cooperation Officer program) established by the Ministry of Internal Affairs and Communication (Sōmusho) in 2009. Individuals are expected to move to structurally disadvantaged areas such as hamlets on the margin for a period between one year and up to three years and engage in activities that promote regional revitalization in cooperation with local municipalities and residents. The program aims to implement revitalization measures at a grassroots level that are difficult to conduct by municipal agencies alone. Officers have considerable freedom in determining their precise activities, although recently, some officers have been recruited for specific projects. Activities are comprehensive and range from branding local products, engaging in agricultural activities with the aim of developing local goods, working in local education, handicraft, food development, and so forth. In contrast to conventional corporate jobs, officers have a considerably larger responsibility for the actions they take; many mention this agency and the resulting sense of satisfaction if the project goes well. For locals, on the other hand, it can be refreshing and inspiring to hear different perspectives about their hamlet and area and unconventional strategies of revitalization. Furthermore, especially in rural areas with a high rate of overaged residents, having an influx of nonlocal youth can make a difference in the atmosphere. The rapid increase of officers dispatched across Japan from 89 in the initial year of the successful program to an astounding 2,625 in 2015 shows the great interest of individuals from all walks of life to join. According to information from the ministry, approximately 40 percent of officers are female, approximately 80 percent of officers are in their twenties or thirties, and approximately 60 percent choose to stay on in the hamlets they were dispatched to after the end of their contract (www.soumu.go.jp/main_content/000405085.pdf, accessed on 4 January 2017).

Many of my informants in all field sites across Japan worked as regional revitalization officers when I met them or had done so prior to our encounter. Some succeeded in starting up their own shops, enterprises, or projects after the end of their contract as officers; others moved on into long-term office work with the local municipal agency. With regard to regional distribution of officers, Hokkaido leads with 369 individuals, followed by Nagano Prefecture with 222 officers, with Shimane Prefecture ranking third with 149 officers and Okayama Prefecture fourth with 118 officers (www.soumu.go.jp/main_content/000425356.pdf, accessed on 4 January 2017).

The logo for the regional revitalization officers shows a female and male officer in business attire, with farm boots, outdoors. Their eyes are gleaming with *yaru ki*—yearning for activity and determination to succeed—although it is not clear whether this is because of the time pressure of neoliberal contract labor or out of true passion.

Given the three-year-period limitation of officers' contracts, the program could also be viewed as a moratorium-like grace period of precarious labor for youth who are uncertain about what they want to do with their lives. Many ultimately fail to establish a means of livelihood in accordance with their ideals and rely on irregular seasonal work to pay their bills.

Figure 3.3. Temporary clothes shop, share house, Tokamachi, Niigata Prefecture.

To sum up, the case studies presented in this chapter show that the rural is "not a unified, discrete and unambiguous space," but "always a complex and contested category and places can only be described as being rural insofar as they exhibit more characteristics of rurality relative to other alternative spatialities" (Woods 2011: 49). Lifestyle migrants have developed a variety of lifestyles that combine positive aspects of the city and the countryside and make the intricate entanglement of the urban and rural even in remote areas evident. The empirical data indicates the enormous potential of rural regions, including remote islands as experimental grounds for developing more personally gratifying and fulfilling modes of working and living for creative and innovative individuals from all walks of life. These examples serve as firsthand empirical evidence of the "rural relationality" approach (Woods 2011: 40) that has recently gained ground in human geography, namely, the argument that relations make spaces (Wylie 2007: 200 cited in Woods 2011: 40). Whereas the general consensus is that the demographic change Japan is facing is inevitable, these cases show that despite the negligible numbers of these migrants, a gradual shift in modes of working and living is occurring in contemporary urban and rural Japan. On the one hand, individuals make choices to relocate; however, institutional and structural measures such as the Regional Revitalization Officer program described earlier have also been partly responsible for individual decisions to move to rural areas. They also make the case that recent trends such as a greater concern with self-realization and work-life balance, less security in the labor market, and generally, more diversified lifestyles have turned seemingly remote rural areas into increasingly dynamic and attractive grounds for experiments of all sorts that are intricately related to urban spaces.

The cases introduced in this chapter highlight the close relation of rural places with urbanity through both material and immaterial links in leisure and work. This chapter has also emphasized the huge potential rural areas hold with regard to providing migrants with more agency and self-determination over their lives, both in terms of work and leisure. Ultimately, the driving force behind these individual stories is the quest for more control over migrants' own lives. Others talk about the purpose in life (*ikigai*) they obtain from engaging in activities that only they could do and the feeling that they are needed in that place as opposed to anonymous urban life. Whereas most migrants grapple with implementing their aspirations in practice, they have made conscious decisions to relocate in order to eventually achieve their dream of a better quality of life, even if this may take time.

Last but not least, contrary to the distinction made in previous research (Sato 2001) between lifestyle and economic migration, individuals depicted in this chapter and volume are predominantly motivated by lifestyle choices, but they nevertheless hedge their bets economically speaking. In other words, while the decision to relocate is not primarily motivated by economic reasons, numerous migrants stated that rural areas seemed to hold potential for professional growth and expansion for them prior to their move, and they mention that finding an economic niche in the countryside has played an important role in their integration and well-being. The continuing recession of the Japanese market and increasingly precarious modes of work in general have cast the countryside in a new light as lower living expenses and more affordable lifestyles due to less pressure to consume imply less need to work and, consequently, more time and space for individuals to do what they want and engage in projects of self-realization in a postmodern world.

Rural spaces have also turned out to be attractive for individuals in the sense that they seem to carry less social and emotional pressures due to the lower density of residents and slower pace of life, at least for those who have relocated there recently. Numerous migrants mentioned that the amount of clothes they purchase since their move to the countryside has decreased dramatically as a result of the lack of shops as well as the lack of need for sophisticated clothes in their daily lives as compared to their previous lives. Whereas the overwhelming majority of migrants' trajectories are characterized by postconsumption lifestyles, the eminent focus of individuals on living (and working) in the moment (Klien 2017) could be categorized as a feature conventionally ascribed to a neoliberalist emphasis on ephemerality (Harvey 2005) and precariousness—the other side of flexibility and creative dynamism.

Chapter Four

Between Agency and Anomie, Possibility and Probability

Lifestyle Migrants and the Neoliberal Moment

My plan from now on? Well, it's all about money . . . if I don't manage to obtain money. Having dreams and talking about them is great, but what counts it convincing others that my dreams are worth pursuing and supporting. Until now, I have always been protected by others, so having dreams and just talking about them was OK. But now, I am by myself and it's here that relations with others come in. I need to focus on turning myself into a brand, but I am not sure whether I should go for one plan or have other plans at the back of my mind in case plan one fails . . .

—Male migrant, mid-thirties (interview on 22 June 2017)

My present mental state? I am not really in a bright mood. I feel that my present lifestyle is healthier than before, but there is a lot of uncertainty about my future and I feel considerable pressure that I have to make a decision about how to go on. Personally, I enjoy my work in forestry, but I am not very happy with the label of a regional revitalization officer, there are a lot of shortcomings to that position. People never know whether I belong to the municipal office or to the forestry company that I work for. Although I work there every day, I feel that they don't see me as one of them ultimately. I hope to either join the company as a full-time employee or set up my own company in the near future.

—Male migrant, mid-thirties (interview on 22 June 2017)

Both statements are excerpts from interviews conducted in June 2017 with two male migrants in their mid-thirties who moved from Tokyo to Hokkaido without having any personal connections to their present places of residence. They work in jobs that are totally different from their previous careers. Makoto—a university graduate—worked as temp staff in a convenience store before moving; Mitsuo was a host manager in a nightclub in Shinjuku, Tokyo. Neither had experienced rural life before their relocation, and both will be depicted in further detail in later in this chapter.

Terms recently circulating in Japanese media such as *kakusa shakai* (stratified society), *muen shakai* (society of no relations, i.e., anonymous society), and *kodokushi* (lonely death) indicate that communication is on the decrease, with "hope having become a privilege of the socioeconomically secure" (Allison 2013: 34). Yet, narratives of lifestyle migrants indicate that rather than the paradigm of a "hope-divided society" (*kibō kakusa shakai*) (Yamada 2004), life in the countryside holds hope for those often dismissed as "losers" by members of conventional society just as migrants that could be categorized as "winners" due to their high educational backgrounds and previous working experience in elite companies turn out to be facing ontological pressures of their self-chosen irregular employment.

Both migrants' statements at the beginning of this chapter could also be taken as pointing to two aspects inherent in migration that have been perceived as dichotomous: Appadurai has distinguished between an "ethics of probability" and an "ethics of possibility" (Appadurai 2013: 299) in humanity's orientation toward the future (Koehn 2016: 153). According to Appadurai, the ethics of probability is evident in the "modern regimes of diagnosis, counting, and accounting," while the ethics of possibility is intricately related to hope, aspiration, and perspective as it "expands the field of the imagination" (2013: 295). In other words, we find the conflicting dimensions of agency (or at least, moving toward agency) and being managed in a system of constraints that is based on the calculation of costs and benefits.

Appadurai's view highlights the two somewhat paradoxical directions inherent in the phenomenon of migration, as governmental regimes across the globe seek to control migratory flows through a variety of measures including detailed statistical documentation of the number of those on the move. On the other hand, media like to focus on the miraculous and dramatic escape of migrants from their war-torn home countries, highlighting the new possibilities that open up to these lucky few. They rarely focus on the fact, however, that in many cases these individuals are bound to end up in precarious jobs and face a multiplicity of barriers on their way to integration in their safe havens.

Even if the situation of the individuals I depict here may seem quite different at first sight, I would like to draw on and depart from Appadurai and propose in this chapter that the migrant trajectories depicted throughout the monograph embody both possibility and probability, yet the line between these poles is not as clear-cut as he suggested. In the case of Japan, governmental actors increasingly like to refer to the paradigm of possibility with regard to rural areas. On the one hand, at the "macro" level, local governments' initiatives are often the result of the pressure to show that they are taking measures to fight against depopulation, regardless of most locals being aware that these measures will not make a great difference in the long term. This also ties in with Love's cogent argument that recent initiatives by diverse actors to revive locality in remote rural areas are nothing but attempts to "convert legacies of marginalization into celebrations of cultural diversity as a way of shifting responsibility for the future of the depleted countryside onto its inhabitants" (Love 2013: 112).

Against this background of increasing despair over the impossibility of turning around the ticking demographic time bomb of aging, depopulation, and lack of offspring in rural areas and sustained attempts of decentralization, programs such as the Ministry of Internal Affairs and Communication's volunteers for cooperation in community revitalization (*chiiki okoshi kyōryokutai*) have resulted in a palpable rise in urban youth residing in rural areas. The two migrants cited at the beginning also work as volunteers for cooperation in community revitalization. As a result of this influx, a partial shift in perspective and thinking what rural areas have to offer has occurred. As mentioned in the introduction, recently, Ishiba Shigeru, Japan's minister in charge of regional revitalization (*chihō sōsei tantō daijin*) since September 2014 argued in the 2015 winter issue of the magazine *Turns* that previously, the conventional idea was to move to Tokyo from rural areas to fulfill one's dream and then move back to one's original home after retirement. Now, the idea that has recently been gaining ground is for people to move to rural areas to fulfill their dreams. Furthermore, Minister Ishiba, himself originally from Tottori Prefecture, the least populated prefecture in a remote part of Western Japan facing the Japanese Sea, explained that the individuals who will change rural areas will change Japan, arguing that in Japan's history, change of the governmental regime always originated in rural areas, referring to the Meiji Reform as an example (*Turns* 2015: 10). The minister predicts that twenty-first-century Japan will be shaped by the regions—Ishiba's statement clearly shows the shifting position of rural areas in Japan's governmental discourse and the high priority it ascribes to the paradigm of possibility, quite in contrast to Appadurai's polarized structure of government as probability and civil sector as possibility. Simultaneously, Ishiba's position could also be interpreted as being in accordance with the neoliberal stance of stealthily delegating responsibility for the viability of remote hamlets to local actors (and those who like to identify themselves with them) (Klien 2020: xvi).

On the other hand, at the individual or "micro" level, many narratives contain elements of hope, vision, and perspective. Yet, these elements of positive outlook and a better personal (and eventually societal) future concur with feelings of insecurity, uncertainty, and risk, although most migrants do not depict these latter feelings as necessarily negative but more as an inevitable side effect of the freedom they have opted for. Migrant trajectories introduced in this chapter confirm Allison's poignant claim that individuals in post-growth Japan are "trying out new tactics (and resistances) to survive precarious times" (2013: 13).

In her fairy-tale-sounding depiction of her move from central Tokyo, to Tono, Iwate Prefecture, that was initially motivated by love for a local farmer, Isezaki Mayumi mentions that she is often asked about feelings of insecurity for the future (Isa 2017: 33). Mayumi gave up her job of seventeen years in a high-end fashion boutique in vibrant central Tokyo to pursue a rural lifestyle in Tono, well known for traditional folklore and unique festivals—an improbable move as her trajectory entails a radical shift on several levels. Mayumi's narrative could be approached as embodying a transition from Appadurai's probability to possibility in the sense that she describes her former fast-paced life as centered on achieving an endlessly updated wardrobe, while she is now living a self-sufficient life with her family and is in the process of setting up an organic farming business with her husband while taking care of her two infants. Mayumi claims that she does not have a sense of insecurity. Work, money, and her children are her main concerns, but for the time being, all are more or less OK (*ima ha dore mo nantoka natteimasu*) as she is well integrated in the local community, she and her husband have several sources of income, and she is thinking about ways of linking farming and her original work of design in the future (Isa 2017: 33).

Furthermore, Mayumi observes that in retrospect her move to Tono made her realize that when she was living in Tokyo, she was always busy and restless (*seka seka*) and could not live according to her own pace. Now that she lives a lifestyle in farming she feels that her life is in accordance with the change of the seasons and that her "self" does not get buried (*jibun ga umorenai*): "If one moves oneself, the world is going to change and one can in fact shape the world according to one's own pace" (Isa 2017: 35). This statement directly relates to possibility and the idea that as an individual one can take control and make an impact despite living a life in harmony at one's own pace and in accordance with one's own values.

"I feel that in the countryside it is easier to realize what I really want to do than in the city."

Risa's story shares a similar departure from self-doubt as the incentive for relocating from Tokyo to a rural area. After graduating from university, Risa worked at a bistro in Shimokitazawa in west Tokyo as well as in a company planning events. However, the longer she worked, the more she felt a growing sense of uneasiness:

> I felt that my way of thinking that should have been flexible turned more and more rigid and that my perspective had narrowed down. I noticed that all I was concerned about was related to money: how much money I needed to earn to make a living, how much money was required to do what. Whatever I did, it was not related to do what I really wanted to do as a passion, so I did not feel a sense of happiness. I thought that if I went on like this I could not realize myself and I could not give my best, so I decided to quit my job. (http://www.furusato-web.jp/iju/niigata-tokamachi, accessed 5 February 2017)

After quitting her job, Risa heard about a program called "Niigata Inaka College" (literally, Niigata Countryside College), which consisted of gaining firsthand experience farming and in other activities carried out by local citizens. Since Risa's father is originally from Fukushima Prefecture, she was interested in moving somewhere north of Tokyo, so Niigata seemed an attractive location. The fact that the program was limited to one month in duration also made it easy to make the decision to enroll in March 2014. The first time she arrived, the three to four meters of snow piling up in Matsudai, Tokamachi, were impressive, and even more so the smooth management of snow that locals carried out daily. Furthermore, she was impressed with the local traditional seasonal customs. When Risa heard about a vacancy for an intern in a lettuce factory for one year when her one-month program was coming to an end, she decided to stay and apply for the internship. While working as an intern, she also did occasional jobs for the German architect Karl Bengs, who has been restoring traditional houses in the area since the mid-1990s when he moved to the area. Bengs remarked that he was thinking about possibly using abandoned houses as restaurants. It all came together then: Bengs's passion for restoring traditional houses and Risa's experience of having worked in a bistro in Tokyo. Furthermore, they encountered a chef from the area who had spent seventeen years as a chef in French cuisine working in Tokyo and Hokkaido, so the project of starting a restaurant in Matsudai took shape. It was opened in June 2015, when the Echigo-Tsumari Art Triennale was held, a contemporary art festival that has attracted numerous visitors from Tokyo and other places. Risa recalls:

> More people than expected visited our restaurant and various things happened that were not anticipated, so a lot of things had to be postponed. It was something like "Wow, things like this happen" and then trying to come up with a sort of crisis management in that situation. In retrospect, it was not so much as if my life changed gradually but it felt as if something would happen, and it was one year and a half punctuated by permanent change. Learning from the mistakes repeatedly, I now feel that we have finally turned into a professional place. (http://www.furusato-web.jp/iju/ niigata-tokamachi, accessed 5 February 2017)

Summing up, Risa's remarks show that in her case as well, a sense of responsibility, uncertainty, and growth all coexist; in other words, hope and risk are both part of her story. This is also evident from her statement that she lives a life in Tokamachi "where every day is filled with fresh surprises and a sense of accomplishment." While she was focused on money when living in Tokyo, she feels that she has changed considerably:

In Tokyo, everything is converted into money. But here, I help others solve problems with their computers, help others in their paddies and in turn get some rice for free. Sometimes locals also leave some vegetables at my entrance. Of course, it takes money to live in Matsudai but there are many other options of receiving and giving and I am very happy about this. I hope that in fifty years, I can also reach a stage where I will be the one to present younger people with vegetables, that's what I am hoping to do. (Interview on 16 June 2016)

She has managed to blend in well with the local community yet constantly meets a stream of nonlocals through her work as the restaurant manager with her boss being from Europe. Although the restaurant is in a traditional Japanese wooden house, it feels like a British pub with some exotic Asian interior elements. When I go to meet Risa in the restaurant in June 2016, her cute puppy dog comes to greet me—usually dogs are not permitted in restaurants in Japan. Risa's place of work is an eclectic mix of Japanese and overseas furniture and design from a panoply of historic epochs and reflects the transnational mind-set held by the architect.

Furthermore, I posit that this close coexistence of chance and control is one of the characteristics of post-growth Japan that most individuals who relocate to rural areas grapple with. The reason for this coexistence of chance and control is the transitional shift Japanese society finds itself in at present, with the postwar system built on high economic growth and "my-home-ism" (Allison 2013: 22) being replaced by a "liquid Japan" characterized by uncertainty, precarity, and overall gloom. The "ordinary lifestyle" and social contract associated with regular employment that used to be taken for granted by employers in postwar Japan has become practicable for only a few (Allison 2013), apart from the fact that many individuals opt for different lifestyles in the first place, as is evident in the following vignettes as well.

"Having dreams is fine but ultimately it all comes down to money and how you can persuade others to support your dreams."

Makoto, who is briefly featured at the beginning of this chapter, is in his mid-thirties and moved to an agricultural town with less than seven thousand residents in Hokkaido as a community volunteer for regional revitalization two and half years ago. He points out that he had previously been to Hokkaido on his bike for leisure and had a vague idea that it could be nice to live there for a while. Having seen a TV program about the community volunteers for regional revitalization program on NHK state television, he decided to apply. For him, it is the first time living by himself as he was residing with his parents back in Tokyo and Saitama where he grew up. Without previous experience as a full-time employee since he only worked part-time in a convenience store in his neighborhood after his graduation from university, he says that he realized the hard way that obtaining professional skills he was interested in was not as easy as he expected. The local government he works for rejected his requests to work outdoors farming as the first community volunteer employed in this town; instead, he was asked to work indoors in the local souvenir shop. In the beginning he made various suggestions to the local government about how the town could promote its revitalization; however, reactions were less than positive. With a sigh, he points out that rumors have it that the local officials expect him to join the local government after his contract expires. However, Makoto confesses that he has no intentions of joining them since his priority is to have control of his own time.

He dreams of opening a manga or internet café in town but lacks the business experience to put this into practice. He also talks about selling photographs of local places online or offering services repairing computers in town. More than anything else, he observes, he is not interested in doing a job where he needs to engage closely with other people. Above all, he wants to work at his own pace as a freelancer. His ideal is to work on his computer, read books, do indoor activities quietly. He indicates that after two and a half years in town, he ultimately feels that he has not been successful relating to locals. He concedes that there are some locals he meets regularly, but on the whole, he has few friends of his age range in town. Given the enormous problems he has experienced when trying to blend into the local community, he has found the network of other community volunteers for regional revitalization in the region valuable: they meet occasionally to exchange views and experiences. Asked about how relocation has changed him, he indicates that he has stopped worrying about what other people think of him, since so many of his suggestions were rejected or met with lack of understanding (interview on 22 June 2017).

Although Makoto is in his mid-thirties, he has neither a partner nor concrete plans to start a family. When I ask him about his ideal lifestyle, he says that he would not mind having a relationship; however, he does not seem to actively seek a partner because he is busy worrying about his own future with only half of the year left until his contract expires. I ask him about his plans for next year. He replies that he intends to stay in town where there are many things for him to do. However, he has not decided on a place to live or work. His ideal lifestyle as a permanent camper who decides from day to day where to go does not seem in tune with his present work, for which societal engagement seems a key prerequisite. In retrospect, his strong reliance on social media and the internet in general was shaped by his urban origin. He says that after moving to rural Hokkaido, he realized that he could only reach most residents through real face-to-face conversation rather than social media. Asked about his long-term dream or vision, Makoto says that he prefers to lead a nomadic (the term he uses is *fura fura*) lifestyle—that is, a lifestyle that does not involve any long-term commitments, either professionally or personally. For him, having time by himself is more important than having a lifelong job and partner, it seems. He says that he cannot envisage himself living permanently in one place (interview on 22 June 2017).

Summing up, Makoto's narrative seems shaped by serendipity, withdrawal, and resistance; given his lack of social skills and lack of interest in engaging with people, his present job as a community volunteer for regional revitalization could be perceived as an ironic twist of fate. However, it could also be interpreted as "moratorium migration" in the sense that the three-year contract allows him to gain time to postpone his decision as to what to do with his life. With two and a half years of the contract being over, he does not seem to have reached a conclusion. Rather, his remark that he is ultimately interested in prolonging his *fura fura* career during a grace period makes him a prototype for post-growth Japanese torn between societal expectations of stable employment, their own ideas about creating freelance jobs for themselves, and the struggle of turning personal fantasies into viable realities.

From the Water Business to Forestry: Moving toward a Start-Up?

> I have realized that money is the key. I was planning on downsizing when I moved to the countryside but some expenses are higher than in Tokyo.
>
> —Mitsuo (interview on 22 June 2016)

Mitsuo, who was also briefly featured at the beginning of this chapter, is a stout male in his mid-thirties with impeccable *keigo* (Japanese polite language) skills who moved to rural Hokkaido in summer 2016. In his white *keitora* (literally, light truck) he looks just like any other local farmer. The reality could not be more different: Back in Tokyo, he was a manager of male hosts in a club in Shibuya, earning 800,000 JPY per month. The salary he receives now as a community volunteer for regional revitalization equals the money he spent on his rent in central Tokyo. The lifestyle of going to bed at 5:00 a.m. every morning and starting work in the late afternoon took a toll on his health and at some point, he remembers, he was ready for a change. At a relocation fair in Tokyo, he encountered a booth with representatives of the town he resides in now. Like Makoto, Mitsuo works as a community volunteer for regional revitalization, but in his case, his work profile is forestry. Like Makoto, Mitsuo says that he did not have any personal connections with Hokkaido—apart from the fact that his former girlfriend was from Hokkaido. But, he points out, they just split up and he is living by himself. Mitsuo just bought a spacious house in the mountains some fifteen minutes' drive from the town center. He is planning to convert this house into a guesthouse and lodge with the aim of attracting urbanites interested in recreational hunting. Deer are prevalent in the mountains and he is planning organized tours and a start-up. The other option for him is to join the forestry company he is presently working in as a full-time employee. Makoto and Mitsuo are both of the same age and both originate from Tokyo, yet they could not be more different. Makoto seems insecure, introverted, and focused on himself; Mitsuo seems confident, driven to turn himself into a success story, and his experience as a host manager has honed his business and social skills. Yet he describes his sense of insecurity about his present position as a community volunteer and his plans to create his own job soon. At the same time, Makoto and Mitsuo both mention difficulties making local friends as there is a lack of residents of their age group. Mitsuo says that he mostly spends his free time by himself, adding that he does not mind being by himself (interview on 22 June 2017).

Mitsuo observes that he misses going out for drinks and eating good food—something that was part of his previous lifestyle on a day-to-day basis. Rural Hokkaido does not offer any places that are attractive for him to go out to eat or drink; paying 3,500 JPY for a good gin and tonic is unthinkable in Hokkaido given the low pay there. He says that ultimately his ideal involves a two-pronged lifestyle with some time spent in Hokkaido and the rest spent in Tokyo. Like Makoto, Mitsuo does not mention any plans of starting a family. His narrative is heavily dominated by work—in fact, he points out that for him the most important identity marker is the job he has. Creating a sustainable mode of work for himself seems his primary concern at present. He observes that if he opted for living in Hokkaido in the long term, he would not have any problems living on minimum wage (*saiteigen de mo yatte ikeru kedo*), but that's not what he is aiming for. The income level in Hokkaido is low, but he does not want to forget his Tokyo experience. The other day, a friend brought a bottle of good wine; it had been months since he had tasted really good wine as there are not places to taste high-quality liquor in rural Hokkaido. Back in Tokyo, he despised supermarket chains like AEON; now, there is no other choice in rural Hokkaido and, due to his reduced monthly income, he feels it is expensive. Before his relocation he had plans to downsize and seek a more minimalist lifestyle; now, after experiencing rural life for one year, he has reaffirmed the importance of money and feels that he is not interested in cutting down his expenses. Above all, he emphasizes, he aspires to a free life, creating the work that he feels is personally fulfilling for himself.

As argued in other chapters, the majority of migrants aspire to a better quality of life by moving away from work as a "structured obligation" (Gratton 2011) and achieving more freedom with regard to how they spend their time. Ultimately, most individuals who relocate to rural areas do so for reasons of work even if they start by talking about leisure, nature, and "the slow life." Many mention their aspiration to a more self-determined way of working, many narrate that their previous stable jobs did not provide them with the long-term prospect of excitement and self-growth they had expected, many say that they were tired and bored with merely executing orders by their bosses; others eventually realized that treading in their father's steps by "opting" for the same job as their father was personally not fulfilling. However, whatever the incentives for the relocation were, the reality migrants face in their new places of residence tends to differ considerably from their expectations and aspirations. Once they have lived in their new rural environment for a few months, many settlers get so busy with their new activities that "the slow life" fades into a distant dream.

The migrants introduced in this monograph can all be categorized as lifestyle migrants as reasons for their move were predominantly
non-economic, yet they all have their respective stories, biographies, and
specific reasons to relocate. Evidently, there is no one type, yet interviews
and participant observation indicate that dissatisfaction with lack of
agency and lack of perspective in determining one's personal mode of
working is a driving force in many trajectories. Many of my interviewees are outgoing, positive, vibrant, and have gleaming eyes when they
describe their visions and aspirations—quite a difference from conventional academic or corporate environments where individuals often trade
their passions or *yarigai* (purpose in life) for safety and order. The large
majority of my interviewees have an above-average interest in asserting
themselves professionally in a way that they perceive as personally fulfilling; many have high levels of education, with experience abroad as
well. However, we also find (mostly male) migrants who appear to lack
confidence, a clear goal, and drive and seem content with lingering with
no clear aim in life—the type I describe as "moratorium migrants," that
is, migrants who choose rural life as a buffer zone to postpone career
choices that they would rather never make if it were up to them. At
the same time, we also find moratorium migrants who wish to experiment with a diversity of lifestyles and modes of working in rural areas
before making an informed decision about their careers and personal
lives.

Between Lifestyle and Livelihood

The search for quality of life and emotional as well as material space
is one side of the coin; the other is making a living in rural areas and
the vitality, sense of strategy, social skills, and persistence required to be
successful against the looming background of an increasingly precarious
labor market in post-Lehman-shock Japan. Another take would be the
search for new forms of work after the end of lifelong employment
that originated in postwar Japan. This is why Korpela's observation that
lifestyle migration "suits the neoliberal agenda" (O'Reilly 2014: 229;
Korpela 2014: 27–45) is so appropriate in the case of Japan as well.
Opportunity and risk coexist in rural areas: the settlers described exude
aspiration and drive; however, only some are equipped with the specific

set of skills required to survive as they have been socialized in a society that prioritizes stability, team spirit, and collective order, with little institutional support for entrepreneurship, self-initiative, creativity, and thinking outside the box. Furthermore, despite their appealing activities and aims, many have been socialized in education and employment shaped and regulated by postwar thinking of material growth and a sense of zero-sum game competition. This is why in many narratives a coexistence of agency and anomie, the ethics of possibility and probability, is salient: Migrants are enthusiastic about the closeness to nature, outdoor activities, and local communities. However, they also mention the lack of entertainment, venues to consume café latte and high-quality Chinese food, and disappointment about the low income of their new jobs and even less leisure time due to a host of unpaid social commitments for the local community. Others indicate that they have the opportunity to meet a broad variety of individuals that urban life does not offer; yet especially in locales with a considerable number of in-migrants, some new settlers mention pressures of having to come up with original ideas for revitalization, selling themselves, finding a niche to carve out a small-scale business for themselves as they are surrounded by other aspiring and ambitious migrants.

A common trait of migrant narratives is that they contain "a breaking point," that is, a time when individuals realized that they wish to proceed in a different direction from their lifestyles pursued until then. In some cases, this breaking point is the result of a job loss, health issues, giving birth, emotional issues, or an extended period of questioning and doubts that "something was missing or not quite right." This decision to change course often meets with a lack of understanding by friends and family, yet migrants nevertheless choose to pursue what they deem appropriate for their well-being and that of their families. They tend to focus on the present rather than pondering and planning their future, like previous generations whose principal aims in life could be neatly recited: finding a job in a good (i.e., lifetime) company, marriage, children, purchasing one's home, secure pension. Representatives of contemporary youth on the contrary say that they do not have plans and that they feel that it does not make sense for them to make plans. They are overly satisfied with their life in the wake of their relocation. Nevertheless, many concede that chances are high that they will not be residing in the same place in five years. Chance encounters are often mentioned as having had a great impact on their lives, serendipity seems a key feature in numerous trajectories. In fact, follow-up fieldwork showed that numerous individuals I had interviewed six years ago had moved on to other places or back to their places of origin for diverse reasons. Many live by themselves, are active members of various communities, or live in alternative communities such as collective housing instead of the classical postwar nuclear family. Only a few mention plans of ever purchasing their own home due to their mobile lifestyles—many rent houses as they move or share accommodation with others; the postwar dream of owning property seems to have disappeared together with the previously uncontested idea of having a family. Yet, despite—and perhaps because of—a lingering and palpable sense of uncertainty, migrants refer to a "lifestyle that they produce in the countryside" (*chiiki de umidasu kurashi*) that is characterized by creativity and a sense of vibrant energy (Isa 2017: 123); this points to agency being the other side of the coin of precariousness and insecurity.

Settlers tend to observe that they have their personal set of principles by which they abide, yet with changing circumstances they may need to change their place of residence and work again. Some consider their time in the countryside to be a limited period of learning and self-growth on their journey to professional independence as entrepreneurs. At the same time, they describe their considerable satisfaction with greater self-determination at work, more time with their families (if they have one), more time for themselves, and time to reflect due to less financial pressure as a result of lower living costs. Many mention more extensive and intense conversations with their new friends and peers in rural areas due to the lack of entertainment and options for consumption and the fact that there is only a small community and limited pool of individuals to socially engage with. Interviewees also describe longer periods of time by themselves after relocation as a positive experience as this allowed them to reflect and ponder in-depth what is important to them, while in their previous urban lives most were so occupied with coping with the daily stresses of professional careers that they never had the time to lean back and reflect on their lives in peace and quiet. Several migrants in remote rural areas mentioned having extended conversations among themselves on a variety of topics for lack of peers they felt they could relate to. Some reveal that this practice has enhanced their emotional maturity, reflective skills, and critical thinking.

Meaningful Mobilities and Mobilities as a
Way of Relating to Neoliberal Reality

Pulling together the various threads that have crisscrossed this chapter so far, geographer Tim Cresswell's notion of "meaningful mobilities" (2001, 2006) comes to mind, that is, his definition of mobility as "movement imbued with meaning." All the migrants introduced earlier have chosen the option of mobility as an instrument to achieve certain goals, mostly associated with career and lifestyle. In many cases, relocation is a prerequisite to achieving a better balance between career and family while improving the overall quality of life for the individual. Cresswell's proposition that mobilities are socially produced, that is, the assumption that understandings of mobilities depend on different societal contexts, also significantly impacts individual takes on mobility. The decisions of the individuals discussed earlier to opt for mobility have been shaped by circumstances such as the Great East Japan Earthquake, the needs of the family, individual dissatisfaction with and the general values inherent in their work and livelihoods. Yet, in many cases, the simplistic dichotomous formula of "sedentarism" versus "nomadism," "settlement" versus "mobility," and "stagnation" versus "dynamism" does not seem to work when analyzing individual trajectories. Many individuals live a sedentary life in the sense that they tend to their paddy fields, engage in farming, live in a spacious house with their family. Yet, at the same time, they engage in other work in another town, make regular trips to other places for professional reasons, engage in conversation on social media, use the internet, and so forth. In other words, despite their choice to live in a geographically rooted place, their daily routine is not ruled by fixity, just as their values and narratives seem essentially shaped by transience and transcendence, echoing Aoyama's findings in his research on Japanese migrants in China (2015b: 23).

I propose that the wealth of empirical data presented throughout this volume illustrates that individuals that can be perceived as "post-modern nomads" in the sense that they "embody societies of de-territorialisation, constituted by lines of flight rather than by points or nodes" (Urry 2000: 27). This generation is resorting to mobility in order to create a perspective for themselves as they are hard-pressed to find employment that makes sense, both in a financial and emotional sense—quite in contrast to the postwar generation of Japanese employees who may have had less choices in terms of lifestyle yet were blessed with greater stability because joining a company was synonymous with lifelong employment. Furthermore, prospective employees in postwar Japan had an entirely different emotional starting point: they were socialized in an atmosphere of pressure to put their best efforts into rebuilding a Japan that was in tatters, which resulted in the individual goal of working toward purchasing a house for their family, buying a car, buying a fridge. In other words, employees sacrificed themselves for the sake of the company, but they also had a clear goal in life: the ultimate aim was to achieve material wealth and stability.

Adey has proposed that "mobilities are a way of relating" as he poignantly argues that mobilities "involve how we form relations with others and indeed how we make sense of this" (2010: 19). Migrants' narratives presented throughout this monograph vividly illustrate that individuals make sense of the world that they have moved to in the process of mobility: They form new relations with locals and nonlocals and thus gradually integrate into their new place of residence. They adopt certain practices that had been unfamiliar to them until then and abandon others; they adapt their communication patterns to local standards in order to achieve better acceptance in the local community—and in many cases, create business opportunities for themselves in the process. The trajectories and narratives of migrants across Japan highlight that mobility is "a lived relation" (Adey 2010: xvii, drawing on McNay 2005: 3–4) as it is their orientation to oneself, to others, and the world through mobility (Adey 2010: xvii). Mobility constitutes a means of making sense of the changing, neoliberal reality of the labor market.

Kana, the student from Tokyo turned farmer in a mountain hamlet in Niigata Prefecture portrayed at the beginning of chapter 3, made her choice to renounce the job offer in an advertising agency in Tokyo six years ago and pursue a career as a farmer in a hamlet with just thirteen residents in the six households remaining instead. On the one hand, her case could be interpreted as the "classic" case of someone opting for the "benefits of slow living over the hustle bustle of big city life" (Iizuka 2017). She mentions the great impact villagers' vitality and values made on her when she came to the hamlet for the first time as a volunteer after a strong earthquake in 2004. Kana mentions how she was impressed by the independence and creativity of villagers growing their own crops. These "rosy" aspects of lifestyle mobility to the rural for reasons of values, traditions, and human relations are usually taken up by media, as in the *Japan Times* article on the "slow life" by Megumi Iizuka. Yet, the other side of the coin is the aspect of migrants strategically investing in rural areas as lifetime employment disappears and corporate jobs entail multiple risks. The aforementioned newspaper article describes Sato as being "quite satisfied with her current life" in terms of both quality and income as she "feels much more secure here than in Tokyo because I built everything myself, such as my job and relations with people" (Iizuka 2017). During my interview with Kana in June 2016, however, she observed with a chuckle that she wished she had had more detailed information on living expenses and average incomes in rural areas before making her decision to relocate. Apart from the evident bias of media on certain aspects in their depiction of rural areas and the individuals attracted to rural areas, Kana's choice to relocate to the countryside can be interpreted as a form of risk management. Even if her income is much lower than Tokyo standards, she observes that social relations contribute to her sense of security. Kana also mentions the sense of ease and comfort that she gained from the fact that locals in the hamlet told her that she is just fine as she is (despite her chubbiness), whereas in Tokyo her friends would always pick on her looks, suggesting that she should diet (Isa 2017: 62). For Kana, moving to the countryside also constituted a means to overcome pressures to look a certain way. In other words, relocation allowed her to emancipate herself to "be herself," even if that meant enjoying eating and looking chubby.

Other respondents referred to this aspect of emotional security, as described in other chapters; for example, the sense of security and emotional consolation migrants derive from cross-generational exchange as well as the emotional and material benefits of receiving vegetables and other food from neighbors (and giving back at times). In the context of this *o-susowake* culture of reciprocity that pervades life in rural communities, comparing salaries and income in terms of black and white figures in rural and urban areas does not seem to make sense. Similarly, many villagers pursue a variety of work throughout the year with seasonal fluctuations instead of holding just one job, as is usual in urban areas. Some of these work activities are paid, others are unpaid but come with communal benefits and do not fall into the leisure or volunteer sector. Some new settlers I interviewed mentioned that they initially came for a visit to the place they were considering to inspect the collective house available and were so impressed that they decided to move right away without having a job in the new place. When they told the local government administering the share house, they were offered a (temporary) job in the local government. This is just one example of the relative ease with which some migrants almost have jobs fall into their laps.

A former male employee in university administration shares a similar story of having a job offer when he was drinking tea with locals after moving from Osaka to Sakaemura in Nagano Prefecture, pointing out that trust plays an essential role in the job search and the help of a key local person one feels comfortable discussing problems with is invaluable (Isa 2017: 82). However, most jobs in the local government are contracted for a limited period, and in many other cases, migrants have difficulties finding a long-term job of personal interest to them and have to get by with manual jobs just to pay their bills. Hence, many think about creating their own jobs, yet few have the necessary vision, organizational skills, business acumen, social skills, verve, discipline, and persistence to go freelance. Other long-term urban settlers hold several side jobs to sustain themselves rather than a main job, as is prevalent in urban life. For example, the male migrant from Osaka who started a new life in Sakaemura just mentioned delivers the local newspaper in the mornings five days a week, works as a part-timer selling vegetables in a shop where farmers' products are directly sold to customers, and works as staff sending out local rice for seven days a month, mostly at the beginning of the month (Isa 2017: 83). There is also seasonal work in agriculture that keeps settlers busy at certain times in the year.

Other migrants, such as thirty-four-year-old Keiko from a small town near Osaka, manage to combine an outdoor rural lifestyle with urbanite entrepreneurship in creative ways: Originally a graduate from an art university in Kyoto, she moved to a mountain village with four thousand residents in Kochi Prefecture with her husband and son eight years ago where they live in a traditional house over one hundred years old. She regularly writes essays, blogs, and manga about her life, has an online shop selling natural food products, and started a café next to her house that attracted the attention of media and has been popular with visitors from across Japan. Keiko's aim is to achieve a form of work and management that affords a balance between family, work, and the local community. Interestingly, Keiko's online store is called Potchiridō (literally, hall of just the right amount), which refers to her aspiration to live a balanced life that is not too busy and not too relaxed and makes her personally happy (Isa 2017: 98–99). In other words, her goal is to create the life she aspires to by herself (*jibun no jinsei wo jibun de dezain suru koto*) (www.pocchiri.com/SHOP/yamacafe-nikki.html, accessed 15 February 2017).

With rare exceptions, local municipalities do not have the necessary human resources to provide effective advice for migrants interested in pursuing a career as a freelancer in the area, such as Keiko, since carving out a niche as a freelancer requires a set of skills and thinking that are not typical of area residents. She mentions her worries in the initial phase of her relocation to Kochi Prefecture that the income available to her and her husband could be insufficient. Her husband, however, emphasized that rather than having disposable cash, building a relation of trust with the local community seemed more important to him (Isa 2017: 105–106) because, in his view, the future would have social relations with other residents emerge as the priority and source of security rather than material income. Others, like lifestyle migrants in Itoshima, Fukuoka Prefecture, take a more pragmatic approach, saying that they aspire to implementing a sustainable lifestyle of self-sufficiency but do not wish to be constrained in their lifestyle options by a lack of disposable cash (Isa 2017: 122)—an attitude that was widely prevalent in many respondents living in post-growth Japan.

Constituting Societal Structures through Mobility

An additional aspect of mobility as a way of relating to one's surroundings is the effect of constituting societal structures through one's decision to relocate (Urry 2000: 49). Migrants may be perceived as a minority that does not make a great difference in terms of Japanese society overall; or the individual trajectories presented throughout this volume may be seen as small steps that add up to a larger whole that will effect larger societal change in Japan and beyond as individuals choose to conceive strategies to create what they consider ideal work, evade unsatisfactory modes of work, and question unfulfilling modes of living as a result of their mobility. Some resort to mobility to play for time and to evade complex personal issues they have not had the power to face—mobility as moratorium if you like. Others resort to mobility as a career path to acquire additional professional skills. Despite the diversity of migrants' motives and trajectories in all cases, mobility is invariably an instrument (used consciously or otherwise) to constitute societal structures, be it by devising new modes of work and hence evading the need to revert to conventional companies or by creating new forms of living by establishing a share house and hence creating an alternative to conventional family structures. Makoto, Mitsuo, Kana, and many other migrants introduced in this book have devised strategic ways of establishing relations with the local and nonlocal (i.e., other lifestyle migrants in the area) community in ways that make sense to them both professionally and emotionally. I agree with Mathews and White's view that historical generational change emerges as "a vast array of individual choices and micro-interactions rather than through organized protest or even conscious generational solidarity" (Mathews and White 2004: 6). In a similar vein, I argue that individual choices of alternative patterns of behavior and life courses will accumulate and eventually form the basis for long-term change in Japanese society toward more diversity. Hence I do not share Furuichi's pessimism about the incapability of contemporary youth of changing Japan. Rather, I contend that change in Japan will happen due to the action of "quiet mavericks" (Toivonen, Norasakkunkit, and Uchida 2011: 1; Furuichi 2014: 200–203) described as individuals who "engage with society on their own terms" (Toivonen, Norasakkunkit, and Uchida 2011: 4). These are individuals who veer from conventional life courses by opting for alternative practices, just as the vignettes of the mobile individuals presented in this book vividly document.

Aspiring to *Waku Waku* Instead of Material Affluence?

> I myself worked in a global company after graduation from university and felt that it was an exciting experience but I did not get the impression that my work made the world more interesting or produced something innovative.
>
> —Koshiba in Teruo Kurosaki's *We Work Here*

Former investment banker turned freelancer and operator of an alternative space Midoriso Koshiba Miho observes that if people start to think that working is fun and produces a sense of *waku waku*, then society can turn into something positive.

Koshiba's statement hits the nail on the head: Youth in contemporary Japan do not share the goal of postwar generations of working to achieve material belongings, nor do most subscribe to the tenet of self-sacrifice for a company whose values they cannot relate to on a personal level. Many find the idea of self-employment attractive but also distant, since many have a broad idea of what they are interested in but struggle to define what they exactly wish to do professionally in the long term and do not have infrastructural support to go freelance. However, this lack of infrastructural support for individuals interested in starting up as entrepreneurs in Japan may be the smaller issue, with the key problem being the lack of serious passion for a given career on the part of most migrants. Many individuals have degrees from reputable universities under their belt, yet they seem incapable or unwilling to settle down to invest themselves in one career. This lack of professional commitment goes hand in hand with a lack of emotional commitment with many being single or having a partner but not families with children. The postwar dream of having a classic nuclear family with two children in a house in suburbia is gone for good; youth in their twenties seem most happy when catching up on news on their tablets and informing others about their activities on social media, as cogently argued by Furuichi (2014: 166); pets have taken the place of offspring for materially affluent couples, and social media fills the void for the less well-off. Functional shopping at low-end chains such as Uniqlo has followed the fixation in the bubble era with high-end foreign brands. Instead of eating out in trendy, expensive restaurants, individuals in post-growth Japan seem to prefer gathering in their own homes with friends. The end of material affluence has been replaced with financial precariousness and emotional uncertainty; individuals are striving to carve out a niche for themselves in their quest for a sustainable future that both provides a livelihood and is emotionally satisfying—a combination that only the lucky few manage to achieve.

Okamoto poignantly describes this situation between going with the flow and despair many Japanese youth find themselves in: "The gap between people who use the information they are surrounded with actively and those individuals who live without hope is becoming salient. I guess we now understand what reality is about. And it is difficult to have hope under these circumstances" (Okamoto 2012: 76–77).

In other words, migrants' narratives reflect personal struggles to balance individual agency and anomie resulting from systemic constraints. They do so by focusing on the moment, on "small happiness," on *waku waku*—a combination of vibrancy, happiness, and positive drive that originates from engaging in activities that are personally fulfilling and inspiring. The recurring element of achieving *waku waku* in migrants' narratives is a distinct departure from the postwar preoccupation with material wealth, although some narratives indicate that individuals prefer to have a comfort zone of material wealth (even if the definition of what constitutes this comfort varies individually). Males in their late thirties talk about the smell of freshly roasted coffee in the morning, energizing music on the radio while they drive to work, or the joys of having a cigarette after finishing agricultural work and being surrounded by the ravishingly beautiful landscape of rice paddies. In contrast, their predecessors were closing down their senses, being forced to commute by train to do a job they did not enjoy in a company they did not personally believe in, despite its being a place that secured lifelong employment.

Some settlers have managed to achieve a successful career in a reputable company—something their parents would probably have been content with; yet many individuals in contemporary Japan cannot help questioning the meaningfulness of pursuing this career path in the long run because they grew up in households with fathers being mostly absent due to work obligations. This postmodern reflection and the resulting decision to choose a different lifestyle for noneconomic reasons is a salient feature of post-growth Japan. I argue that this option for change in individuals will transform Japanese society, just as Okamoto has proposed (2012: 9). The other side of the quest for *waku waku* is an emerging acceptance of risk, as Rosenberger incisively argues: "A sense of risk and an ensuing search for new ways to live life and solve problems have captured the imagination of the young people in the nation" (2014: 131).

Serendipity, Surprise, and Sharing

An interview published in the 2015 winter issue of the magazine *Turns* with the nomad worker and web designer Nishimura Haruhiko similarly contains a mix of control and constraint as he refers to a rediscovery of the senses, serendipity, surprise, and sharing inherent in post-growth youth and middle-aged individuals. In his mid-forties and having twenty years of experience as a corporate employee in Tokyo, Nishimura has set up several collective housing projects and coworking spaces across Japan after retiring from his corporate career and feeling in need of a third place for working and social relations. A rising star on the nomad work and collective housing scene, he cleverly promotes minimizing material belongings and sharing facilities in order to reduce living costs, promoting serendipity and the emergence of relations through ad hoc encounters and a sense of surprise and *waku waku* through leaving things to evolve naturally (*chokkan ya nariyuki ni makaseru*) (*Turns* 2015: 52–53). He also calls on individuals seeking to successfully set up work in the country-side to actively engage with the local community, with an eye on using abandoned material belongings that locals may have; the line between sustainable lifestyles or parasitic living is fluid, but Nishimura has managed to carve out a niche combining nomad working, the development of IT applications, and leisure at his own pace in a remote rural hamlet in Niigata Prefecture, where he is based at present. As Nishimura's narrative simultaneously contains calls for creativity, curiosity, and vision as well as risk management and strategic hedging—neoliberal *waku waku* elegantly framed in appealing catchphrases of community and communication—I argue that he could be considered a key representative of post-growth Japanese visionary reformers with a well-defined sense of appeal to the general public, specifically, the up-and-coming generation of aspiring entrepreneurs in their twenties and thirties.

Meaningful Mobility and Downshifting

Last but not least, to return to the idea of "meaningful mobilities" coined by Tim Cresswell discussed earlier in this chapter, the individual trajectories depicted show the comprehensive shift in thinking that is under way in contemporary Japanese society: Mobility is now increasingly perceived as a positive sign of mature and responsible individuals centered on making a worthwhile contribution and achieving a life that makes sense to them individually, just as Morley had suggested that mobility "is increasingly seen as a social good and immobility increasingly acquires, by contrast the connotation of defeat, of failure and of being left behind" (2000: 202). Both settlers in their twenties who have only worked a few years as well as more senior employees at the top management level have started to actively weigh their options by reflecting carefully on their work and lives and, in many cases, choosing mobility. A geographically and territorially fixed lifestyle with the home at its center has given way to a more hybrid lifestyle of "individualized mobility," to borrow Elliott and Urry's term (2010: 87) that combines home and mobility, in a vein that reminds us of Urry's "post-modern nomads" who embody societies of deterritorialization (2000: 27).

In the majority of cases, mobile youth in one way or another refer to practices of "downshifting," that is, practices that aim to reduce living expenses, the amount of material belongings, clutter of all sorts, with the ultimate goal of facilitating a focus on meaningful things and practices. Ultimately, thinking about individual decisions to drop out of corporate careers, many narratives suggest that the lack of meaningfulness in material abundance was a major incentive. The shift from material wealth to the personal freedom to use one's time is perhaps the greatest societal transition that is presently taking place: Takasaka, the owner of the bar Tama ni ha TSUKI wo nagamemasho (Let's gaze at the moon sometimes) in Ikebukuro, Tokyo, used to work in a major department store with an annual income of 6 million JPY. Now he earns a bit more than half of this; however, he has much more time available to himself. Takasaka is not interested in making a fortune; all he wants is to make enough money to keep himself going so that he can do what he likes. Recently, after earning too much, he has increased his days off to three a week. He spends his free time with his family and works growing vegetables in Chiba Prefecture (Furuichi 2014: 209–210). Takasaka calls himself a downshifter, that is, someone who puts priority on slowing down his lifestyle, distancing himself from the consumption society, and emphasizing personal values; his bar attracts other downshifters. Takasaka's case shows that there are numerous urbanites who pursue a lifestyles based in two locations to engage in practices that make sense to them and their families while earning a living—meaningful mobility at its best.

The choices of the individuals portrayed earlier entail a complex postmodern combination of sedentary and nomadic lifestyles, of freedom and constraint, creativity and subjection, agency and subordination, resistance and compromise, a sense of vibrant energy and vision with an underlying lingering feeling of uncertainty. While I do not consider anxiety in migrant narratives in post-growth Japan to be "debilitating" in the way Yoda describes the fizzling out of the bubbly economy and the overall atmosphere of "unbearable fragmentation, opacity, and paralysis" (Yoda in Yoda and Harootunian 2006: 34–35) since some individuals clearly hold distinct visions and hope despite their struggle with self-doubt and uncertainty, the consciousness that the magic formula of life-long employment and self-sacrifice of the individual to a range of societal institutions is no longer sustainable has gained ground and social anomie is palpable. No clear direction of a new formula has emerged, so it is no surprise that migrants draw on postwar terminology and lifestyles while seeking novel approaches that seem to linger between stasis and aspiration to change, societal engagement and withdrawal, hope and resignation. Hence, the coexistence of contradictory features in one and the same fragmented experience of a single individual may ultimately be what is the essential trait of post-growth Japan and what is bound to emerge in other postindustrial societies in the near future. Perhaps the remark by a thirty-year-old female lifestyle migrant originally from Chiba Prefecture who has embarked on life on Itoshima Island illustrates the concurrence of disparate themes in a nutshell: "Personally, I think that if we manage to acquire skills to live without relying on capitalism, establish a community we can rely on and find ways of earning cash living in this way, we can solve most of the issues that we are faced with today" (Isa 2017: 122).

As argued by Rosenberger drawing on Foucault, the resistance shown by migrants to values favored by postwar mainstream life and their ensuing attempts to live according to their own values is never completely outside of the generally accepted truths and power dynamics of the times but is always present in a society (Rosenberger 2014: 107; Foucault 1980b). Such nascent confluence of resistance to and appropriation of mainstream societal values, possibility and probability, aspiration and subjection, societal engagement and withdrawal, regeneration and stagnation is all intrinsic to the fuzzy experiences of mobile subjects grappling to negotiate their lives in shifting contemporary Japan.

Chapter Five

Convergence of Work and Leisure

Blessing or Plight?

"I felt that life in the countryside holds many chances."

"Since my wife is originally from Shimane, we started a life with work and life in the two locations of Tokyo and Shimane. I found myself setting up a café and restaurant in Shimane while organizing events and working as a web designer with a few days in Tokyo every month." In November 2016, I visit Kazu's booth at the Shimane U/I-Turn Fair 2016 in Tokyo International Forum in Yūrakucho. In his early forties, he is one of the fifteen newcomers who are there to share their experiences of relocation with the fair visitors. With his wife a professional chef, it naturally turned out that she is in charge of their organic restaurant, whereas Kazu is involved in the organization and PR of the café while working in IT. The local town they relocated to three years ago has some twenty-five thousand residents. He says that when he drives in his car to work in the morning, listening to the music he likes and drinking delicious freshly roasted coffee, he feels so happy he cannot describe it. He says that his satisfaction rate with his present life is 120 percent as he is in the fortunate position of making a living from the things he enjoys doing. In the beginning he relied predominantly on clients based in Tokyo; now he says that he gets 80 percent of his work commissioned by local clients in Shimane, with only 20 percent in Tokyo. In retrospect, he says that he felt that "life in the countryside holds many chances"; depopulation in rural towns means that there is less competition and pressure. His narrative overlaps with recent advocates of a new role for rural areas in the vein of the OECD's *New Rural Paradigm* (2006) that envisages new possibilities for rural areas (Shikida 2014: 70) and Ōminami Shinya's "creative depopulation" (Matsunaga 2015: 44), a term that implies grassroots initiatives geared toward the empowerment of rural areas by creating niche functions that turn aspects that have been interpreted as disadvantages into advantages.

Kazu's vegetarian café was opened one and a half years ago; the menu is available in English and Japanese and comprises smoothies, wraps, soya yogurt, ethnic food such as Asian soya meat salad, and exotic dishes such as vegetable taco rice. When I ask him about the local reaction to the organic café opened by his wife and him, he says that rather than quantity, they are interested in attracting select regular customers who appreciate macrobiotic food as a lifestyle. The café also includes a bakery with sophisticated menu choices such as "rice mugwort nan bread," "soybean flour bean jam donut," "pizza nan dog," or "croque monsieur." These dishes are evidently influenced by French, Indian, and Japanese culinary cultures and thus constitute fusion creations. Kazu and his wife are planning to expand staff beginning April 2017. They also have scheduled a one-month winter break when the entire family intends to travel across Southeast Asia. I ask Kazu how he envisages his life and activities in twenty years. He replies that all he knows is that he will be self-employed since, regardless of all the insecurity and pressure that comes with working freelance, he prioritizes having control of his time. What he disliked most about working for an employer back in Tokyo were the frequent phone calls from his boss checking in on him just for the sake of surveillance. He also says that now that he works for himself, he feels so good waking up every morning, thinking about how he is going to make an effort to achieve satisfactory work. When he thinks back to his early thirties, he remembers often wondering, "What do I really want to do, what am I really into, what makes me feel really good" (*boku ha ittai nani ga shitain darou, nani ga suki de, nani wo suru to jūjitsu shita to omoeru n darou*). While he was enjoying himself in some ways, he also faced frequent days of depression and he says that he never wants to go back to that period of his life.

Spending money to escape his sense of emptiness ultimately did not solve his personal issue of feeling lost, and he got to the point that he felt he needed to seriously rethink his way of life. He mentions that at some point he noticed that purchasing one clothes item after another did not make him happy. Some six years ago he realized that he could only get somewhere by taking concrete action and started making efforts to disseminate something personal even if it was small. He felt that he needed to look for a way that allowed him to do what he enjoyed. If he could not manage that he strongly felt that there was no way of spending an exciting second half of his thirties and forties. If he could find a way of turning what he really enjoyed doing into work, he felt that could be a way of getting over these depressing days. When these thoughts occurred to him, he got the impression that the world opened up to him and that he had some hope. Discussing his decision to relocate from Tokyo, he observes that he did not move because he does not like his hometown; after all, he still spends 20 percent of his time in the capital and conducts regular business meetings there. When he asked himself why he keeps living in Tokyo and thought about his wife's hometown in Shimane, he felt that this constellation is more than a reason to relocate. He points out that when he thought about himself and his family, his ideal mode of work and life and the extent of freedom he aspired to, he somehow felt that it was worth living somewhere else apart from Tokyo as he could learn a lot by moving to the countryside. Even if Shimane is geographically quite far from Tokyo, it is still the same country, and he has moved back and forth by car many times transporting goods and material.

Kazu's narrative is a mix of serendipity and planning, aspired lifestyle in the sense of relocation geared toward securing more agency with regard to work and more time with the family, gauging business chances and having an eye on niche markets. Thus, his lifestyle embodies the coexistence of the need for personal growth and transformation with the workings of the neoliberal market and the pressures of the changing Japanese labor market. At first sight, Kazu seems like an easy-going, happy-go-lucky person who happened to have the chance of marrying a chef from Shimane—someone who has good social skills; yet, the other side is that he is planning to spread his business to Asia and talks about his explicit priority on self-determination, leisure, and family. He seems to fit the mold of young and midlife entrepreneurs who, rather than "finding themselves," create and adapt themselves both professionally and personally depending on circumstances in a very Baumanesque sense of liquid modernity and identity (1996). It is a new generation of Japanese individuals who, rather than opting for large-scale changes, make a clear statement in favor of change through their lifestyle choices, in Kazu's case, by quitting his corporate job and going freelance (Mathews and White 2004: 6). This lifestyle and career change coincided with corporeal movement from an urban to rural environment despite the fact that Kazu returns to his hometown Tokyo regularly. As stated in chapter 2, mobility is an ongoing process with a further relocation to a third place being a realistic option for many interviewees. Just as Mathews and White have observed in their seminal volume about Japan's changing generations, youth use a variety of strategies and tactics to pursue lifestyles that personally make sense to them and to not enter "the adult social order" (2004: 2), and mobility is a valid instrument in this process for some individuals.

On another note, the organic café Kazu and his wife have opened could be perceived as a venture that shares features with "creative tourism" (Sasaki 2014: 15), that is, emerging forms of tourism that contribute to overall regional change by bringing in new values and attracting first-time visitors. Creative tourism envisages regular forms of exchange between creative cities and rural areas, ideally with the aim of producing some sort of medium that connects both sites and leading to new initiatives of mutual interest. The term "creative village" (*sōzō nōson*) coined by Sasaki implies economic self-sufficiency and local initiatives (2014: 21). Whereas the organic café in rural Shimane evidently does not fall into the category of classic tourism, its establishment per se is bound to add momentum to the diversification of values in the small town where it is located—a crucial prerequisite for creative rurality (Sasaki 2001). Diversified lifestyles and values as a result of an influx of a variety of migrants, including IT workers in satellite offices, craftsmen, artists, among others, also form the basis of the revitalization policy shaped by NPO Green Valley in Kamiyama Town, Tokushima Prefecture (Noda 2014: 191).

"My dream is to be a farmer while engaging in activities as a musician."

Moving on a few booths at the fair, I talk to Taka, who settled further south in Shimane Prefecture in a local town with 7,834 residents. Originally from Kyushu and forty-two years old, he attended university in Tokyo to study journalism. He had initially wanted to become a professional musician but was not successful, ended up as a *freeter*, and eventually moved to Shimane sixteen years ago to pursue his ideal lifestyle as a self-reliant (*jikyū jisoku*) organic farmer focusing on the cultivation of brown *genmai* rice. He aspires to a lifestyle that requires few expenses and helps cultivate survival skills in the sense of vitality (*ikiru chikara*). In fact, since he uses cut wood for heating, the heating costs are low and he points out that living costs of 30,000 JPY per month are sufficient, although expenses have risen since he and his wife have had children. Taka remembers that he also considered Hokkaido as a possible place of relocation, but he eventually chose Shimane as it seemed more exotic and he felt that he could relate immediately to the local town from his first visit. His vision is to link agriculture and culture, that is, spend time on cultural activities when he is not busy with farming: for example, he has organized live performances of his band in the greenhouse usually used for the cultivation of vegetables. He explains that he approaches farming as a philosophy (*tetsugaku*). He shares a spacious house that is one hundred years old with both Japanese- and Western-style rooms with his wife and three children, and his mother has recently joined them from Kyushu to cohabit the spacious house. He says that in the winter, he focuses on music, his grand passion. Occasionally, he performs as a solo musician in the genre of folk rock. Initially, he had moved to Tokyo to become a professional musician but eventually took an interest in agriculture, although he adds that being in farming requires hard work, despite acquiring the survival skills to make a living as a farmer. Nevertheless, he still feels that he needs to improve his skills. However, the positive aspect of working as a farmer in a remote rural area is the fact that one works by oneself and is surrounded by nature. One needs to devise means of surviving entirely by oneself, but it is also possible to live without relying on the capitalist economy, since Taka produces the vegetables he and his family require. Taka observes that most people who work as corporate employees do not seem to have the time to reflect and thus do not even have time to question their lifestyles. What he enjoys most about his present life and what gives him energy and drive (*waku waku*) is the fact that farming provides concrete results. But the moment he feels happiest, he adds with a smile, is when he looks around and realizes he is surrounded by beautiful landscape after finishing work and taking a break to smoke a cigarette. He also seems happy about his social life, mentioning that he has set up a loose network of newcomers in the region who meet once or twice a month. The local town where Taka lives has recently seen an influx of some sixty students (mostly from Tokyo) who engage in diverse activities that link urban and rural areas;

hence, the town has seen changes in population and lifestyle. Nevertheless, Taka states that in order to live in Shimane, it is important to find
ways to derive fun from activities that are not related to earning money.
Options for conventional entertainment are limited in rural areas so it
is essential to create one's own entertainment in one way or another, but
Taka points out that the positive thing about the lack of entertainment
is that there are hardly any chances for spending cash. On the down
side, he remarks with a laugh, there are no select record shops for music
maniacs like him in the countryside.

Urban migrants in the countryside tend to engage in several activities to earn an income; individuals often mention the terms *nisoku no
waraji* or *sansoku no waraji* (two pairs or three pairs of shoes) to describe
their multifaceted professional careers. Since jobs are limited in rural
areas, new settlers tend to engage in seasonal work and pursue their
original (often creative) activities in a gray zone between work and leisure. Individuals opt for such surprising combinations as, for example,
outdoor guide with graphic design, Airbnb host and restaurant manager,
ecotourism guide and seasonal work, book store operator and guest house
manager, or making shoes and seasonal work after relocation to rural
areas. Numerous migrants who were working as regional revitalization
officers at the time I interviewed them mentioned plans of starting their
own small-scale shop or business and combining this with some other
activity to earn an additional income.

The reason why I have chosen to start this chapter with these two
vignettes in rural Shimane Prefecture is these migrants' focus on self-determination and agency that has resulted from diverse circumstances:
inherent dissatisfaction with the predominance of work in the everyday
lives of employees in urban Japan in the first case and lack of success
obtaining a job as an urban employee in the second case. As diverse as
they may be, both male migrants have chosen to pursue lifestyles that
emphasize freedom in daily routines that allow time for leisure. Both
have chosen professions that are closely linked with their interests and
ideal lifestyles. Neither had initial plans to engage in lifestyle travel, but
it "had come into being," as also described by Erskine and Anderson
(2016: 132). Both could be categorized as "circumstantial migrants" (Sato
2001) in the sense that their circumstances shaped their actions and
relocations. Kazu mentions his plans to take several weeks of vacation
with his family over the winter and travel to different Asian countries
as he aims to branch out into Asia in the long term, since he thinks

that economic growth there holds many chances for freelancers like him. Taka has chosen agriculture as a lifestyle choice of self-autonomy that allows him to engage in his pastime of playing music during the winter. In other words, both do not refer to the lack of holidays in corporate employment, yet their trajectories indicate their inherent departure from a mode of work and life that compromises leisure and family and tends to be regulated and controlled by others. These narratives suggest that migrants are highly satisfied with their daily lives after relocation, and the representation of migrant stories in magazines and TV often emphasize the positive elements as they pick up "success stories" that focus on outgoing individuals who manage to relate successfully both in professional and emotional terms to a rather rustic countryside in the conventional style of a "rural idyll." Yet the reality is often more nuanced: Feelings of liminality and precariousness coalesce with a sense of freedom and self-determination; creativity and inspiration are the other side of the coin of insecurity and fragility. Many migrant trajectories contain experiences that may objectively be dismissed as "failures" or, at least, a sense of restlessness and lack of satisfaction and vitality; yet these experiences initiated the decision to relocate and, in retrospect, are not necessarily perceived by the migrants themselves as negative experiences but, rather, as a source of reflection and incentive for growth and self-development.

Similarly, the border between leisure and work is getting ever more fluid. According to Smith and Godbey, "Leisure, as a modern concept, was first conceptualized as free time" (1991: 90). Dumazdier defined leisure as "the time free from productive work, thanks to technical progress and social action, for man's pursuit of a non-productive activity before, during, or after the period of his productive occupation" (1960: 526). Instead, scholars from various disciplines have started to take a more flexible approach to the definition of work and leisure. According to Green, Hebron, and Woodward, for example, "work and leisure are no longer regarded as separate spheres but instead as a complex set of experiences involving degrees of freedom and constraint" (1990: 19). Many activities migrants engage in cannot be categorized clearly as work or leisure but fall somewhere in between. When Taka offers his handmade bacon from the grill to visitors of the remote hamlet where he has chosen to be an organic farmer, this could be perceived as hospitality, yet it could also be understood as an act to advertise his produce. At first sight, these two individuals may be dismissed as slackers whose sole aim is to drop out from mainstream society. In fact, their families often struggle to understand their lifestyle choices. Kazu tells me that his relatives back in Tokyo were critical at first; however, with the passing of time, they have noticed the positive change in his well-being and sense of energy and drive since his relocation and have come to accept his decision. Many lifestyle migrants observe that their parents took time to come to terms with their decision to abandon "safe" jobs and move to "marginal villages." Corporate employers based in urban areas may shake their heads at Taka's choice of living a life that requires few expenses and focuses on nonmaterial leisure activities. Both have not entirely dropped out of the capitalist economy but have chosen to opt for a small-scale approach that targets a niche clientele emphasizing sustainability and high-end products and services. Younger generations in Japan, like Kazu and Taka (even if they are over forty years old), have clearly started to question the self-sacrificing work ethic associated with lifelong employment in corporate institutions, yet some modes of work seem deeply ingrained in the societal psyche. Their backgrounds may be very different: some individuals have worked in secure full-time positions for many years and made a conscious decision to quit. Others aspired to such a position but did not manage to obtain one for various reasons. However, they are united by their clear intention that they will not work at the expense of their private lives, as has been cogently showed by Nagatomo (2015, chapter 4), and make active efforts to pursue a work-life balance while engaging in activities that personally make sense to them. None of these or other migrants depicted in this volume or encountered over the years seemed to have aspirations for upward social mobility; in fact, many came from relatively affluent backgrounds or had worked in stable employment for some time. Even those who clearly had no savings and were in precarious working conditions did not mention aspirations to move up economically or otherwise and instead talked about meaningful ways of spending their lives and having fun for the time being. While previous research into migration primarily focused on forced movement, more recently scholars have interpreted migration as voluntary (Glick Schiller, Basch, and Blanc-Szanton 1992), with the line between migration and tourism being increasingly dissolved (Nagatomo 2015). Rather than being motivated by material affluence, all migrants depicted here aspire to certain lifestyles and visions of what for them constitutes a meaningful life. In implementing these lifestyles and visions, individuals tend to become so engrossed in their work that in many cases there is no divide between work and leisure anymore.

In the next section I discuss three trajectories in more detail to illustrate the following points: First, precariousness and the struggle to achieve one's ideal lifestyle often coexist. Second, individuals are going to great lengths to improve their work-life balance but often struggle to shed familiar habits and modes of working, living, and thinking from their previous lives. Third, whereas individuals seem altogether satisfied with their present lives, a lack of commitment at the private level is salient as they are not sure where they are going in the medium and long term.

"I feel like I am on the cusp of something."

Okinoshima Town office: On a rainy day in September 2016, I meet up with Chiharu, who is originally from the Tokyo area and in her late twenties (although she does not wish to specify her age when I ask her). The section in charge of promotion of in-migration at the municipal office has kindly agreed to introduce migrants between twenty and forty years of age. Chiharu and I talk in a quiet meeting room, just the two of us—she seems shy, introverted, and avoids eye contact during the entire conversation. Having studied international cooperation at university, she was active in an international NGO and worked as a volunteer during her student days. Most jobs she worked after graduation were in sales and as an office assistant in companies before her move to Okinoshima as a regional revitalization officer. The reason for her move was the job announcement and her wish to contribute to rural revitalization (*chihō wo genki ni shitai!*)—she was also considering a similar post in Shimanto in Kōchi Prefecture, Shikoku, but eventually chose Okinoshima for its location by the sea. After her three-year contract as a regional revitalization officer (*chiiki okoshi kyōryokutai*) ended, she returned to Tokyo for three months but eventually returned to Okinoshima and took up various seasonal jobs, such as an assistant for film production teams or food processing work.

Now she regularly works at the souvenir shop at the harbor four days a week to earn her livelihood. In her free time she looks after her vegetable field and learns textile weaving since she has an interest in traditional culture. She expresses her hope to contribute to the preservation of local and regional traditions and vaguely talks about the impressive skilled handicraft found in Japanese culture, but she does not specify how this could translate into concrete projects in her own life. When I ask her what her goal is, she replies that she feels that "she is on the cusp of finding something. Tackling challenges every day and moving around actively as I do now gives me the feeling of being myself" (interview on 13 September 2016). All the different activities she engages in make her feel alive. Her satisfaction rate with her present life is 60 percent because she spends time on the things she is interested in, such as weaving or making soap. Presently, she is trying her hand at Mandarin soap-making, but this kind of activity does not translate into cash and she also needs money to pay her bills. She hopes that she will eventually have more time to do what she is interested in, such as regional revitalization and traditional local culture, but she does not have any concrete plans of getting out of her present situation. Right now, the reality is that she does not have sufficient time to pursue the things she is interested in. Presently, she lives in a house with two rooms, a kitchen, and a bathroom by herself with a spacious garden and field to cultivate vegetables. When I ask her about her plans for marriage and family, she says that she does not have the ambition to get married, although if there were someone appropriate she would consider that option. Chiharu adds that she would be interested in living in a share house with others, but she does not know anyone interested in sharing. Most other in-migrants have families or a partner and, in any case, she does not know many other settlers in Okinoshima Town. She says she only has a few local friends she occasionally meets with but otherwise is busy with work and taking care of her vegetable field. When we discuss work and life in Okinoshima as compared to Tokyo, her view is that in Tokyo the pressure is much greater to achieve certain things at given times, regardless of the circumstances. For example, in Okinoshima, when there is snow, people agree that it is acceptable to delay work until the next day, while in Tokyo you are expected to walk if the train is out of service due to snow.

I ask Chiharu about her ideal work—she replies that she has never thought about this but adds that she would like to engage in work that combines craft work in the classical craftsman style with that of a coordinator, designer, and creator, which also involves communication and PR. She concedes that she does not even have appropriate internet access at present, only through her mobile phone, but the mobile network is weak in the hamlet in the northern part of the island where she lives. When I ask her about her medium- and long-term plans, she laughs, saying that she has none, although she has a goal, although it is somewhat vague as mentioned earlier. The countryside is the place, she notes, "where I feel I can tackle challenges in a relaxed manner . . . although I have no money" (*Kigaru ni challenge dekiru no ga inaka ka na . . . okane ha nai kedo . . .*). As for her culinary habits since relocation, she observes that during her three years as a regional revitalization officer she mostly ate food similar to that of her life in Tokyo, purchasing most of the food at the local supermarket. But since she now works at the souvenir shop at the harbor, she manages to get all kinds of food at the end of her working day, such as grapes, lunchboxes, and so forth. Now, she regularly receives various things from locals so she does not need to go to the supermarket so much, which also means a reduction in her food expenses. Chiharu's lifestyle unites abstract urban aspirations to "revitalize the countryside" and "to preserve local traditions" with local reliance on *o-susowake* (receiving things—and giving things back at another point).

Chiharu has ideas about what she is interested in but does not seem to translate these ideas into something concrete that fits her own life. She is so busy earning a living that she does not have sufficient time to think of ways to bring her ideas to fruition. Living a socially withdrawn life, she has no partner or family and says that she is not particularly interested in having a relationship. In a way, Chiharu can be considered the vulnerable embodiment of youth in post-growth Japan characterized by irregular work, focus on the here and now, and lack of concrete vision due to being caught up in precarious employment in order to earn a living. Individuals who for various reasons have only the choice of irregular jobs in urban areas choose to move to and stay in remote rural areas, even if they ultimately do not seem to manage to implement the visions they initially had and lead rather similar precarious lives in the cities they left, with the only difference being the more affordable living expenses in the countryside.

Chiharu's narrative clearly illustrates the recent shift in contemporary Japanese youth from corporate familism and "my-home-ism" (Allison 2013: 22) to post-growth embracing of individual responsibility and risk, be it from neoliberal constraints, individual choice, or a combination of both. Individuals settle for life in rural areas out of a combination of individual ambition (that is often unfulfilled and turns out to be a never-ending project) and crisis management (living a life that cuts down on expenses and offers more free time), which makes it altogether a very post-growth lifestyle decision.

"Not having the pressure to continue
this work and be liked . . ."

Naoto is my host during fieldwork on one of the islands that make up Okinoshima. A contact on the island introduced me to Naoto since he works in the local tourism association and is in charge of a share house located in a remote fishing village where short-term residents such as student interns are accommodated. From the numerous emails we exchanged prior to my arrival, I imagined a socially inward, intelligent person who pays meticulous attention to small details and is highly sensitive. When I meet him, it turns out that he is more outgoing than anticipated and very much immersed in his work. Although we live in the same house for two weeks, we hardly meet. Naoto works long hours and, in many cases, also on weekends when some event takes place. In his late twenties, with a bone-dry humor that makes his origin from Osaka palpable, he attended a top private university in Tokyo and worked in corporate employment in what he calls a "traditional company" for four years. The work he envisaged in the company did not match the activities he had to do every day. He eventually quit the job when one of his senior peers from university introduced another job opportunity to him, only to find after he had quit that this did not work out. The three months of unemployment that followed seem to have deeply affected and shaped him into the person he is now. He says that getting up every day at noontime, sitting on a bench in a park, and thinking about his life was useful since he thoroughly thought through various things (*mushoku no toki iroiro jikkuri kangaeta*). He has now worked as a volunteer for cooperation in community revitalization (*chiiki okoshi kyōryokutai*) in the local tourism association for half a year. The main reason for his relocation from the capital is work: he plans to move to Europe to pursue a career as a dairy farmer before the age of thirty and was looking for a job that would offer him the chance to acquire further skills that prepare him for the big step of moving abroad and starting out as a dairy farmer. So quite in contrast to the prevailing image of lifestyle migrants as aspiring to a slower life, he sees the present job as preparation for being the boss of a company, since establishing a company from zero all of a sudden would be too risky. In other words, Naoto is a lifestyle migrant in the sense that for him work is totally equivalent with his lifestyle. In his present phase of life, work constitutes the most important factor as he has moved from corporate position to another form of work that may not look so different from his former job at first sight, but that he himself perceives as an exercise for the next step of professional independence. "I think that here, I can practice and get myself prepared for this next job for three years" (interview 15 September 2016). His salary is significantly lower than in his previous job in Tokyo but so are the living costs on the island, and he seems prepared to accept lower pay for the sake of long-term career progression; he sees his present work as a place to grow and he appreciates his considerable self-determination, although he also remarks that he would like more flexibility over the place and mode of working. For example, staff at the office are expected to come in everyday, although many activities could also be conducted at home more efficiently, since in the office they also have to respond to tourists' inquiries while working on other tasks, which often slows down the process. He states that in the long term he would prefer to have his own company rather than be employed as the latter implies that everything is decided by someone else, and one would have to put up with this. If one made decisions oneself, it would not be hard to live with the consequences.

His ideal form of working would be a small-scale company with staff like a family with himself being the boss and making the decisions. He sums up that, ultimately, he thinks that for him there is only the option of starting an enterprise by himself (*hitori de yatteiku shika nai ka na*), since in most companies employees just carry out the orders they receive even if they doubt the meaningfulness of these orders. He thinks that once he has made the step of going abroad, he will find like-minded peers naturally. What he likes about his present work is that he does not have the pressure to continue to be a stellar employee, like in the previous company. He was always working hard to be the employee who excels since he wanted to get promoted in order to achieve his aim of going abroad. He concedes that he had actually chosen the company because it involved employees being dispatched abroad for a while just to find out that even abroad employees had little contact with local workers and mostly socialized among Japanese coworkers. Naoto adds that one of the advantages of his present work is that he is not afraid of being disliked (*kirawaretemo ii kanji da shi*) and having emotional space (*kimochi no yoyū*). He is not particularly interested in Shimane as a place or in living in the countryside—in fact, when he came to the island for the first time, his immediate reaction was that he could not put up with living in this place in the long term as it was surrounded by the sea and he felt a sense of isolation and constraint. But compared to his previous work, he is much happier with his present job and he says he feels more satisfied with the activities he is engaged in, although he wishes his salary were higher. Nevertheless, he has not had a holiday as long as he can remember because there are many events scheduled on weekends when visitors have time to visit the island.

In hindsight, Naoto's experience of studying Russian in Moscow for one year when he was a student seems to have left a great impact because he refers to this experience many times throughout our conversation, and it turns out that he chose his previous job for the chance of going abroad. His goal is to set up a dairy farming business abroad as well. For an unspecified reason, he has decided that this needs to be done by the age of thirty, so time is running out as he is in his late twenties. The implementation of the project that he is in charge of on Okinoshima has been delayed for various reasons, so he observes that he may stay longer than planned, but on the whole he does not see himself on the island beyond the three years of his present contract. As regards his private life, he has a partner but seems emotionally uncommitted and the frequent residencies of interns from various universities in the share house where he lives and works leave little time for his private life and leisure. Naoto's excessive focus on work (despite or because of his experience of unemployment) seems to go hand in hand with a lack of commitment in the private arena. I ask him about his social life on the island; he says that in Tokyo, it was much easier to strike up a conversation and become friends with complete strangers. Here it takes time and there are only few occasions to meet new people. Whereas there is always something going on in the remote hamlet where he lives, such as preparations for local festivals, drinking parties, and so forth, he observes that this environment has narrowed his perspective (*shiya ga gyaku ni semaku natte kiteiru ka na*), but the lack of people also means that he has more time to himself to think thoroughly about things and discuss things in more detail and depth with close peers (*fukabori*). At the same time, he says that living in the small hamlet in the southern part of the island means that he has had the chance to meet socially with members of the fishing community, a group of people he has never had contact with so far and, as he adds, where communication works in different ways from his workplace, where a large part of the staff are nonlocals from across Japan. His recent participation in local dance practices have provided the occasion for him to meet local residents unrelated to his work and talk to individuals he would not meet otherwise. He observes with a chuckle, true, chances are slim that a graduate from a top university in Tokyo would drink extensively with a former host from Osaka.

Whereas Naoto has spent considerable time deviating from the conventional corporate trajectory and states numerous times that he could not imagine himself going back to corporate employment for the lack of self-determination, certain fixed ideas about when he needs to achieve certain goals, such as moving abroad and starting out as a farmer and entrepreneur by the age of thirty, suggest his being entrapped in conventional rigidities of life course planning. When I meet him again in November at a migration fair in Tokyo, he seems tired. He concedes that he has only slept two hours prior to his departure as he was preparing materials throughout the night. He explains that he is not the kind of person who can work regular hours but always ends up working late hours before a deadline or business trip since he feels he needs to compensate for the time out of the office—a rationale that seems oddly familiar to postwar salaryman thinking and reminds us of James Clifford's concept of "traveling cultures" (1997), implying that individuals often partially hang on to their familiar modes of working and living despite a change of physical locality.

> "I wonder why I have been attracted to this place
> as I never had plans to settle on a remote island . . .
> it just happened."

Forty-one and originally from Sapporo, the capital of Japan's northernmost island, Hokkaido, Haruki is a neighbor of my host Naoto and lives just around the corner in the idyllic fishing village in the southern part of the island. I meet him in the evening of a muggy early autumn weekday as he was busy working during the day. He seems exhausted from factory-like manual work, which he does regularly to earn his living. Tall and gaunt, his life has been dominated by mobility: Tokyo, Kanagawa, Saitama, Hokkaido, Australia, Ghana. His initial dream was to become a medical professional in the manner of Albert Schweitzer to contribute to development in Africa. However, he did not manage to make it through the entry exams for medical studies. He thus decided to study IT at a private university in Tokyo and went on a one-year working holiday in Australia during his studies. For twelve years he worked as staff in a supermarket and pachinko gambling parlor to pay back the debts he had accumulated from attending university. But eventually, after applying three times, he was accepted as a paid volunteer youth to be dispatched by Japan International Cooperation Agency (JICA) for two years to Ghana. Haruki set up a school there to teach children how to use computers. He came back to Japan from Africa in October 2015 to realize that it was difficult to find employment at the mature age of forty. Haruki observes that the age of thirty-five is the borderline—after that it becomes virtually impossible to find a job in Japan. For people like him who are not willing to do work that does not make sense to them personally, the hurdle is even higher. His assumption that his overseas skills would be an asset that could also be used in Japan did not prove true. Haruki did not have any personal connections with Shimane Prefecture but received information from Naoto, since he had registered on a page related to his JICA affiliation as a volunteer abroad.

In April 2016 he started working on the island as a regional revitalization troupe member, just like Naoto but with a focus on agricultural activities. Haruki receives 120,000 JPY per month for one year but needs to cover the lease for his car, rent, and all other living expenses from this. He lives in a share house that belongs to the town, where interns also stay, with his own room, but all other facilities—kitchen, bathroom, living room, and toilet—are shared.

Compared to his previous life in Tokyo, his satisfaction rate is higher, around 80 percent. The remaining 20 percent is due to the fact that his present life is characterized by challenges and that he has chosen a life that is fundamentally full of risk. Right now, he has just started his career as a farmer and needs to do some temporary *arubaito* work to support himself since the income from his vegetables is not sufficient. In Tokyo, he was mostly working to pay back his student loan and was forced to accept work that he was not really interested in. Hence, in retrospect, his satisfaction rate for that time amounts to only 50 percent. As for his social life on the island, he observes that he feels he can relate to locals better than to people in Tokyo. In fact, he states that when he started working in Tokyo after his experience abroad, he felt more of a culture shock about the fact that in Tokyo there was a clear-cut divide between work and private life in his working environment. In Africa his experience was that everyone was part of a big family and things were shared as a result. Haruki felt that people in (urban) Japan were quite cold, since everyone was only looking after themselves, but in the countryside, people seem closer to the African lifestyle.

I ask him about his change since relocating to the island. He says that it is only a few months since he has arrived but he feels that if one makes an effort, one can find means to achieve what one aspires to. Before, he had certain ideas about what he needed to do and was anxious about what others might think, but now he thinks that if he wants to live in a certain way, he can do it. He has done what he promised and despite all the insecurity and challenges his lifestyle entails, he thinks it is OK to live the way he does. After all, he has shown that he has not ended up homeless and he will live like this all his life (interview 18 September 2016).

About his everyday life, he says that working in the field is not really work since he likes agriculture. He does not do it as work but more because he feels like eating the results and, therefore, agriculture is more like life and his way of life. Hence engaging in agriculture is a way of life and there is no divide between work and life.

As for his private life, my initial impression is that he does not have a partner. When I meet him, a girl is cooking dinner in the kitchen; it turns out that she is a coresident and friend who worked as a volunteer in Thailand, is originally from the Tokyo area, and is spending some time on the island to relax. However, a few months later, Haruki announces his marriage on Facebook to the girl who was cooking in the kitchen in both Western and Shinto wedding ceremonies, and a trip together to Ghana follows.

The house has rooms in Japanese tatami style but the furniture seems urban—Haruki sits on a lounge sofa on the tatami, the perfect cultural fusion between urban and rural, Ghana, Hokkaido, and Shimane. I get the sense that in the case of Haruki, his ideal lifestyle of freedom, self-determination, and social contribution are intricately related with precariousness and he has accepted this lifestyle of uncertainty in a way. Drawing on his extensive experiences from working in development in Ghana, he sees common features between the African and Japanese countryside and also mentions that he would like to eventually live a lifestyle spending the winter in Africa and the rest on the island once he gets settled with his present agriculture project. Rather than "finding himself," Haruki is creating ways of pursuing the work and lifestyle he envisages for himself, and he has experienced abroad. Broaching the subject of the lack of understanding for his lifestyle choices by his family and the general public, Haruki implies that he does not mind, but he states that he has fulfilled his promises, managed to get by so far, and hopes to keep on living in the same way. Hence his relocation was not so much about "shedding societal expectations and roles" (Erskine and Anderson 2016: 134), but rather Haruki had already departed from "the conventional lifestyle" centered on corporate employment, family, and home prior to his relocation with his decision to work as a volunteer in Africa for two years.

"I am just so into this way of life here."

Originally from Mie Prefecture, Junko exudes gleaming vitality and down-to-earth practicality. With a degree from an elite university in Tokyo under her belt, she worked as a journalist for several years—a well-paid but fast-paced and very stressful job she enjoyed. Yet when eight years ago, after a brief visit to the island, she was approached by a representative of the tourism association from the island where she lives now and asked whether she was interested in working on the island, she took the opportunity and never returned. In retrospect, she says that growing up in the countryside herself, she never felt completely at ease in Tokyo and spent all her time on work. Thinking back, she cannot remember any leisure activities she engaged in at the time. Furthermore, the stress level and pressure were so high that she did not have regular menstruation. Compared to that, her present life on the island is not entirely stress free, but her work-life balance is considerably better. She has worked in the municipal office since her move and is in charge of public relations and presswork plus coverage for the local television station. What she enjoys about her present work is that she gets direct feedback from the locals—back in Tokyo, she did not receive reactions to her articles from her readers, they "had no face"; now, she knows most residents—an unexpected benefit of depopulation. In her leisure time, she takes care of a small field that she cultivates with ten other settlers. She observes that she is engaged in numerous (unpaid) activities besides her job, such as participation in local festivities, community activities, and social meetings with other migrants to share experiences. Despite a failed marriage to a local, she has chosen to stay on the island, saying that she prefers the lifestyle here to Tokyo where she had no relations with her neighbors at all. She mentions that the countryside allows her to get together with similarly minded peers to engage in activities they enjoy together. Furthermore, she remembers that in Tokyo she did not have any relations with individuals from other generations such as senior citizens. Due to the high rate of elderly residents on the island, Junko says that she enjoys meeting senior locals who share their experiences and knowledge with her and also offer her advice on a wide range of issues. She is happy about the fact that she has managed to make good friends and can also share experiences with other nonlocal migrants like her.

When she goes back to West Japan to see her parents, they say that she has changed since her move—she laughs more and looks healthier—whereas before, she was tense and pressured due to her work obligations as a journalist. In fact, she has put on considerable weight since moving to the island as she enjoys the fresh vegetables, fruit, and homemade foods she receives regularly (*o-susowake*) from her local neighbors. Since she has made friends with local senior citizens, life on the island has been so much more enjoyable because she gets advice on healthy eating and maintaining vitality and she feels reassured after talking to them (*iyasareru*). Junko likes the fact that in the countryside there is something beyond material wealth and money, the mind-set that "things we don't have we just don't have" (*nai mono ha nai*), and that the scarcity of things actually enriches people in other ways—the official catchphrase of the local tourism association on the island. In retrospect, she thinks that her mental health has improved greatly since her relocation. While her salary is less than half compared to the amount she was earning in Tokyo, she indicates that she is receiving so many things now that money cannot buy: above all, a sense of security and emotional support. She says that back in Tokyo, she would definitely have died a lonely death one day and, thinking back, she felt an underlying sense of permanent insecurity. I ask her about her ideal lifestyle—she replies that would be freelance work and having sufficient time for leisure activities such as agricultural work and time for reflection. She observes that compared to her previous job as a journalist, she has come closer to her ideal lifestyle, but at present she feels that she is not using her expert knowledge to the full and does not have enough time to work with the earth, like tending the field. With her present work at the municipal agency she is too busy to work on her field every day, and on the weekend, if the weather is not good or if she has some job related to the local television, she cannot work in the field either (interview on 15 September 2016).

Junko altogether proves a lifestyle migrant in the true sense of the world: Highly satisfied with her private life and leisure despite her divorce, she is not totally happy with her work, mentioning that she feels that she is in charge of a lot of issues that any generalist could do, and that she would prefer to be responsible for more specialist work that allows her to use her expert knowledge as a journalist. Furthermore, she is working more hours than scheduled every day and also needs to work regularly on weekends. Still, compared to her job as a journalist in fast-paced Tokyo, her present workload is still an improvement. Nevertheless, Junko mentions that she would like to work freelance, but thinks that after working for the municipal agency for so many years, she doubts whether she could manage and revive her old contacts in Tokyo. At the same time, she concedes that she does not have any passion or vision that would be worth mentioning—apart from her interest in partaking in outdoor activities with other nonlocal friends and feeling seasonal changes through having direct access to nature. This relatively high sense of satisfaction with the present life (especially compared to her previous life dominated by work) combined with a lingering awareness that more is necessary to reach the ideal lifestyle is echoed in numerous narratives by migrants, regardless of their age, background, or present activities.

But ultimately, Junko aspires to a "free" lifestyle rather than the constraining, tightly regulated mode of working she has to cope with presently. She expresses her high satisfaction with her social life, point-ing out that having a network of similarly minded nonlocal migrants adds greatly to her satisfaction as she can discuss issues of integration into the local community. She points out that in the initial years after her relocation, she made great efforts to interact mostly with locals, but these days she feels most comfortable with other nonlocal residents her age. Altogether, she emphasizes her satisfaction with life in a rural setting where there are plenty of opportunities for social exchange in a small-scale community of people where everyone knows one another's face and, possibly, name.

Thinking about common threads that pull together these three very diverse vignettes, we find that idea of "transformative travel" inherent in all narratives. Individuals have relocated to achieve personal growth, self-realization, search for the self, and change through movement. Two of the three individuals introduced had traveled extensively to other countries before—these experiences featured in their observations of their present everyday life and testified to the global outlook that char-acterized their perspectives. The notion of a "global career" (or in the case of Junko, translocal career) is inherent in most of these trajectories and seems to be the result of an exposure to foreign countries at an early age. Rather than "finding themselves," their narratives suggested a permanent process of malleable selves that were adjusted to the respective circumstances they found themselves in. For example, Naoto remembered that one of the things he enjoyed most in Russia was drinking with strangers at hours of the day that were unthinkable for Japanese and not knowing at all what people were thinking. Clearly, his social life on the island is measured not only in comparison to urban life in Japan but also his experience of studying in Moscow. The same holds for Haruki, who elaborated about the similarities between rural Japan and rural Nigeria, as well as Chiharu, who talked about her trips to various Asian countries during her student days. Among the subjects of the three vignettes introduced in this chapter, Chiharu is the only one who continues to be in the process of self-search in the sense of creating an identity based on individuality rather than societal structuring (Beck and Beck-Gernsheim 2002), as her expression of "being about to find something" implies. Naoto has a clear idea what he is aiming for but seems somewhat at a loss of how to relate this idea clearly to his own life and trajectory. Furthermore, because he enjoys his work on the island as it holds challenges and ways of professional growth unknown to him in his previous job in Tokyo, he keeps postponing his own project of moving abroad, although he has a personal deadline for this by the age of thirty. None of these migrants are spontaneous travelers, although all of them observe that they did not plan to live in the place they are based now, but the relocation happened; all of them mention an element of chance in their lives, although all migrants seem to have spent considerable time reflecting on their lives and careers (some less so).

One more trait that features in all trajectories is the ambiguity of mobility and sedentary elements in their lives as both fixity and fluidity of the place they have relocated to coexist through the interactions and social relations as migrants with their environments. Their narratives illustrate that place "is no longer seen as wholly fixed and static, but dynamic and subject to change" (Erskine and Anderson 2016: 136). The share house that Haruki lives in may be the same house that it used to be forty years ago from outside, yet the furniture and lifestyles inside the house are a fusion of urban and rural, Japanese and international features. Similarly, the café Kazu has opened with his wife in a rural hamlet in Shimane Prefecture offers dishes that draw on global and local influences and could remind guests of the wide choice and diversity often found in cafés in stylish districts in western Tokyo.

The fact that individuals tend to perceive their new places of residence in a comprehensive way, that is, by comparing it to other places they have lived before or they have traveled to, shows that one and the same "place" has a different connotation for each and every migrant. Furthermore, all of them leave their new places of residence regularly for business or other purposes, thus keeping their former networks and developing new ones beyond their place of residence. Chiharu briefly mentioned that she usually buys shoes when she has something to do on the mainland as the choice on the island is limited, and Amazon is not an option for her as she has limited internet access and does not like the idea of ordering shoes without trying them on. Naoto states that his perspective has narrowed since his relocation in social terms since the number of strangers he can meet in public places is limited and he spends more time with less people and more time by himself. These observations implicitly take his previous lifestyle in Tokyo as a measure and thus show the wide scope of his perspective beyond one locality and, in some cases, beyond one nation. The same applies to Kazu, whose choice of menus in his café shows his underlying cosmopolitan approach apart from the fact that he is planning to expand his business to Asia in the future. Other individuals place regular orders on Amazon to access products that are not available on the island or in their region of residence. Junko likes to engage in social activities with other nonlocal migrants despite her extensive network of local friends. "After all," she says despite or perhaps because of her long period of living on a remote island, "I feel most at ease talking to other nonlocals." She observes that the close-knit local community that gives her a sense of security she missed when she was living in Tokyo also has serious downsides, such as complex human relationships and social pressures that she also does not know much about even after eight years of residence on the island. All these statements by a diverse range of migrants provide empirical evidence for and highlight the fact that "localities need not necessarily be limited to the shared social relations of local histories, experiences and relations, but can connect to wider geographical histories and processes—in a way that articulates a 'global ethnography of place' " (Brickell and Datta 2011: 3). The statements in this section also indicate that many migrants lead thoroughly multisited lives that transcend previous notions of distinct "rural" versus "urban" or contingent "national" spaces.

Many of the migrants discussed in this chapter have a past of moving to places for a given purpose, so it is not the first time to relocate; many seem to have developed a taste for "testing themselves in new places" as a personal challenge and have "morphed into [relocation] junkies" (Butler and Richardson 2013: 254) rather than "expat junkies" (Collings et al. 2011: 364)—and a certain extent of lack of emotional commitment to the locality is palpable in their narratives even if they work hard and enjoy their daily activities at the workplace. Lise Gundersen has intriguingly pointed out the coexistence of mobility and sedentary features in the ways migrants envisage their notion of "home": "Home is where you are; home is the moment you are in" (2008: 27). The trajectories of individuals discussed in this chapter may only constitute a tiny drop in the ocean of depopulation that is prevalent in rural areas and tends to feature in the media; yet, these trajectories make evident that despite the first associations and social imaginary of the countryside as stagnant backwaters of the old, the senile, and those who have given up on their future, "fixity" as a notion itself does not apply any longer at several levels. Cresswell previously argued that mobility itself cannot be defined as an antagonism to the notion of fixity because individuals are moving between different spaces but continue to engage with spaces they lived in previously in both material and immaterial ways. "Accordingly, they [translocal actors] do not cease to be attached to the real places they moved from, but they add the place of arrival to the place of departure (along with other, previous places where they lived)" (Hedberg and do Carmo 2012: 3). The emergence of croque monsieur in an organic café in rural Shimane, freshly roasted espresso in an Italian café on a remote island in Shimane, and a lounge sofa in a tatami room in a fishing hamlet in Shimane are all firsthand evidence of these cultural flows and of rural areas as constantly changing spatial entities. The fusion of local and nonlocal elements in the everyday lives of the individuals described here shows once more the appropriateness of Doreen Massey's argument about a relational understanding of places, namely, that every locality is positioned in relation to others rather than by itself (1999, 2005). The implication is thus that every locality belongs to a larger network of places (Stenbacka 2012: 57 in Hedberg and do Carmo 2012: 3).

The diverse stories and mobility practices of these talented, engaging, highly driven (in most cases), and courageous individuals propose that rural areas are increasingly perceived as spaces where they can pursue niche enterprises, try their first steps as an entrepreneur, live lives that offer both time to think and pursue personally fulfilling work, or prepare themselves for future activities with an eye to career progression. We often tend to associate mobility with dynamism, aspiration, and hope—not features that rural areas tend to be associated with conventionally. Yet this chapter has shown that contrary to the social imaginary rural areas offer individuals from a broad range of backgrounds, either with clear visions or migrants who are about to find something, the freedom and space to reflect, experiment, and implement their ideas or think about their next career step. Rural areas also offer nonlocals merits of tightly knit communities that community members may detest, that is, social capital that evidently is just the other side of social surveillance, reciprocal obligations, and pressures of all sorts. As described earlier, a career woman who previously lived in Tokyo is bound to perceive the opportunity to receive advice from senior locals differently than someone who has spent all his or her life on the island. In the same vein, familiarity with everyone in the neighborhood and even on the island was mentioned as a plus; many locals who have grown up on the island may tend to perceive the small scale as a negative aspect of rural living—in fact, Naoto's observation about his perspective having narrowed as a result of his relocation is related to these effects of demographic regression. Depending on the number of in-migrants in a given locality, new settlers may find similarly minded peers to exchange their experiences with and ask for advice about interaction with the local community.

The stories presented in this chapter ultimately show that precariousness and vision are closer than generally anticipated; the narratives of numerous migrants indicate that precariousness and a lingering sense of uncertainty is the price they have to pay for the potential of pursuing lives they want to live and visions they are aspiring to implement.

Finally, the narratives introduced in this chapter propose that despite their relative high satisfaction with their present lives, the majority of migrants struggle to pursue their ideal life—the life they have in mind as their personally ideal way of life that has motivated them to relocate in the first place. Some spend a large part of their time pursuing activities other than the work they are ultimately most interested in. Some justify this by arguing that this work will improve the professional skills that they need to reach their ideal work. Others openly admit that they need to do this kind of work to make ends meet. Some are aware of the gap between aspiration and practice yet feel incapable of changing their lives for various reasons. While many work less and some face less pressure than in their previous lives, only a minority actually manage to pursue their ideal lifestyles, with many making compromises and ultimately living a life that is not so different from the life they gave up before relocation.

Chapter Six

Liminal Belonging and Moratorium Migration

Lifestyle Migrants between Limbo and Purpose of Life

I wish the locals would not call me an *ijūsha* (migrant). Once you are called that, you end up having this label forever.

—Male migrant from Tokyo, 53

I am spending more and more time on communal affairs and have less time with my family as a result. As someone who cannot drink, I don't really see the point of these gatherings with locals drinking for hours and hours, but I have to put up with it.

—Male migrant from Osaka, 37

Locals do not ask us to make commitments about staying here forever [literally, burying our bones here] like in other places, I find that very reassuring.

—Female migrant from Tokyo, 40

Quite in contrast to the stories presented in the media about lifestyle migrants who manage to find happiness and comfort in rural communities through the pursuit of "healthier" lifestyles in organic farming, textile weaving, and ecotourism, many interviewees discussed their difficulties of integration into local communities, their uneasy position as mobile subjects who have come from outside and find themselves dependent on residents' support, as well as their continued ambition and ideas about moving elsewhere.

This chapter explores the concept of "liminality" (originating from the Latin *limen* or "threshold") as defined by Victor Turner (1974, 1982, 1996) and draws on several theoretical concepts approaching liminality in a more nuanced way, such as Patricia Hynes's proposal of a continuum between the concepts of liminality and belonging (2011) and Szakolczai's idea of liminality as a permanent condition (2000: 220).

According to Turner, "liminal entities are neither here nor there; they are betwixt and between the positions assigned and arrayed by law, custom, convention, and ceremony. As such, their ambiguous and indeterminate attributes are expressed by a rich variety of symbols in the many societies that ritualize social and cultural transitions" (Turner 1996: 512). Turner defines liminality as a transitional phase that allows for an inner process for personal growth and individualization; others have defined liminality as "the paradoxical and potentially productive condition of being situated between two locations" (Zavala 1997: 9).

As the third statement made by my informants at the beginning of this chapter reveals, migrants rely on the cooperation and trust of local residents; yet, they often find themselves in a zone of "socio-cultural non-identity, non-existence" (Rapport and Overing 2000: 230). The ways interviewees handle their ambivalent position varies considerably, with some perceiving it as a major disadvantage since they take it to imply that they are not seen as full-fledged members of the local community. Others, however, seem to enjoy this "nonidentity" since it affords them freedom and choices that they would not have as regular community members who generally face "constrained adulthood" (Suzuki 2015: 245).

In this chapter I argue that the narratives of many lifestyle migrants indicate that liminality—the state of being "betwixt-and-between" (Turner 1996: 512)—is a key element of migrant identities and that heightened mobility (both physical and virtual) has resulted in a multiple sense of belonging and an extended sense of limbo. These modes of becoming are experienced differently by individuals: for some, they are part of the process of reinventing themselves professionally and personally; for some, they are necessary periods of reorientation, even if they are not sure what awaits them; some talk about the stress and restlessness (*sowa sowa*) they experience as a result of the pressure of having to find something, come up with something original; others again seem to have given up on finding what they are genuinely interested in and simply aspire to an easy and comfortable life. These narratives resemble McRobbie's incisive observations about "mobility, which does not quite know where it is going" (2016: 90) in that we find a sense of lingering movement without a clear direction, movement for its own sake as it were. A male migrant in his mid-thirties with four years of experience of rural living observes that he "feels more relaxed now as I have found my place in the local community and have a better understanding of how locals are connected"; yet, he talks about his ideal lifestyle of traveling while creating his own site-specific work, ideally with his two children and wife by his side (interview on 13 March 2017). He seems to share a similar mind-set with other migrants I encountered during my fieldwork at multiple sites across Japan who have made a conscious decision to move to a place to evade tedious, uninspiring work and exhausting relationships, achieve personal goals, but do not necessarily envisage themselves there in the long term.

In a similar vein, Hynes argued in her study of asylum seekers that the concepts of liminality and belonging are intricately related by revealing that individuals pursue subtle policies of resisting policy-imposed liminality in strategic ways and "remake" belonging through "recourse to pre-existing and creation of new social networks" (2011: 176). At the same time, individuals were contained in the liminal space due to their legal status as asylum seekers. Integration of asylum seekers is described as going hand in hand with a sense of resistance to being ascribed integration by local representatives (Hynes 2011: 176). Lifestyle migrants are by their very nature bound to differ fundamentally from asylum seekers, yet the multiple narratives presented throughout this book epitomize similar experiences, that is, the complex and often contradictory coexistence of liminality and belonging. Just like asylum seekers swerve between integration and resistance, lifestyle migrants often retain and draw on their professional networks from their previous careers while making efforts to establish a new career and maintain multiple identities and functions in the process. They engage in actions that appear to emphasize their affiliation with and integration into the local community as well as actions that could be interpreted as introversion and withdrawal.

Liminality is generally understood as a state in which "the usual order of things is suspended, the past is momentarily negated and the future has yet to begin" (Pearce 2013). But what if things are suspended for good, the present (moment) is all that life revolves around, and the future never starts? Turner observed that "liminality is both more creative and more destructive than the structural norm" (1982: 47). What if liminality were an extended, even permanent condition that denotes a process of negotiating between aspiration and inner void, between freedom and precariousness? What if liminality and a sense of belonging coexisted to form a phenomenon that I call "moratorium migration," that is, migration that is used by migrants as an instrument to gain time to postpone rethinking what they wish to spend their lives on due to a lack of more appealing alternatives? I argue that the trajectories of migrants discussed in this chapter and throughout this book indicate that this postliminal condition, that is, extended liminality and ensuing "nonidentity" as belonging, is the key feature characterizing "post-growth" societies. According to Thomassen, liminality amounts to unstructure, that is, a lack of fixed points in a given moment (2015: 55). However, Turner also argued that the liminal needs to be understood as the origin of structure (1979: 95). In other words, in Turnerian terms, structure and unstructure are mutually constitutive. I draw on this condition of "permanent liminality" as coined by Szakolczai (2000: 220). Szakolczai refers to a concept that contains deeply paradoxical traits yet forms a unified social process: "Liminality becomes a permanent condition when any of the phases in this sequence (of separation, liminality, and reaggregation) becomes frozen, as if a film stopped at a particular frame" (Szakolczai 2000: 220). This "deep-rooted sense of ambivalence" (Thomassen 2015: 55) inherent in individuals' narratives and trajectories forms the core theme to be explored in this chapter.

Respondents frequently refer to their being "different" from locals who have grown up in the community they have moved to, not understanding unwritten rules of conduct that residents have orally passed on from one generation to the next, having different social values that make it difficult for them to relate to residents. Many interviewees who relocated only recently explain that they feel pressure to behave like residents since they are conspicuous as individuals who have come from elsewhere. For example, Takako, a migrant in her early thirties from Kagoshima, emphasized that she makes an effort to greet everyone in the small town where she lives now to avoid being perceived as rude. She puts this into stark contrast with Prague, where she lived before: she avoided greeting others since she got the sense that "Asians" were not generally perceived positively and she did not want to stand out (interview on 8 March 2017). Nevertheless, Takako mostly socializes with her coworkers who are all nonlocals, like herself. Either way, her narrative could be interpreted as indicating that she finds it difficult to reach out and engage with local residents at a deeper level although she would like to. However, the reality is that she does not and all her friends are nonlocal settlers just like her.

Migrants also refer to aspects of their previous lives in their hometowns that they miss presently, such as having daily contact with their families, eating out, drinking at *izakaya* (Japanese-style pubs), living by the sea. Given the strong consciousness of migrants (and locals) of their different origins, it seems natural that they resort to liminality as a permanent lifestyle (Kelly 2008), a way out of the conundrum of being eternally labeled a newcomer in the community, or at least a way of keeping their awareness that they are labeled as newcomers to a minimum. Kelly described liminality as a permanent way of living in patients with a terminal illness. Tying in with Kelly's argument that liminality may turn into a state that sometimes becomes impossible to leave, lifestyle migrants across rural Japan like to keep to themselves. Comparing lifestyle migrants with patients suffering from a terminal illness may strike the reader as somewhat inappropriate; however, numerous narratives by lifestyle migrants introduced in this monograph indicate that migrants tend to be labeled as nonlocal neophytes by residents that make it difficult to leave this category—a status that corresponds to being stamped as outsiders. In places with a sizeable number of migrants, newcomers often like to resort to networks of similarly minded migrants; they thus engage in social relations with other nonlocals. In places without a migrant community, integration seems even more difficult, as suggested by Makoto's narrative in chapter 4. Many locals do not seem to understand the nature of work that community volunteers in regional revitalization (*chiiki okoshi kyōryokutai*) engage in. During an interview, Makoto shared his experience with me of having been picked on by a local neighbor for leaving his home around lunchtime after working at home in the morning. Flexible modes of working are rare in rural areas, where most employment involves nine-to-five office jobs or agriculture; hence, a lack of understanding and ensuing suspicion about different modes of working is not surprising. Such lack of understanding of and sympathy with migrants' professional activities may encourage "liminality as a way of life" (Pearce 2013), with migrants withdrawing to social relations with other migrants while engaging in a minimum of relations with the local community for reasons of work.

The experiences of my interviewees suggest that the border between local residents and nonlocal new settlers seems distinct, even for individuals with many years of experience living in their place of choice. For example, a female lifestyle migrant called Junko in her late thirties who has lived in her present rural place of residence for eight years shares her experience of trying to make as many contacts with local residents in her initial phase of rural living; however, now after eight years and a divorce from a local, she admits that, after all, she feels most comfortable spending her leisure time with other (nonlocal) settlers just like herself. Despite this insight, she indicates that she enjoys rural life and has no plans of reverting to urban life.

A male lifestyle migrant from Kumamoto Prefecture called Jun describes his everyday life in Tokushima Prefecture where he holds a full-time position in an electric shop; he seems comfortable with his social network that consists mostly of other nonlocal migrants. Nevertheless, he also mentions that he returned to his hometown recently for one month because he was longing to see the sea and sun there, yet he chose to return to Tokushima. Jun elaborates on his lack of vision about what he wants to do in the long term; all he aspires to is living an easy and comfortable life. Despite being close to forty, he has no partner or family and finding a partner does not seem a pressing issue. He seems to live a life that is betwixt and between, wishing to go back to his hometown yet remaining in this new place of residence for the mostly reassuring network of similarly minded peers, having a full-time job, yet no plans of starting a family. Jun complains that locals are always busy working and taking care of their fields where they grow vegetables and there is no place to go drinking in town. Despite his dissatisfaction and criticism, he chooses to stay in town and seems to maintain close relations with other migrants like him who came to the town for a retraining work program a few years ago. He describes himself as "indoor," implicitly setting himself apart from local residents who like to spend their leisure time in nature.

He touches on his inherent lack of confidence about his vision and long-term plans, especially compared to his peers, many of whom have already set up their own shops and enterprises; in a group interview conducted with other lifestyle migrants in March 2017, he asks in a half-joking manner whether he is going to be OK (*Ore, daijōbu ka na*) since he does not have any grand ambitions in his life. He is a regular customer at 503, a local lunch box takeout started by one of his peers, a female migrant from Nagoya—which is incidentally also the place where we meet for the interview that seamlessly unfolds into a three-hour-long drinking session. Jun has the habitus of a freelancer: avoiding eye contact, engaging in a high degree of mobility, being hesitant to talk about himself. Still, he holds a full-time job. He has a history as a freeter living in Tokyo but is reluctant to elaborate on his experience. Jun could be considered the embodiment of deep-rooted ambivalence about what he aspires to, incorporating mainstream views of what is socially acceptable by refusing to verbalize his freeter experience. Resembling a run-of-the-mill *shakaijin* (working member of society), his values are shaped in large part by resistance to societal expectations; yet he fulfills the minimum role as a full-fledged member of the working class.

In other words, liminality pervades Jun's narrative and manner, both with regard to his position in the local community as well as in the community of migrants. The condition of being in permanent limbo started before relocating to Tokushima Prefecture—our interviewee concedes somewhat hesitantly that he spent two years living in Tokyo, being here and there, doing this and that—all expressed by the convenient Japanese term *fura fura* (literally, being unsteady on one's feet, tottering).

Jun does not seem unhappy, yet life could be better—he aspires to a life close to the sea with more sunshine, having a family, having a (more interesting) job. He has lived in Australia for one year, but he ultimately feels content living in Japan because he thinks the food tastes best in his home country and life is convenient and easy. Some may perceive his narrative as sobering since he does not seem to have a personal passion in his life, neither professionally nor privately. Others may consider him to be the typical representative of Japan's post-growth generation who aspire to nothing but living small without emotional commitments or investing in the future: "Japan is a small country, and we're OK with small. It's perhaps a sort of maturity" (Kato 2010). Jun's experience echoes the findings of previous research that mobility is often perceived as a "temporary arrangement" to evade constrained adulthood (Suzuki 2015: 243). It seems to showcase of suspension of time, dislocation, and exemption from societal obligations despite Jun also fulfilling expectations of male adulthood. His narrative contains elements of liminality as a permanent condition as described by Szakolczai and mentioned at the beginning of this chapter (Szakolczai 2000: 212), and it indicates the complex coexistence of structure and unstructure.

Haru, a former corporate employee working in IT in his mid-forties, has opened a collective housing project in a mountain hamlet where he lives with ten other residents. Like Jun, he describes himself as "indoor," preferring to spend his time on computer games and developing new computer apps. He laughs, saying that he only ventures out rarely to buy tobacco and occasionally joins common local activities in order to maintain good relations with the local community. He admits that despite having moved to Niigata Prefecture, one of the rural areas in Japan known for its abundant snow throughout its long winters, he rarely goes out in the winter; instead, he prefers to have extended conversations with his coresidents and visitors over shared food and drinks. Like Jun, Haru seems to enjoy living in the countryside, but he mostly interacts with nonlocals. In a region that is known for agriculture (rice farming) where residents engage in a panoply of strenuous outdoor activities, individuals like Haru stick out like sore thumbs in various ways: Despite his age (forty-six) he married only a few months ago and prefers to live in collective housing; he spends all day at home, indoors; he does not work in an office, nor, in fact, does he work regularly in a conventional manner. He does not own a car, which is remarkable in rural Japan where there is hardly any public transport. Like Jun, his narrative contains many elements of downsizing, that is, going small scale and focusing on the people immediately around him (i.e., in his share house) rather than developing grand visions. His main interest is "to have a great time until he dies" (*jibun ga shinu made tanoshiku suru*) (interview on 9 August 2016). Since living expenses in the countryside are much lower than in urban areas and collective living implies a further decrease of costs for Haru, he can afford to work only 10 percent of the time now, spending the rest of his time on things he enjoys doing. As someone who cannot cook and used to rely exclusively on food from convenience stores back in his days as a corporate employee, living in a share house also makes sense from a culinary point of view since there is always food available and ready to eat at home.

Haru does not have any plans of moving to other places, but he also admits to not having any medium- or long-term plans really, describing his life as 10 percent planned and 90 percent serendipity. Haru's narrative contains elements of both withdrawal and engagement: He concedes that he engages with local residents to the necessary degree to ensure peaceful coexistence. Yet his priority every day seems focused on indoor activities that have clearly been shaped by urban nerd culture: playing computer games, developing computer applications, reading manga.

Hence, just like with Jun, the fact that Haru has opted for rural living simultaneously constitutes structure and unstructure: He quit his corporate career, yet he has taken on another career as the manager of the collective house. He explains that there are no rules, except that everyone should do what he or she deems appropriate—a rule that in itself seems an embodiment of neoliberal freedom: preordained "freedom." Haru has opted out of the corporate normative lifestyle but is also successful in branding himself as a charismatic lifestyle migrant and advocate of the sharing economy who has been featured in representative magazines such as *Sotokoto* or *Turns* several times. He may look like someone who lives a day-to-day existence with no stable job, who defies societal expectation about adult behavior, but he also makes public appearances in business suits at presentations in Tokyo to talk about his lifestyle.

A female migrant called Masae from Tokushima Prefecture had attended university in Tokyo and worked there for several years before choosing to relocate to her home prefecture (if to a different region from the place where she had spent her childhood). She joined as a community volunteer in the regional revitalization program and also hinted at her condition betwixt and between by explaining that her parents (who still live in Tokushima Prefecture, although in a different part) did not seem particularly happy about her decision to move back, asking what had gone wrong in her career in Tokyo. After all, she had landed a permanent and well-paid job in an elite company. Masae shares the sense of pressure arising from being surrounded by other highly educated migrants with ambitious visions. She explains that her sense of self is low (*jiko kōteikan ga hikui*; interview on 14 March 2017) and adds that she always sees the glass half-empty rather than half-full. She remarks that now she prefers to stay at home with her two children and spend her days in peace and quiet rather than taking part in the numerous events held by migrants for other migrants in the community and disseminating photos and messages on social media to show how fulfilling her life is in the countryside. With a degree from a top university under her belt and experience working in an elite company in the capital, she indicates that her life with her partner who works in IT and spends considerable time abroad for his work tends to be perceived as "glamorous" by many friends and acquaintances; yet, the reality is that they are not sure about their lives beyond her three-year contract as a regional revitalization officer, her income is less than half of that in Tokyo, and Masae indicates her sense of insecurity. Furthermore, their original plan was to ensure some financial security for the family with her pursuing a stable job in IT at an elite company, where her partner works, which tends to be an industry that entails high returns but also high risk. However, this plan did not seem sustainable from a family point of view as Masae hardly had time to spend with her children due to frequent overwork.

Referring to her experience of living in Australia and Bolivia, she remembers that when she turned thirty she felt that if she did not leave the corporate path then, she would be stuck there forever. At the time she was planning to marry an elite salaryman, but she eventually quit that path because she could anticipate the way her entire life would evolve and felt that something crucial was missing. Masae's narrative illustrates that more mature migrants with abundant experience of living and studying abroad tend to make informed and strategic choices; carefully weighing their options, they eventually pursue lifestyles that combine work and family in a work-life balance that makes personal sense to them even if that option entails considerable risk and insecurity about their future.

Interestingly, Masae reveals that she feels little connection with her home prefecture since she spent her formative university years and work experience in Tokyo and abroad; hence, she seems to consider herself more as an in-migrant than a returnee, also because the town she has relocated to is several hours' drive from her place of birth. Masae's narrative epitomizes the diversified lifestyle choices highly educated women with overseas experience increasingly make in contemporary Japan. Masae has lived in South America and Oceania and looks back on extensive working experience in Tokyo. In purely biographical terms, she has "come back" to her home province, but she does not seem to feel at home emotionally. Rather, rural life seems a strategic step for her to take time out from her busy career to spend more time with her infant children. As with other moratorium migrants, Masae's sense of insecurity about the uncertain future of her and her family feature side by side with hope that life in the countryside will provide her with the opportunity to create her own niche business.

Shōichi, a thirty-nine-year-old manager from Western Shikoku who worked in Tokyo for ten years and relocated to a prefecture close to his hometown for work-related reasons similarly mentions the inherent sense of liminality he felt when starting out in the small town: As a migrant, one is inevitably labeled and perceived as someone coming from outside of the local community. One's sudden arrival out of nowhere means that one needs to prove one's worth and earn the trust and respect of residents who have lived all their lives in the community (interview on 13 March

2017). He observes that this starting point can be quite a mental burden. Individuals who start working in a company or network that has been active in the local community for some time tend to have an easier time because they are perceived more positively in comparison with individuals like Shōichi, who started their own projects and company and are hard to understand from the perspectives of local citizens. Shōichi observes that he is proud of having established solid relations with local residents through his work; however, he emphasizes that for him, continuing to maintain his work and professional network in Tokyo (and abroad) is at least as important as his start-up company in the small town to which he has relocated. This statement suggests that in a classic postmodern fashion, Shōichi envisages himself as part and parcel of multiple places and cultures, fusing local and global arenas. He draws on professional networks from previous jobs in diverse fields (IT, design, venture) to a considerable degree and works hard to the point of self-exploitation in order to create a job for himself that entails a personally fulfilling lifestyle. As seen in other (specifically) male migrants, Shōichi's entrepreneurial ambitions mean that he sacrifices his leisure and time with his family. Spending one week working in Tokyo every month, he pursues a life-style that entails a working situation based in two extremely different locations. In addition, he talks about his strong emotional attachment with peers on the US West Coast. He seems so focused on making his present enterprise a success that he does not even have time to reflect for one second about the meaningfulness of it all in the long term. In that sense, Shōichi's case incorporates both mainstream references in terms of his work style and alternative approaches. He seems well integrated into the local community through his work, but he also makes it clear that work is his priority and he may move on to some other place with his family, if professional goals require it. He observes that he feels ashamed about the many job changes in his life that made it clear that he evaluated himself in accordance with conventional career norms despite his highly mobile career trajectory that involved moves to the United States and frequent job changes, one only after three months because he felt that "he was a mismatch for the job" (interview on 13 March 2017). Clearly, Shōichi's mind-set straddles mainstream salaryman thinking that prioritizes lifelong dedication to the company with the desire to break out, start an innovative enterprise, and do something different that is also personally fulfilling.

Rootless: Or, Routes to Pursuing Professional Aspirations in Changing Locations?

Home is the moment, and the moment is now, here, and gone.

—Lise Gundersen, "The Place You Left, the Latitude of Home,
Music as a Home and the Coordinates of Here"

The process of migration per se tends to be depicted as an epic event, as a decision of momentous importance. However, in practice, interviewees tend to refer to their choice to relocate more as a fleeting moment, one step in their lives that naturally happened (Aoyama 2015a). Yoshi, a male lifestyle migrant in his fifties, indicated that he does not feel like he has moved to a rural town in Western Japan as his relocation only happened recently and he goes back to Tokyo, his hometown, frequently, for work and to see his father, who lives there by himself. Many migrants even go so far as to say that they do not remember the moment of having actually relocated, with individuals often moving rather lightheartedly to a place for a short term initially, and their stay is simply extended successively afterward (especially in the case of disaster volunteers). Numerous former disaster volunteers mentioned that they were planning to engage in pro bono work for around two months in the beginning and then ended up staying for various reasons, but many mentioned the community of similarly minded peers from across Japan that have made their activities worthwhile. Interestingly, female migrants often argued that rather than feeling attachment for the place they have relocated to, it happened to be the place where they can do what they want professionally. In some cases, practical reasons such as finding convenient accommodation, a good reaction of the children to a place, or good timing of a deadline for a regional revitalization officer post were mentioned as reasons. Migrant narratives generally featured relatively strong commitment to work, although some migrants did refer to leisure activities (surfing, mountain climbing, fishing) as a driving incentive to relocate, even if it turned out that they hardly had time for the regular pursuit of such activities. Many also added that they could envision themselves moving on further to other places if it were for work.

In other words, work was a dominant factor for these migrants and being eternally on the move for career reasons seemed an evident feature of their mind-set. In addition, time with the family (if they had one), for leisure, and in nature were also mentioned as key factors of importance in their decisions to move to rural areas. Hence work was generally accorded high priority, but lifestyle also featured high on the agenda of individual migrant narratives. Some lifestyle migrants with distinct professional skills that are sought after in rural areas such as IT or those in the medical profession choose to relocate for financial benefits and quality of life; however, many also turn out to aspire to frequent job changes as part of their lifestyle, that is, reinventing themselves with each relocation while improving their careers in the process. Interestingly, migrants without a family or partner showed little commitment to their private lives, seeming content with ersatz families, such as networks with other migrants, or indulging in leisure activities of various sorts. These single migrants indicated that they "were not personally apt for marriage" (interview on 13 September 2016) like Chiharu, a single female lifestyle migrant originally from Tokyo introduced in chapter 5, who indicated rather passively that she is "not particularly interested in marriage, but would not be opposed to life with a partner if she were to encounter someone appropriate" (interview on 13 September 2016). Chiharu narrates that she would like to establish a collective housing project with other migrants as it makes more sense to share accommodation; however, she could not find other migrants interested in sharing because they are either married with children or not interested in collective living, Chiharu adds that she has few local friends in the community she has moved to. Having a job that pays her bills but not much more, Chiharu is too busy working and hardly has time to reflect on what she wants in the long term. Not the social type, she seems content spending time by herself and observes that she has few local friends and does not relate to other in-migrants. Precarious, socially somewhat isolated, but with a network that keeps her going, Chiharu has a life trajectory that is heavily infused with living on a day-to-day basis and suggests liminality as a "permanent condition" (Szakolczai 2000: 220), like other lifestyle migrants.

Hisa, a male respondent aged twenty-seven from Yokohama, points out that family is very important for him; that said, Hisa does not feel ready for marriage as he does not earn a stable income at present and describes himself as *fura fura* (interview on 22 September 2016). Hisa dropped out of university for financial and other reasons, eventually sold Hawaiian food from a mobile food stall in Tokyo, and engaged in a variety of other temporary work. He heard about his present place of residence from friends and moved there despite not having any personal connections. He lives on prefectural subsidies (120,000 JPY per month) that he receives for engaging in agricultural and other work he does for farmers in the neighborhood (30,000–40,000 JPY). He says that his diet consists mainly of *natto* (fermented beans) and vegetables that he gets for free from friends and neighbors since he does not have any savings (despite the fact that, on good days, he made as much as 200,000 JPY per day with his mobile food stall in Tokyo). This constitutes quite a change from his lifestyle back in Tokyo when he was constantly eating out and going out frequently at night. Now he gets up at 6:30 a.m. (4:30 in the summer), works from 7: 30 to 5:00 p.m., and goes to bed quite early at night.

Hisa's narrative suggests a lack of medium- and long-term planning: "I am not sure how long I will stay but for the time being I will stay here, but I don't have plans to move anywhere else" (*Toriaezu iru kedo . . . kaeru yotei ha nai ne*) (interview on 22 September 2016). Characterized by a lack of planning and lack of commitment, his narrative is replete with liminality; his lifestyle contains elements of the sharing economy and downsizing as he indicates that all the clothes he wears he got from friends—he only spends money on gasoline, tobacco, utilities, and books since he is not very interested in material things. He is presently in the process of restoring a spacious abandoned house with the help of local neighbors so that friends visiting him from across Japan can stay at his place. Hisa mentions that after relocating to the countryside, he felt lonely as he missed his family, but now many friends from Tokyo, from across Japan, and abroad keep visiting him. It is worth noting that most of his friends "do what they like" and few have stable employment. Asked whether he plans to open a guesthouse or hostel-like accommodation since there is none on the island where he lives, he remarks that he is not interested in working in the service industry. Yet a few months later he announces on social media that, restoration of his house being complete, he now accepts short-term visitors through Airbnb. Hisa farms now although he has no prior agricultural experience. He says that he does not have any plans for his future and mostly lives his life "from day to day" (*nagare de iku*; interview on 22 September 2016).

Different as Masae's incentive for moving and trajectory may be from Hisa's, since she is forty and has two children and a partner, she describes herself as a "chameleon that changes depending on the place" (interview on 14 March 2017). Looking back on her extensive experience of corporate employment in Tokyo and experience living in South America, she observes that for her personally, the most appropriate mode of working and living may be to have a space where both can be done together rather than belonging to some work institution, since she wants to take time to spend with her children but also engage in professional work—something that did not seem possible back in Tokyo. Despite their differences in age and educational and professional background and values, both Hisa and Masae appear to be constantly adapting to the changing circumstances of their lives.

Kei, a thirty-six-year-old IT expert, was dispatched eight months ago by his Tokyo company to the rural town where he now resides in order to manage the newly founded satellite office there. Having spent all his life in the Tokyo area, Kei remembers that he was less than positive about this order as he associated "countryside" with inconvenience and remoteness, but he could do nothing about it. To his surprise, he has liked rural living so much that he asked to stay on beyond the initial period of dispatch. First of all, he felt that his health improved because he did not have to commute to work for hours on the train every day: his constant hip pain disappeared. Furthermore, the rural environment is so quiet that he feels he can concentrate better on work and get more things done. He has also lost over eight pounds as he stopped eating convenience store food and started cooking by himself and eating mostly local vegetables. Kei argues that for him, rural life has turned out to be a valuable opportunity to reflect on and rethink his life (and work).

Although Kei is clearly enjoying his first experience of rural living, he concedes that at present he is not sure whether he wants to spend the rest of his life in the rural town where he resides now. He indicates that he feels comfortable living there, and it is good place to get work done. However, there are drawbacks, such as having to go and meet some clients personally in Tokyo. He has to go to the capital for work-related appointments once every two months. Asked about his plans for the future, Kei admits that he does not have plans but would like to start a family and have children within one year. He admits that he has no idea where he is going to be living one year later (interview on 7 March 2017). As for work, he reveals that he has no concrete plans either but rather waits to see how things are going to evolve. If there should be disadvantages for work, he would probably choose to go back to Tokyo, but he would like to live a lifestyle based in two locations.

Kei's case illustrates that recent changes in perception of rural areas, along with emerging policies of opening branch offices in the country-side as a means of reducing risk in case of a major earthquake in the

Tokyo area and cutting costs, have resulted in individuals who are not initially interested in rural life moving to rural areas. However, despite his surprisingly positive reaction to being dispatched to the countryside, Kei's narrative also makes clear that he still focuses primarily on work and engages with the local community only to a limited extent. Furthermore, his lifestyle is still thoroughly urban (although he points out that it has become healthier) as the pace of his life seems in step with Tokyo: dinner at 10 p.m., going to bed late, and getting up relatively late for local standards. Kei's trajectory is an example of salarymen moving to the countryside for a limited period for career purposes rather than for leisure and the lifestyle. On the other hand, he has switched from commuting by train to relying on his car to get from his home to his office, has started to cook for himself, and feels "life" more than before when his life was centered on work. He states that he is "in the process of experimenting" (*jikkenchū*; interview on 7 March 2017). In other words, his narrative is dominated by surprise that as someone who never questioned urban life or even imagined a move to the countryside, he actually enjoys rural living, but also by a feeling of transience and lack of commitment.

Going Over the Edge and Looking Back?

Liminality has conventionally been interpreted as resistance or a form of counterstatement to conventional societal structures and norms. As Foucault has poignantly argued, resistance occurs in and refers to the system (1980b). Numerous lifestyle migrants who lived abroad for an extended period experienced difficulties blending into Japanese society after their return as they realized that their experience abroad was not perceived as a plus by potential employers. Many of these returnees decided to apply for the regional revitalization officer program offered by the Ministry of Internal Affairs, which would permit them to live in rural areas for one to three years and seek ways of making a living while contributing to regional revitalization. This program affords individuals considerable freedom to rethink what they wish to do with their lives in the countryside; the program allows them to grapple with their status "in the interstices of social structure" (Turner 1996: 517). At the same time, as pointed out by former corporate employees, the salary is relatively low and they are referred to as "community volunteers," which misleadingly suggests that their activities are unpaid. Furthermore, the pressures that come with the program are considerable, as migrants have to establish ways of making a living by the end of the program period. While this step constituted a way of "opting out" from orthodox career trajectories, many migrants referred to conventional views throughout their narratives, assessing their own life courses and decisions through the eyes of mainstream representatives of societal order. For example, a male interviewee who had spent several years in Ghana, and had been on the move across Japan before that, tried to legitimize his nomadic life; he said that he has proved that despite all the hardship and insecurity that his life has entailed, he does not live on the streets, manages to make a living, and has fulfilled all the promises he had made to his family, who seemed skeptical about his nonnormative lifestyle.

Taku, a thirty-six-year-old migrant from Chiba Prefecture, has relocated to rural Western Japan after working in central Tokyo for ten years. Having lived in the small town for several years now, Taku has established solid relations with the local community and talks with passion about his activities engaging for the preservation of traditional local folk arts. He describes, on the one hand, the easygoing and positive atmosphere of residents as a big plus since nonlocals are encouraged to try new things, even if this may involve failed attempts. He points out, however, that the easygoing nature of locals could also be seen as a lack of commitment and discipline, on the other hand. This observation implies that long-term life in the small town could turn out to be a career disadvantage since work does not reach a professional level comparable to places like Tokyo. Taku's initial incentive to relocate to rural Japan was a job retraining program where he lives now; he had turned thirty and somehow felt constrained by his work in central Tokyo. Nevertheless, he concludes pensively toward the end of our conversation that despite the growing numbers of young migrants relocating to the small town that he lives in, ultimately, stable life in urban areas may be the right choice, although, he adds, it is too early to tell (interview on 8 March 2017).

At the same time, he mentions that he has established an archive for old photographs in the town and says that he would like to create a place where citizens could see these photos, meet others, and digitize the photos. Like many mobile subjects, Taku seems to be on a path with two divergent strands that are actually more on a continuum, as elaborated earlier: positive and outgoing engagement with the local community on the one hand, as signaled by his engagement for the local archive, and insecurity about one's position on the other, along with the nagging feeling that urban life could be the better choice in the long term after all.

In addition to these emotional issues, climate differences also seem to constitute a source of stress for some migrants in West Japan: Migrants described the humid and hot summers with centipedes, cockroaches, and snakes in the home and long and harsh winters with minus-degree temperatures in one's home due to a lack of central heating. Some urban settlers mentioned that they have no heating in the kitchen, which means that during the winter season they only use the kitchen for obtaining hot water to eat junk food like cup noodles, or they prefer to eat out if possible in order to limit spending time in the freezing kitchen.

Hiro, a forty-five-year-old male migrant from Gifu Prefecture, relocated to rural Western Japan after working in Osaka and Tokyo. After a period of extensive nomadic life (five years, which is very rare in Japan, where there is no notion of "gap year") spent in Hokkaido, Hiro says that his long-term dream has always been to go freelance, rent an abandoned factory in a rural area somewhere, start a new creative enterprise, and have enough leisure time to spend fishing and enjoying outdoor activities. At the same time, Hiro observed with pride at some point in our interview that he managed to make a career as a top designer and be acknowledged in Tokyo despite his unusual CV, which includes his period of nomadic traveling and lack of education (he never attended university or vocational college). He has not only managed to relocate with his family to the countryside, but he has also taken his business from Osaka with him. Now into his fifth year of rural living, he laughs about the fact that he is busier than back in Osaka, with design shows abroad and collaboration projects with governmental agencies. He hardly has time to enjoy leisure, so he is thinking about taking a break from work for two to four weeks when the weather is nice. Hiro is an interesting case because he seems to cross borders of genres of work and people constantly, with diverse contacts to bureaucrats, hippies, organic food caterers, architects, among others. He has pursued an unconventional lifestyle that resembles the American dream of entrepreneurship yet also successfully relates to governmental actors, and he has recently been increasingly commissioned with local governmental projects as well. His unusual habit (for Japanese standards at least) of taking holidays for weeks in a row in a season when he can practice his favorite outdoor pastime of fishing and spending time with friends also shows his individualist way of carving out his own way of working and living.

Mia, a twenty-nine-year-old female interviewee from Chiba Prefecture, has relocated to a rural town in Western Japan in spring 2016 after spending two years in Bangladesh as a youth volunteer for Japan International Cooperation Agency, the governmental development agency. She also worked as a company employee in Tokyo for several years, where she remembers that she was so busy at times that she did not have time to go to the toilet (interview on 9 March 2017). She seems satisfied with her present life, saying that she is facing a low level of stress and thinks that she lives in a balanced way that is not taking a heavy physical and emotional toll on her health, like her previous job in Tokyo. She remembers that after living in an Asian developing country, she felt that people in Japan are quite cold toward others. Back in Bangladesh, everyone would stop work to ask her whether she was homesick since she came to Bangladesh by herself. Mia points out similarities between her life in Bangladesh and in the Japanese countryside: people always taking time for a chat (sometimes excessively), being invited for meals to other people's homes; even her work now as a regional revitalization officer shares feature with her activities in Bangladesh when she was in charge of providing support for a group of citizens trying to grow organic vegetables as a development youth cooperation officer.

She is busy making efforts to secure a livelihood once her contract as a regional revitalization officer expires in two years. She feels that her present work fits her personally as she meets people from different walks of life and has opportunities to talk to farmers, senior citizens, and many other residents. Mia frequently compares her present life with life in Bangladesh, teasing out surprising similarities between living in rural Japan and living in Bangladesh. Like many other lifestyle migrants, Mia narrates that most of her close private friends are other nonlocal migrants just like herself. Her local contacts are by and large limited to the people she meets through her work as a regional revitalization officer and through her participation in a traditional dance group. There is a gap between this lack of local contacts and her aspiration of engaging in work the effects of which she is in a position to notice directly (rather than working in a company where interaction is mostly anonymous). This brings us back to the inherently liminal position of these lifestyle migrants in rural areas, negotiating between residents' expectations for what nonlocal youth like them can do and facing the harsh reality of creating social contacts and livelihoods from zero. Just like Masae, Mia did not have any personal connections with the rural town she now resides in, and both have extensive experience living in a developing country.

In retrospect, Mia says that she was impressed with the sophisti-cated homepage of the town office and decided to apply for a three-year regional revitalization officer position. Mia states that her long-term aim is to engage in the field of tourism or create connections between chefs in the Tokyo area and local farmers. Due to her experience living in Bangladesh, Mia has both an external and internal view of Japan. Given her encounter with a totally different approach to work, for example, Mia chuckles that nothing really throws her out of her comfort zone and she feels that rural life fits her well.

Summing up the diverse vignettes introduced in this chapter, the preceding cases illustrate that many migrants pursue lifestyles that differ essentially from the trajectories of corporate employees; they contemplate the idea of "going over the edge" (Pearce 2013) but keep looking back to societal order. Some have adopted diverse values during trips abroad or have been shaped by their work experience overseas. Others have traveled widely across Japan. Regardless of their backgrounds and previous lives, all migrants depicted seem highly driven in pursuing personally mean-ingful lives yet also seem caught up in orthodox values. The argument by Hisa serves as such an example as he has clearly departed from the conventional life course by dropping out of university and relocating to the countryside while still referring to mainstream familial structures. Some migrants even play with the idea of rejoining corporate careers if opting out proves unsustainable in the long term. Others discuss their lower salaries in comparison with their former corporate employment but hasten to point out that they are willing to accept this situation for the experience and skills they can gain. Some migrants argue that the low living costs in the countryside are a strategic benefit as this allows them to work less and hence affords them more free time to reflect on their lives and live a slower pace of life.

These examples also reveal Foucauldian mechanisms of sustained contextualization of resistance within societal order and norms at play in the sense that the resistance shown by migrants to values favored by postwar mainstream order and their ensuing attempts to live according to their own values are never completely outside of the generally accepted truths and power dynamics of the times. They are always contextualized in society (Rosenberger 2014: 107; Foucault 1980b). These narratives clearly illustrate that migrants' modes of living and working in the coun-tryside emerge from aspirations to alternative lifestyles yet are contextualized in mainstream societal values. Not surprisingly, numerous narratives contain elements of pressure and anxiety, which may be interpreted as reflecting the "high level of anxiety among today's job seekers" that has become evident with the precaritization of employment in Japan (Osawa and Kingston 2015: 68). Few migrants choose to discuss these feelings of pressure and anxiety explicitly (and if they do, they happen to be predominantly female); even lifestyle migrants with a past of mental or physical breakdown only touch on this in passing during extended interviews. This tendency to disguise fragility and vulnerability could be interpreted as a reflection of the sense of risk and liminality that comes with precarious work and an emerging sense of responsibility ascribed to the individual in a neoliberal environment (Scharff 2016: 220–221). The tendency to avoid any topics related to fragility and vulnerability could also be perceived as a continuing sense that "failure" is not socially acceptable in Japan. In neoliberal interpretation, the notion of the "responsibilization of the self" (Peters 2016: 300) means that failure is conceived as the responsibility of the individual and hence understood as a double stigma in contemporary Japan. Migrant narratives often revolve around terms such as "aspiration," "dreams," "ambition," "purpose of life," self-realization, and *waku waku* (feeling of energetic drive and happiness from fulfilling activities). At the same time, the daily practices of many migrants dedicating an overwhelming part of their lives to work-related activities rather than family and leisure can be understood as empirical and implicit evidence of the enormous pressure individuals face.

Moratorium Migration: Living in Permanent Limbo

Wrapping up this chapter, I return to the notion of "moratorium migration," which in my view brings liminality and a sense of belonging together in a way that captures the post-growth—and neoliberal—age. Notwithstanding the diversity of the migrants introduced in this chapter and throughout this monograph, the majority of narratives indicate a departure from the alleged stability and safety of corporate employment. Some respondents worked in corporate jobs for a while; others never took this path. However, a recurring theme in all trajectories, regardless of their age or gender, is a lack of planning and anticipation of what the future will bring; most individuals seem to prefer to focus on the moment, carving out what is (or could be) in their eyes an ideal job.

Many settlers fleetingly touched on the fact that their present place of residence might not be permanent; others openly talked about their plans to move on at some point in the future. A feeling of transience and permanent limbo pervaded many narratives: interviewees described their sense of satisfaction about their present place of relocation yet added that they will probably move somewhere else in a few years (Aoyama 2015b: 23). Narratives introduced in this chapter also contained trajectories that combined a high extent of local community engagement with pronounced doubts about rural life in the long term. Others observed that for them, life and work in the countryside constituted just "another experience," outlining their plans of returning to their hometowns (interview on 8 March 2017).

I contend that the trajectories of my research participants discussed in this chapter and throughout this book indicate that this postliminal condition, that is, extended and permanent liminality, is the key feature of "post-growth" societies. Moratorium migration is perceived by many to be a necessary stage toward reinventing themselves on their way to implementing their aspired lifestyles. However, vision often goes hand in hand with pressure, a sense of vulnerability, and lingering emotional void. The depicted narratives indicate that, somewhat paradoxically, the shift of contemporary Japan toward a more diversified society goes hand in hand with persistent references to ingrained societal behavioral patterns such as the fear of standing out, being different, and falling outside the norm. Many lifestyle migrants grew up in protected middle-class households with housewife mothers and breadwinning fathers, and they find themselves in a position to fend for themselves for the first time. Having eschewed the safety nets of lifelong employment or urban networks, many individuals find themselves in a "no-man's-land betwixt and between the structural past and the structural future as anticipated by the society's normative control of biological development" (Turner 1986: 41).

Moratorium migration hence seems an appropriate mechanism to which individuals in different life stages resort in order to hedge their bets, gain time, and seek assurance, inspiration, and courage to do (or to further postpone doing) what they ultimately feel makes sense to them in a neoliberal age. Empirical data discussed in this chapter also indicate that side by side with aspirational moves, that is, mobility motivated by the wish to experiment with novel lifestyles, we find ingrained patterns of mobility where concrete aspirations do not feature explicitly. The latter type of migrant often describes him- or herself as *fura fura* (lingering, implying that there is no clear goal). Regardless of whether they refer to aspirations, migrants mention considerable pressure they are exposed to while pursuing nonnormative lifestyles; in many cases, their families and friends only show limited understanding for their decisions to relocate to the countryside. Just like the example of the female lifestyle migrant in her early twenties who discussed her sense of restlessness and pressure to come up with original ideas illustrates, the decision to depart from corporate trajectories comes with the double burden of proving oneself and one's individualized professional or lifestyle choice in Japanese society that does not appreciate departure from the norm and proving a success in the neoliberal age marked by self-enterprise and a "prevailing and powerful ideology of 'passionate work'" (McRobbie 2016: 88).

Having grown up in well-protected households in urban areas, few of my interviewees ultimately possess the experience, acumen, vitality, and courage to pull through all the way; many end up opting for the rather convenient state of permanent limbo as they are faced with their aspiration or lack of it, opportunities, responsibility, risk, and self-exploitation in the creation and pursuit of independent work. Those few who do, however, manage to perpetuate liminality and belonging in strategic ways. They oscillate between drawing on the benefits of sustained liminality through emotional dislocation and engaging with the local community in intricate and multiple ways. Coming full circle, the daily routines and mind-sets of these mobile subjects are characterized by a "deep-rooted sense of ambivalence" (Thomassen 2015: 55). Lifestyle migrant narratives indicate that respondents like to fantasize about their visions of the good life, yet its ideal form tends to lie out of reach—it seems just one step ahead—but self-exploitative practices that interviewees have been inscribed with in former employment often prevail, a "cruel optimism," to finish with Berlant (2011), that ultimately results in the prevalence of permanent liminality.

Chapter Seven

Social Entrepreneurs between Self-Determination and Structural Constraints

Examples from Miyagi and Tokushima Prefectures

"The enterprising subject"—to borrow Nikolas Rose's term (1992: 142)—can be seen from the angle of agency, self-determination, and individualization as well as a phenomenon intricately related to the neoliberal enforcement of competitive individualism. On a positive note, Yoshitaka Mouri has written about the "creativity of the age of *furiitaa*" (part-time employees often subjected to precarious modes of production) (2010: 52). On a darker note, Michael Hardt and Antonio Negri have argued that we are seeing the transition from a disciplinary society to a society of control, in which "mechanisms" of control become more "democratic" and are "distributed throughout the brains and bodies of the citizens" rather than through the operation of specific disciplinary technologies (2000: 328–329). These claims about societal pressures and neoliberal constraints circulating through individual bodies and mind-sets as a Foucauldian *dispositif* in the sense of self-monitoring mechanism (1980b: 194) tie in with the ethnographic evidence of lifestyle migrants' pressures to succeed and persistent fear of failure depicted in the preceding chapter. The emergence of self-directed and entrepreneurial work provides hope as this new form of labor constitutes "a flight from unrewarding, mundane work" in many cases (McRobbie 2016: 93). However, the narratives of lifestyle migrants also indicate the complex entanglement of aspirational and self-exploitative labor, which reminds us of Bauman's ideas about neoliberal modes of production and capitalism resulting in a shift of responsibility to the individual (2000).

The term "social entrepreneur" (*shakai kigyōka*) is still unfamiliar to many despite the fact that postwar Japan is often associated with successful entrepreneurs who made considerable societal contributions, such as Sōichiro Honda and Akio Morita (Haghirian 2016: 125), and recently individuals who refer to themselves as social entrepreneurs have started to appear in Japanese media (Oshima 2009: 10). Furthermore, if two out of ten people say that they have heard the term, their interpretations of its meaning vary. Miyagi Haruo, the founder of the nongovernmental organization ETIC (Entrepreneurial Training for Innovative Communities) argues that individuals in their twenties and early thirties do not feel any passion for the money-centered values of their predecessor IT venture types; the lifestyles proposed by the latter do not fit into the realities of their own lives (Oshima 2009: 23) because the younger generation has grown up in a materially affluent environment. This is why many of the younger generation have been looking for ways of linking their activities to creating social values. This is where social entrepreneurship comes in, a term that denotes business activities linked with achieving social change for the improvement of society by tackling societal issues (Yamamoto 2009: 65). Miyagi and others hold that social entrepreneurship shares common ground with NEET, that is, individuals who are not in education, employment, or training, as both groups do not feel comfortable in conventional working and learning environments (Oshima 2009: 231). Similarly, social entrepreneur Yamamoto calls on everyone who does not know what to do with their lives to consider social entrepreneurship (Yamamoto 2009). ETIC has contributed enormously to the increasing acknowledgment of social entrepreneurship by offering a great diversity of internships and projects that are geared toward individuals interested in engaging firsthand in social entrepreneurship. Interestingly, in contrast to non-Japanese interpretations of social entrepreneurship who define social entrepreneurs as "people who take reasonable risk on behalf of the people their organization serves" (Brinckerhoff 2000: 12), Japanese authors do not make explicit mention of risk as an element in such undertakings, although most social entrepreneurs tend to embrace risk as an inevitable (and positive) part of their activities. In fact, one of the projects described later in this chapter did not receive funding from governmental sources because it was perceived to be "too risky and without prospect" since it was located in a marginal village facing depopulation and aging.

As outlined in previous chapters, rural areas in Japan have been commonly referred to as symbols of shrinkage and stagnation, with terms such as "marginal hamlet" (*genkai shūraku*) being used that focus on their limits rather than their potential. This chapter outlines examples from Miyagi and Tokushima prefectures of how individuals used social capital embedded in networks to implement their entrepreneurial ideas with limited means to achieve surprising results. In this sense, this chapter confirms the oft-claimed role of "the young as representative and reservoir of this frontier of potential or the future yet-to-be" (Gevurtz Arai 2016: 155), even if some of the migrants introduced may not fit the category of the young in terms of biological age.

Furthermore, these cases show the important, often underestimated role of in-migration in so-called peripheral rural areas. They also highlight the fact that rather than being peripheral, rural areas provide opportunities for networking due to various factors such as compact size, close-knit communities, coexistence of various cultures (especially if there is an in-migrant community of palpable size), and ingrained local customs of community meetings of various sorts (which some migrants have also described as a major downside of rural life since these meetings are not financially reimbursed, time-consuming, and do not seem meaningful at first for performance-based urbanites). The entrepreneurial activities described in the first half of this chapter range from starting a DIY design brand, creating local work for women who lost their employment due to the Great East Japan Earthquake by conceiving a design accessory brand, managing a café and event space, and creating a textile design brand from abandoned resources of the disaster—these initiatives are all taking place in Ishinomaki, Miyagi Prefecture, one of the worst-affected areas of the earthquake and tsunami in March 2011.

The cases introduced all have in common that they involve local and nonlocal project members, showing the importance of endogenous entrepreneurs as driving forces of these inspiring activities. Many of these entrepreneurs obtained long-term experiences as disaster volunteers in the area before they started their entrepreneurial activities. This is why despite (or because of) their relative youth, these individuals draw on a wide network of collaborators that they gained from their volunteering experience. As volunteering attracted a large range of individuals from various backgrounds, these emerging start-ups resemble the network society defined by Castells as "work[ing] with a multiplicity of cultures" due to its global nature (2005: 39), which in turn creates the potential for "complementarity and reciprocal learning" (2005: 42) between cultures. For the cases described, this holds true both for actors from geographically different contexts as well as varying professional backgrounds and, often, varying generations. Such collaboration between heterogeneous actors forms the basis for the harnessing of local resources from an endogenous perspective. Such collaboration of diverse individuals coincides with strong levels of trust and shared values between nonlocal actors (often former disaster volunteers); so we find both diversity and ingrained shared value, a balanced mix of which seems one of the factors accounting for the success of these ventures.

As pointed out in previous research into in-migrants in rural England, "the embeddedness of entrepreneurship differs significantly between in-migrant and locally born entrepreneurs" (Kalantaridis and Bika 2006: 125), with in-migrants making better use of extralocal opportunities. Many of the nonlocal entrepreneurs draw on networks from previous professional activities that extend well beyond the place they find themselves now; this use of external resources provides extra (and critical) value for their emerging start-ups. Many of the individuals described are either already engaged in a variety of professional activities that transcend the locale they have migrated to or they mention plans of doing so in the future. Yet at the same time, the cases indicate that local embeddedness is a crucial precondition to success, an insight that has also emerged from previous research (Bosworth and Atterton 2012: 265). The extent of this embeddedness varies, but all the projects described in this chapter involve local contacts and collaborators and have hence obtained the understanding and support of the local community, even if the emergence of acceptance took time.

Ishinomaki Laboratory:
DIY as Local Revitalization Tool and Business Creation

"Energising people and society with the spirit of DIY (Do it Yourself) and design. The world's first DIY label, direct from Ishinomaki." This is how the up-and-coming furniture design label presents itself on the homepage (http://ishinomaki-lab.org/, accessed on 1 April 2017). Ishinomaki Laboratory (Ishinomaki Kōbo in Japanese) literally rose from the rubble of the 2011 Great East Japan Earthquake: Tokyo architect and designer Keiji Ashizawa founded the workshop as a sign of support and community building. Just months before the tsunami shattered Ishino-maki, Ashizawa had completed a restaurant conversion project; soon after the earthquake he revisited the town to see how he could help. In the beginning, Ishinomaki Laboratory was merely a common utility space for locals to conduct DIY activities, with lumber and repair materials provided by volunteers, mainly designers from Tokyo. But the staff of Ishinomaki Laboratory also provided assistance for the restoration of local shops. As a result, the Fukkō Bar (Recovery Bar) and a community space called Irori (open fireplace) were established with the aim of contributing to the revitalization of the town, which had seen demographic stagna-tion well before the earthquake and tsunami. Right after the earthquake, Ishinomaki Laboratory's core activities focused on the implementation of design workshops to provide practical DIY skills to the local community. The founder of the initiative, Ashizawa, observed that he realized that a short-term volunteer initiative would not change the bigger picture and thus decided to conduct workshops where locals could obtain hands-on knowledge of how to repair their houses and restaurants. "At first we wanted to teach people how to fish, not just give them the fish," explains Chiba, a local who heads Ishinomaki Kōbo (Wilson 2017: 105). Whereas the material aspect of *monozukuri*, making things, for instance, furniture, catches the eye, it is actually the immaterial aspect that often tends to be overlooked: the aim of Ishinomaki Laboratory to spread a DIY spirit and sense of independence and self-help in the local community and hence contribute to an overall restoration and revitalization of the town.

In the autumn of 2011, the global furniture manufacturer Herman Miller joined the workshops, with the CEO of Herman Miller Japan, Ben Matsuzaki, regularly visiting Ishinomaki Laboratory and offering his advice to the budding initiative. Matsuzaki recommended a focus on excellent quality from the very outset rather than engaging the volunteer spirit in which the initiative started out. Now, six full-time employees are working under the supervision of Chiba Takahiro, a sushi chef turned wood craftsman who observes that he thoroughly enjoys his new work, more so than his previous work taken on from his father, which was not his own choice. Originally, Chiba had planned to move to the United States with his family; however, when his visa application was rejected, he took on the post of full-time manager of Ishinomaki Laboratory instead. Some of the initial designs such as the Ishinomaki Bench or the Ishino-maki Stool have become classics, the latter having become a part of the permanent collection of the Victoria and Albert Museum in London.

All products of Ishinomaki Laboratory can be purchased online through Yahoo Japan, showrooms have opened in Tokyo, and items have recently become available in London and New York. Hip cafés in Tokyo like the new branch of Blue Bottle Coffee in Nakameguro use furniture produced by Ishinomaki Laboratory. In 2012, Ishinomaki Laboratory was awarded the well-respected Good Design Award, a comprehensive design evaluation and commendation system in Japan that has existed since 1957.

In other words, Ishinomaki Laboratory's story is a success story of a volunteer-based community project that has turned into a full-fledged commercial enterprise and new business model that has met with both national and global acclaim. Gone are the days when it was possible to win the fruit tray—a good DIY starter piece designed by Shigeki Fujishiro—by lottery at some event or take home a prototype model of the mini-stool left over from some earlier workshops, as I had a few years ago during fieldwork in Ishinomaki in 2012. The story of this DIY workshop initiative turned business model reaffirms the innate potential that often lies uncovered in many local towns and that, given the right circumstances and set of people, can effectively change the atmosphere of a place by linking it to international sites through professional contacts and creating local workplaces in the process. Whereas in the beginning, the full-time members of the furniture label were locals, its international acclaim has resulted in nonlocal staff joining. The team uses a durable Canadian red cedar for the majority of its products as this type of cedar ages beautifully, with the wood taking on a darker nuance over the years (as the author can attest, having purchased the Ishinomaki bench for her office back in 2012). Hence, the story of Ishinomaki Laboratory is not only about the recovery of a local town devastated by a natural and man-made disaster, but also a story that illustrates the intricate relationship of local and global, material and immaterial, as well as process and results (i.e., products). In this sense, Ishinomaki Laboratory seems to fall into the category of one of many emerging social design enterprises that seek to combine business interests with social issues and bring local concerns together with global outlooks. Even if the history of this project only spans a few years, it provides hope to up-and-coming entrepreneurs and confirms the possibility of projects located outside of Tokyo that seek to bring out local pride through work and create jobs in the process. In short, it is a story of hope and aspiration for rural areas in a very new sense of experimental ground for individuals with ideas that have yet to be tested (Klien 2019).

OCICA: Of Deer Horns, Social Design, and Job Creation in Remote Rural Regions

Makinohama, Oshika Peninsula, is located in Miyagi Prefecture, one of the three prefectures in Tohoku devastated by the Great East Japan Earthquake in March 2011. Although now that the roads have been repaired, the drive from Ishinomaki to Makinohama takes only some twenty-five minutes, after the earthquake, the hamlet was isolated for a whole week (Tumugiya 2012: 26). Makinohama once had a flourishing oyster farming industry, but the earthquake and tsunami brought an end to fishing and oyster farming. Before 2011, the hamlet comprised twenty-three households and the port had an oyster processing factory where the freshly harvested oysters could be processed by workers from the hamlet and environs. The processing factory and twelve houses were destroyed in the disaster. In July 2011, Yuichi Tomohiro, representative of the NGO Tumugiya, visited Makinohama during work on a project to evaluate the situation at evacuation facilities. Many of the local women indicated that rather than continuously receiving support, they were hoping to contribute something themselves as they had lost their jobs in the oyster processing and fishing industry and were hoping to find some kind of new work; many also mentioned that having no work made them feel lonely, struggling to find something to do all day (Tumugiya 2012: 21). The chief of the hamlet also made a similar point: "We appreciate that we keep on receiving goods and volunteers from across the country, but at the same time we think it is important for us locals to get back to our feet again" (Tumugiya 2012: 27).

The key theme of Tomohiro's group Tumugiya is "bringing various people together"; the Japanese verb *tsumugu* literally means to spin, to make yarn. According to Tumugiya's homepage, the aim of the group is to create new forms and shapes of the resources that lie uncovered in the regions, create relations between the people who create and receive these new products and enrich everyone involved in the emerging small-scale sustainable project (http://tumugiya.org/about/, accessed 3 April 2017).

Hence, Tomohiro came up with the idea of using deer horn and fish net to create a brand-new accessory, the deer horn dream catcher. As the Oshika Peninsula (literally, Deer Peninsula) has an abundance of wild deer, deer horns are available in great quantities. Accessories, for instance, necklaces and earrings, are made by making notches in pieces of deer horn and winding fishnet around them. Every Tuesday and Thursday, from 10:00 a.m. to 12:00 p.m., about ten local women aged between thirty and seventy gathered in the local community hall in Makinohama to make these eye-catching accessories. By August 2013, as many as 10 million JPY had been earned by OCICA's total sales, which amounted to essential support for the livelihoods of local women in the coastal hamlet. The women had initially been skeptical that anyone would be interested in buying their hand-made products: "Who would bother to buy stuff made by elderly women in the deep countryside like us?" (Tumugiya 2012: 036). At the beginning of the project, some participants expressed their deep sadness about family and friends they had lost in the disaster and pessimism about the future. Since some of the participating women lived in temporary dwelling (*kasetsu jūtaku*) at the time, the work sessions and tea breaks were a welcome change from their routine lives.

The OCICA project consists of a continued collaboration between Tomohiro, an economics graduate from a top university in Tokyo, a designer named Eisuke Tachikawa of the NOSIGNER label in Tokyo, a photographer name Nitta Rie from Osaka, and local women who were interested in spending time on the project. Tachikawa put great priority on the fact that the design should be conceived in a way that made it relevant to the local community. According to Tachikawa, deer horn was a difficult material to work with as its core is porous and its surface rough. Extensive attempts of slicing the deer horn eventually resulted in a product that looked like a doughnut—the item that was later named "dream catcher" as it resembled a traditional Native American accessory believed to "catch" bad dreams. Since ancient times, deer horn has been believed to serve as an amulet on the Oshika Peninsula that protects its owner from water-related disasters. The local women shared this local belief with their collaborators when they were making the accessories.

While Tomohiro selected the materials and designs used for OCICA products very carefully, he mentions that he does not intend to maintain the brand forever as the needs of the local population may change: "When people in the coastal communities are trying to change, we should not become a burden to them" (www.earthmanual.org/p22en, accessed 2 April 2017).

Another important aspect of the OCICA project is its focus on communication apart from its emphasis on economic support. After the sudden end of the oyster processing and fishing industry in Makinohama, local women had no place to get together and exchange information. The regular gatherings for women to work on the accessories aimed to produce the design items; however, they also meant that locals could engage in talk while working—an important source of stress release and entertainment. In fact, after the two-hour stretch of intensive work, women always hold a tea break called "Ochakko" with homemade snacks and tea. Some women apparently got involved in the project initially because of the relaxation time after work. In other words, the communication aspect of the project is intricately linked to the revival of the community and prevention of emotional issues such as depression, a severe problem across the disaster area. During the work sessions in the morning, the noise pitch in the local community hall tends to be high as women laugh together, share recent gossip, and exchange ideas about how to improve the quality of the products they are working on. In this sense, the work created by OCICA resembles traditional *naishoku* piecemeal work that women in rural areas do at home when they have a few hours left; yet the social aspect of people coming together and the material with strong local references creates the added value here. One member of Tumugiya, the group that Tomohiro established in late 2011, ensures that the quality of the products reaches a certain level so that they can be sold at various shops across Japan, mostly in Tokyo, Osaka, and Sendai. In 2015, OCICA has conceived a new design item, a leather pen case that consists of wild deer leather and whale tails. According to the website of Tumugiya, the rare leather is obtained from local deer hunters and part of the work is carried out by disabled individuals (http://tumugiya.org/project/2016/03/01/ocica-deer-leather-pen-case/, accessed on 2 April 2017).

To sum up, the OCICA project evidently contains a strong focus on site specificity through its inclusion of items related with local industry and nature; the project also features social design, that is, bringing a contribution to local societal issues and design together. Community revitalization is the aim of the project and design is used as a tool to create work for the local women and to contribute to their well-being. The fact that the project has continued for six years attests to the ongoing need and meaningfulness of OCICA to the local collaborators. Last but not least, the exchange between the local women, the majority of whom are elderly and nonlocal individuals who are mostly in their twenties and thirties, greatly contributes to the expansion of mutual perspectives and experiences across generations—in terms of age, the local women could be the grandmothers of the urban organizers of the project and this is one of the reasons why the women seem to enjoy engaging in the project (Tumugiya 2012: 38). Projects such as OCICA entail the encounter of diverse individuals who would probably not meet otherwise—local women who were working in the oyster processing or fishing industry before the disaster, graduates from urban top universities, designers also from urban areas, experienced local deer hunters, and local owners of companies processing deer meat. Ultimately, one could even claim that as beautiful as the design accessories may be, it is the process of making the accessories that is most enriching for the project participants as they exchange invaluable information and experiences. The OCICA project provides inspiration at several levels: Tumugiya was started by Tomohiro, a student graduate with no professional experience—so it is a story of what inexperienced graduates can achieve. Second, this project shows the great potential diversity holds as project participants come from extremely heterogeneous backgrounds, yet all collaborate toward a common goal. Third, the project, just like Ishinomaki Laboratory, shows that the process is at least as important, if not more important, than the actual end product. Designer Tachikawa observes that making beautiful things tends to hold therapeutic value—this is why he felt at the very beginning of the project that making the design accessories would take on a meaning exceeding the economic sense of creating cash for the local women (Tumugiya 2012: 52).

Fourth, the project shows that there are ways of linking the empowerment of local communities with the creation of new small-scale business models, although in this case the commercial success does not seem to be the ultimate aim, only a means of achieving the end of empowering the local community. Furthermore, as refined as the accessories are due to designer Tachikawa's input in the collaborative project, the goods carry a value that goes beyond the material level: when the goods are displayed for purchase, the faces of the women who created them are also added as well as the story of Makinohama and the region after the disaster. Whereas OCICA is a model case of the creation of a livelihood for local women in a remote rural region where employment is scarce, the establishment of a meeting point for intergenerational exchange seems all the more important in a region that continues to make headlines with higher than average suicide rates and occurrence of mental issues since 2011.

Last but not least, since the project organizers are all in their early to mid-thirties, OCICA illustrates that contemporary Japan is facing a new generation of relatively young entrepreneurs with creative ideas, robust social skills, and the capability to work across genres and boundaries with a diverse range of people. Tomohiro observes in retrospect, "The members of Tumugiya were all inexperienced—so it was all a first for us and it was natural that we could not do things the way we wanted. Our way was to move on forward while learning and not being afraid of failure" (Tumugiya 2012: 98). Another member points out that the low expenses of the project meant that everyone was prepared to risk a potential failure of the project. Interestingly, he remembers that local women were cautious about joining the project in the first place as they feared failure. In their words, they "did not have a place to evacuate to if the project should fail" (interview on 19 May 2017); in contrast, the nonlocal project members could withdraw and move back to Tokyo at any time. Hence, risk was unevenly distributed even among members of the same project.

As diverse as the perspectives of all participants involved in the project may be, they share a common feature, that is, the creation of *ibasho*, a place to be, for the local women as well as the nonlocal organizers.

Hamagurido Project: Doing the Impossible or Opening a Café in a Marginal Village

The hamlet of Hamagurihama is located on an idyllic small bay some thirty-minutes' drive from central Ishinomaki. The Great East Japan Earthquake enforced the ongoing demographic decline of aging and depopulation: in the case of Hamagurihama, only two households were left after the disaster; since the tsunami had wrecked a large part of the village, it was thus designated as a "danger zone" (*kiken chiiki*). Residents were permitted to live in their existing houses, but it was legally forbidden to build new housing. Yet, March 11 also brought in thousands of disaster volunteers, many of whom were planning to stay a few days to offer help but ended up staying for years. The Hamagurido Project is the story of a collaboration between former disaster volunteers in their twenties and thirties and locals of the same generation who needed to reorient themselves after the disaster; the project was established in November 2011 and includes seven members. The starting point of the café project was to help Tsutomu, who lost his wife in the disaster and who had dreamt about opening a café with her after retirement. Now, opening the café aimed to provide Tsutomu with a new *ibasho* (place to be) and meaning of life—an opportunity that he took on with enthusiasm. I ran into

Tsutomu's father at the café who expressed his deep gratitude for the project members of having set up the café as his son has now a new source of *ikigai* (purpose in life) as well as a new community of peers. Yet, when Tsutomu and his peers, who were mostly former disaster volunteers who had stayed on in Ishinomaki to engage in their various projects, applied for funding from governmental bodies to support the project, they were rejected on the grounds that it did not make sense to open a café in a marginal village (*genkai shūraku*). Hence the group had no option but to rely on their own resources, which meant that all equipment and infrastructure were improvised from recycled matter in order to keep down the costs. Tsutomu carefully selected the furniture used in the café and combined vintage items with self-made objects, traditional Japanese architecture with American furniture classics—a mix that has added a unique atmosphere to the café. Concretely, the café was opened in a traditional Japanese family home (the grandparents of Tsutomu), and guests are now sitting on midcentury seats on the wooden Japanese *engawa* veranda (see figure 7.1). Visitors enjoy home-made bread, looking out on the quiet bay with occasional deer vocalizations echoing from the nearby woods. It is hard to believe that this bay is only twenty minutes from downtown Ishinomaki—time seems to run at a much slower pace here.

On weekends, the café is crowded—many guests are from Ishinomaki City; others heard about the café through social media and are friends of friends living as far away as Tokyo. The success of the café is remarkable as it has attracted visitors to a place that used to be a quiet fishing village with no tourism. Yet, the participants of the project indicate that they are planning to spin out the project further: they recently organized an outdoor wedding for an acquaintance, they are planning to open a guest house in an adjacent space, and in the long term they are planning to organize water sport tours. In other words, the Hamagurido Project is a strongly site-specific comprehensive enterprise that aims to make use of available resources in a remote rural hamlet at a grassroots level and bring together a societal contribution to the reconstruction of a former disaster area with an attempt at regional revitalization. Each of the project members has his or her own skills and priorities and engages in work other than the project, so there is a high degree of flexibility: one member is in charge of roasting and preparing the coffee to be served; another bakes fresh bread, having had a professional career in bakery; another is in charge of interior design and restoration; and so on. Since most of the members have known one another for several years

Figure 7.1. Midcentury chair on Japanese-style porch (*engawa*), Hamagurido Café, Oshika Peninsula, Miyagi Prefecture.

due to their experience as disaster volunteers and are friends, there is a high level of trust among them, which facilitates the conception and implementation of the project. Several of the members involved have spent time living and studying abroad—for example, one of the local members, Takashi, was studying at the University of Hawaii when the disaster happened. He came back as he felt that supporting his hometown at such a time was more important than studying. He considers the café and the planned activities that come with the entire project, such as marine sports, a form of coming to terms with the disaster through sport activities (interview on 15 August 2014). He expresses his satisfaction that the senior residents from next door in the hamlet also come to the café to enjoy some coffee, and one staff has joined who is originally from the hamlet. He also points out that the fact that a place like the café has opened means that there is a meeting point for locals and nonlocals and that the hamlet will not vanish in the near future.

Another volunteer member in his early twenties whom I interviewed on site is originally from the greater Tokyo area but spent some time working in Sydney; he is planning to go back to Australia in the near future. Ryo is a former disaster volunteer from Kobe in his mid-thirties who used to work as a chef before coming to Ishinomaki. Outgoing, friendly, and with great organizational and social skills, he has a strong network in the local community due to his long-term volunteer experience. He spends 80 percent of his time working for Hamagurido and 20 percent sleeping, observing that work amounts to life in his case. Ryo indicates that he understands himself as a "person of the wind" (*kaze no ningen*) who brings in fresh ideas and then moves on—an observation that implies that he is not envisioning himself to be in Ishinomaki in the long term. In fact, at the time of the interview he is single but marries a year later and moves to Tokyo to start his own restaurant that introduces local resources from Ishinomaki to urbanite gourmets. When I meet him in Tokyo one year later in 2015 for a follow-up interview, he says that even if he has physically moved from Ishinomaki, he maintains close relations with his friends and peers there as he relies on fresh fish from the region for his restaurant in Tokyo.

Three years later, I head back to the village to interview the project members. Some of the members in charge of the café are unknown faces to me; Tsutomu later tells me that the staff have shifted from nonlocal former disaster volunteers to U-turners, that is, locals who came back after the disaster to seek employment in their home regions. The café is packed on a Sunday noon, with a waiting list at the entrance and friendly, but business like taking of orders and serving of food. Many of the guests have come from afar, some as far as Tokyo. During the week, locals make up the larger share of the guests. Whereas the café seems highly popular with a good turnout of guests, Tsutomu observes that with five staff in charge of the café, there is little profit despite the popularity, and staff seem tired. In contrast, Takashi has started his marine leisure project, offering various activities in the sea such as diving, canoe, and surfing lessons with a barbecue of local delicacies in the boathouse members have recently built in the idyllic bay. Takashi's leisure project enjoys high popularity and, unlike his efforts at the café, he manages to earn much in comparison just by himself, although there is no work in the winter.

While he admits that he would like to have a higher income as he is married and has offspring, he says that he is slowly trying to build up a stable salary rather than going for a large income quickly. He has started to go hunting for deer with one more project member during the winter as the region has an abundance of deer and he needs to create an income for the season when marine sports cannot be practiced.

The other project member Takashi goes hunting with is Satoru, who is in his late twenties and from Kagoshima. Having come to Ishinomaki as a disaster volunteer, he has remained ever since, relinquishing his former well-paid work as a crane operator. A quiet person who exudes a sense of balance and well-being, Satoru chuckles that his rate of satisfaction with his present life amounts to 120 percent, as he does not have any complaints and does things that he likes doing for work. As a result, there is no line between work and life for him. Six and a half years have passed since he moved to Ishinomaki; asked about how long he intends to stay, he says he has no idea, but it could well be that he finds himself here for his entire life. Still, he does not like the idea of settling in one place (interview on 6 August 2017). In addition to his project work in the small hamlet, he is thinking about starting a share house in Ishinomaki and also makes small functional designer objects for sale. Occasionally he organizes a morning coffee service in downtown Ishinomaki, where he offers coffee to customers who can give as much as they deem appropriate or do something they feel skilled at in return. Satoru's narrative makes evident that he draws heavily on features of the sharing economy and no longer subscribes to the tenets of consumerist society as he did during his days as a crane operator. He hardly buys anything these days, only high-quality equipment that he needs for work.

Funade Project: Entrepreneurship, Networks, and Work-Life Balance

Tetsuya, a forty-two-year-old male from Tokyo, had been working in Kyoto as a designer for two years when the earthquake struck. While he was volunteering with the NGO group On the Road, he came across abandoned *tairyōbata* (literally, "big catch banners," ship flags). These flags from fishing vessels were hoisted on special occasions or when an exceptionally good catch had been made. As the owner of the ruin where he had discovered the flags with his fellow volunteers gave him permission to take away the flags, he decided to start a small-scale shop that makes use of these local resources and create something new in the process. Tetsuya now runs his own shop and brand called Funade311 in downtown Ishinomaki offering products made of these recycled ship flags. Funade means "departure of the ship" and refers to starting a new life after March 2011. Seven local women and a (nonlocal) former volunteer assistant are involved in the project doing *naishoku* (home-based piecemeal work), so the project has also resulted in the creation of local employment. He observes that his values have changed considerably as a result of volunteering. He used to be focused on material concerns, whereas now he concedes the importance of money but emphasizes that it is important not to be focused exclusively on making money. He states that he is earning more now in Ishinomaki than he used to earn in Kyoto and feels more satisfied with his social life, too, since he has a network of like-minded peers around him.

Like most of the other newcomers, he says that since he is really enjoying his work there is no clear-cut division between his work, leisure, and private life—a mode of life that resembles the lifestyle advocated by Honda Naoyuki, who introduces various individuals in the creative industry who have recently moved out of Tokyo and started a new life and career in rural areas (2015). Tetsuya's narrative resembles that of other lifestyle migrants: His extended volunteer experience in Ishinomaki made him realize the limitations of a consumerist way of life focused on material concerns and he now lives a life that is more concerned with having control of his time rather than accumulating money; nevertheless, he concedes that his entire life is focused on turning the products offered in his shop into a successful brand. His mode of life is characterized by downshifting and concerns for sustainability. The interior of his shop was self-made with the help of his former volunteer peers, and the products he sells draw on abandoned local resources, an approach that brings site-specificity and sustainability together. Like other narratives, Tetsuya's narratives also contains an inherent gap between his overall aim of slow life and the reality of turning his work as a freelancer and owner of his own shop and brand into a sustainable livelihood.

Furthermore, Tetsuya's life course has been characterized by extensive mobility: Born in Copenhagen, he has traveled to Thailand and regularly travels across Japan for both work and inspiration. He makes a point of taking holidays, in contrast to the widespread custom in Japan of working without taking any days off, as he believes that taking time off affords him time to think, which in turn results in new ideas—a mind-set that may be related to his experience of living in Thailand. However, like the narratives of many other migrants introduced throughout this monograph, Tetsuya's narrative suggests that his work, life, and leisure are all wrapped into a seamless entity as he has created his own work and mostly engages in work that he personally identifies with. His trajectory reminds us of Hoey's definition of lifestyle migration as concerning "individuals and families who choose relocation as a way of redefining themselves in the reordering of work, family, and personal priorities as they seek a kind of personal moral reorientation to questions of the good" (2005: 593). After all, this lifestyle migrant from Tokyo has established his own small-scale enterprise reusing abandoned textiles in a unique manner that aims to benefit the local economy apart from securing his own livelihood.

In retrospect, Tetsuya observes that he is financially better off compared to his time in Kyoto as a designer, and he adds that he is highly satisfied with the social relations in Ishinomaki as he has a network of like-minded peers from his volunteer days. However, he also points out that despite this high satisfaction, he is aware that it is important to keep on working on his own self-growth: He always thinks about his

7.2. Funade shop, Ishinomaki, Miyagi Prefecture.

next step (interview on 15 August 2014), an observation that reminds us of the "reflexive self" coined by Giddens (1991) as well as of Beck and Beck-Gernsheim's terms "reflexive biography" and "do-it-yourself" biography (2001). Work takes up the majority of his time, yet he also makes efforts to dedicate more time to leisure and seems to permanently evaluate his mode of life, which also carries Baumanesque features of self-realization projects in postindustrial societies (Bauman 2000). Tetsuya's experience of constant reevaluation and remaking of the self (Bauman 2004) features in many narratives of individuals of his generation.

When I head back to Ishinomaki three years later in August 2017 to meet Tetsuya for a follow-up interview, he looks unchanged, his face perhaps a bit fuller than previously. Having started surfing for leisure in the early morning hours before going to work, he seems pleased with his overall life in Ishinomaki. Still critical about the small town, which he describes as *chūto hanpa* (a mixed bag of compromises), he does not have plans of leaving as his shop is going well; in his own words, he is "earning loads" (*kasegimakutteiru*) from the rising number of customers due to the Reborn Art Festival that started in summer 2017 (interview on 9 August 2017). His staff in the shop has increased from one to three assistants and he has started renovating a house close to the shop for his atelier and studio. As for his private life, in his early forties now, he is single after a failed relationship and says that he would like to get married if there were an appropriate partner, as it is hard to be a single, with locals pitying him for his status. However, with a comfortable income, fulfilling leisure activities, and extensive social relations, he does not seem to be making active efforts to start a partnership and family. Rather, he concedes that he likes to spend free time in the evening in his favorite *izakaya* in the neighborhood drinking and snacking.

In sum, Tetsuya's experience and narrative could be interpreted as a coexistence of postwar focus on self-assertion and self-growth with post-growth concern with sustainability, networks as ersatz family, and down-shifting combined with a continued interest in material belongings. In fact, the values and thoughts of the majority of lifestyle migrants gleaned from interviews and participant observation indicate the coexistence of a rather paradoxical set of priorities in one and the same individual narratives, which may be the characteristic of post-growth contemporary Japan as it is clearly a transitory period, with individuals making efforts to adjust to and carve a niche in permanently changing circumstances.

Shizq Water Conservation Project: Sustainability, Community Engagement, and Social Design

Nobu, an outgoing, straightforward, and down-to-earth designer from Gifu Prefecture in his mid-forties, is smoking a pipe sitting on a wooden bench in front of the entrance of his office located in a picturesque traditional house in the center of Kamiyama Town, Tokushima Prefecture. His army pants combined with his pipe smoking make him stick out like a sore thumb in the local town that is known for its *sudachi* citrus fruit production. Nobu remarks with a smile that the community here is very close-knit and that "it's a good idea to keep in mind that everyone will notice the color of your pants when your washing is out in the garden to dry" (interview on 14 March 2017). At the same time, he recently became the proud owner of a *keitora*—the ubiquitous white light trucks that characterize rural life in Japan—and posted a short video of his first drive on the narrow winding mountain roads on social media. This episode illustrates his chameleon-like skill of adapting smoothly to various social milieus: Nobu points out during the interview that he has many hippie friends from his period of nomadic traveling in Hokkaido, yet he also has long working experience in web and graphic design in Tokyo and Osaka and widespread connections with the local community due to various collaborative projects that will be described later in this section. At first sight, the pipe-smoking Nobu may strike one as a bourgeois bohemian; yet further on in the interview that is interrupted by visits of customers, since the interview is in his showroom and shop, he appears a strategic entrepreneur with excellent communication skills. At the same time, he maintains good relations with other lifestyle migrants who come from the reggae and hippie scene and organizes occasional club events in town.

Nobu moved to Kamiyama with his wife and two children in October 2012 as he had long aspired to life in the countryside, and an attractive house that was over 150 years old and in good condition came up for sale in the town. In fact, one of the reasons why he decided to pursue a career in web design (rather than continue to focus exclusively on graphic design) was the fact that he expected the development of broadband internet connections to facilitate life and work independent of urban locations. At the time when he was starting out internet was still in its infant stages, but he anticipated that the time would come when people could choose where to work (and live). He was dreaming about establishing a creative base in a spacious abandoned factory building somewhere in Wakayama Prefecture, working there, and fishing in the nearby river in between. So in retrospect he consciously chose internet-related work since he expected that working in such a manner would become possible in the future.

He did not have any connections to Kamiyama but initially heard about the town from the president of a company with a satellite office there and decided to inspect the place. Even after his move, he maintained his web design office in Osaka, eventually deciding to move his office and staff to Kamiyama in August 2016 as the monthly office rent in Osaka was 200,000 JPY and staff were willing to relocate. He restored the cottage separate from the main building (*hanare*) before the relocation and is using it as his office and showroom now.

Nobu's life course seems like the classic American self-made entrepreneur story: He engaged in nomadic work in Hokkaido for five years, traveling and doing a variety of jobs in farming whenever he ran out of money. In retrospect he feels that he got valuable insights into rural life in Hokkaido from Akan (in the east) to Rebun Island (in the northwest), learned how to live in the countryside by observing firsthand how fishermen and farmers worked and lived, and noticed that everyone was not financially well off but had a rich lifestyle as individuals (*hito no kurashi no yutakasa*). Subsequently, he worked in graphic design and web design in Tokyo and Osaka for some ten years and was totally immersed in fast-paced work. Nobu never attended university or technical college and remarks that he occasionally feels that obtaining some specialist education would be helpful as he feels "he has no backbone" (interview 14 March 2017) but managed to pursue a successful career in design with shows at the Design Hub in Roppongi, Tokyo.

When I ask him how his expectations about life in the countryside matched reality, he replies that there was a gap between his image and reality; his greatest surprise was that 80 percent of Kamiyama Town consisted of forest, but that 70 percent of this forest was man-made. For a long time, residents had planted trees as a longtime "harvest." However, when wood could not be sold as a local resource at competitive prices anymore due to the influx of cheaper Asian wood, the forest was not taken care of any longer; this led to darkness due to trees no longer being cut and an ensuing decrease of water in forest areas. The volume of river water flowing through the lush verdant town is now only a third of what it was thirty years ago. This decrease has been the result of a deterioration of the water-retaining capacity of the local mountains. Nobu started his water conservation project called Shizq (*shizuku*, meaning "drop of water" in Japanese) in June 2013. The project entails a collaborative undertaking with a local craftsman who handshapes soft cedar from the mountains around Kamiyama using a lathe technique into tumblers, cups, bowls, and plates. The project is an attempt to ascribe new value to Japanese cedar wood and restore the water-retaining capacity of the local mountains through the medium of design.

Asked about his level of satisfaction with his present life, he replies that he is still not entirely satisfied, but he is convinced that something worthwhile awaits him if he carries on like this. When he was living in Tokyo and Osaka, he was mostly doing work in order to earn money but the work he was doing did not have as much of societal meaning as the Shizq project he has started now. He observes that he loves fishing and that's why he is happy to live in Kamiyama. However, his work has increased—which he appreciates—and he gives his best when he is busy; yet last year, he took a holiday in May and June when the weather was really good as many friends were visiting and he wanted to enjoy outdoor activities. Rather than having a work-life balance every day, he is more interested in concentrated work at some periods with an extended holiday season at other times of the year. He feels that not enjoying the best season in early summer would make his relocation to Kamiyama meaningless.

On a typical day, he gets up at 6:30 a.m., eats breakfast with his family, takes his kids to school, goes for a walk in the neighborhood for one hour, and starts working from 10:00 a.m.—relatively late for local standards. When he is busy, he keeps working all day; if not, he goes fishing, cuts wood, or spends time at home. His vision is that there are times when you focus on earning money and other times when leisure comes first. However, he concedes that his present reality is that he has insufficient time to reflect on things thoroughly since he is overwhelmed with work, which means that he has too little time for leisure and private life: for example, he has a field at the back of his house but he hardly has time to cultivate any vegetables.

In other words, the attractions of the imaginative pull of the countryside continue to remain mostly out of reach for him. His short-term aim is to create time to take care of the field and link it to his design work by creating a work style like a farmer (literally, "hundred works" in Japanese) who engages in a variety of professional activities; this would be his contribution to a more enriching way of life. His long-term aim is to tie in manual work in agriculture with other projects, like starting a bar or guesthouse, with the ultimate aim of creating a panoply of professional, self-sustained activities. He poignantly observes that designers working in cities conceive various designs, yet many of them are not capable of designing their own lives. This lack of control over one's own life was the starting point for him to consider pondering a move to the countryside. He plans to open a field/creative bar and guesthouse in November this year and provide a place where people can obtain information about high-quality products from Tokushima ranging from design to food—this project is based on his own idea and initiative but will be carried out with the support of funding by Tokushima Prefecture, as Nobu has recently become a member of various collaborative projects with prefectural and town agencies. He shares an episode about the growing trust that the local government seems to hold in him as he has started working together with them on issues related to forest management: In the beginning, the representatives of local government in charge of the forest did not seem to understand his ideas, but after four years, he was asked to design the logo and poster for Kamiyama cedars, which turned out to be highly popular. The other day someone from the forest authority in the local government told him that many residents feel they get a positive boost from the poster, and the fact that Nobu has focused his perspective on the mountains has changed local awareness of the forest. As someone who only moved to Kamiyama four years ago, Nobu was so happy to hear that that he had tears in his eyes. It had been exactly his aim to enforce a change of mind-sets and thinking in this town as a designer, so he was highly pleased with this feedback. Furthermore, he has been involved in design projects abroad as well—in Paris and Amsterdam—so his base is firmly rooted in Kamiyama, yet his activities are spreading out at a fast pace both within Japan and abroad.

Nobu's case is simultaneously encouraging and sobering as it shows that individual drive can make a noticeably positive impact on larger society despite being a migrant from a different societal and geographic background. His observations also indicate the difficulties he faced at the beginning of his integration into the close-knit local community. Yet, while Nobu's main incentive was an improvement in his work-life balance, the reality is that, somewhat ironically, due to his success, his work load keeps growing and his initial motive of achieving more time for leisure and private life continues to be a distant aim. At the same time, Nobu indicates that despite his growing workload he feels the overall direction of his projects makes sense to him personally and that he is "getting somewhere worthwhile" (interview 14 March 2017).

Nobu's trajectory is a timely story of how Japanese middle-age workers manage to successfully create their own small-scale businesses independent of place yet pursue professional activities that involve deep engagement with the local community while being embedded in networks that comprise other locales across and beyond Japan. On the downside, Nobu struggles to balance his professional career with his growing consciousness that life is not only about work, and it also illustrates the great challenges Nobu and his peers encounter on the way to making time for leisure and social activities while engaging with the local community, because being a fully acknowledged citizen of a small town involves a great number of time-consuming activities such as parent-teacher association (PTA) work and committee work for the town due to the lack of residents compared to urban areas. Nobu observes with a dry smile that it took him a while to get used to work on the PTA as everyone else knows one another from early childhood, calling each other by nicknames, and it seemed difficult to get over this wall as a neorural. Furthermore, no clear instructions exist for how to do things since knowledge has been passed on orally from one generation to the next; so for someone who arrives all of a sudden in town, it seems impossible to get things done due to the lack of this knowledge, and the fact that due to a series of municipal amalgamations the geographic area one is in charge of keeps changing every year does not help either. In retrospect, now that he has managed to find ways of coping with this work he can laugh about it, but he remembers that getting used to this kind of (unpaid) but unavoidable work was really hard, "like hell" (interview on 14 March 2017). Nobu's narrative shows the underlying gap between the geographic imaginary of "slow life in the rural idyll" with the reality of rural life that is permeated by societal obligations enforced by traditional decision-making practices and increasing depopulation.

Food Hub Project:
Creating a Future for Local Agriculture
by Branding Local Food

Supporting the agriculture of Kamiyama Town by eating. Kamaya is a restaurant that aims to link farming in Kamiyama to the next generation. We use organic vegetables produced by our own agricultural team as well as vegetables from the local group Satoyama no Kai as much as possible. Since we hope that locals of Kamiyama Town will use our restaurants, we are offering a discount price for residents.

—From the Foodhub home page (http://foodhub.co.jp/ daybook/521/, accessed on 22 April 2017)

The food hub project started in April 2016; Kamaya restaurant was officially opened in March 2017 (although it had a prerun test trial limited to residents) and has a cosmopolitan touch to it. For lunch, customers pay first and then choose the dishes they like and take them to the table as a one-plate lunch. As there is a considerable discount for residents as well as for company employees of IT satellite offices, most days the lunch menu is sold out by 12:30 or earlier. It took me three attempts to actually get lunch—and indeed, the meat loaf is delicious, as are the incredibly fresh local vegetables like radish and watercress salad that come with it. Tofu comes with tartar sauce, pork with chili sauce—definitely not the average local fare. Close to the entrance of the restaurant, there is a blackboard providing information about all the local providers of the vegetables used on that day for the meals.

Evenings are somewhat more relaxed, but the restaurant is only open on Thursdays and Fridays. Motoki, the director of the project, is an ambitious thirty-nine-year-old originally from a small town in Ehime Prefecture who has an impressive array of professional experiences in Tokyo and the United States. After a one-year exchange during high school in Iowa, he studied design and management for four years at a liberal arts college in Iowa. After graduation, he felt that he had to work in Japan, otherwise he would forget about being a Japanese after being abroad for such a long time. He worked for a Dentsu venture *doburaku* (literally, totally black) company in advertising and he describes the totally exploitative work practices there for eight years and at another company for one year in Tokyo before coming to Kamiyama for the first time in 2012. In fact, he still works for an IT company in Tokyo, receiving his salary there and spending one week a month in Tokyo to make sure that everything is going fine in his absence. Looking back at the time of working for the venture company, he observes that it was all about "testing one's limits"—doing business abroad although he was not confident about his English-language skills but just going ahead with it (interview on 13 March 2017). Motoki remembers that he was so busy that at some point he just put cardboard on the floor below his office desk and slept in the office; there was just no other way of managing work, even if he did not like this situation. Motoki points out that he would not ask his staff to work in that manner, yet he gained valuable experience by working in this way and he would not be able to do what he does now if he had not gone through this hardship. Motoki observes that he felt there were several points that did not make sense to him when living in Tokyo: working in advertising, it was all about creating an experience that went beyond everyday life (*hinichijō*). Furthermore, money was necessary to do anything. Being from Shikoku, he discussed the option of relocating to his home island with his wife who agreed that for the sake of their two children, a relocation would make sense.

Due to his widespread connections with professionals in various sectors, including the deli provider Dean & DeLuca and Google Japan, Motoki was asked whether he had any ideas for a revitalization project in Kamiyama Town to implement with *chihō sōsei* funding for regional revitalization purposes. Motoki had wanted to do a project as a producer rather than a consumer that brought everyday life, food, and regional revitalization together in novel ways. He felt that after working in large-scale advertising and design, he was ready for a small-scale project that involved close cooperation with locals while raising their local awareness through approaching local ingredients in a different way. Kamaya offers local vegetables as the main attraction of the meal with a certain twist: watercress—one of the most ubiquitous seasonal vegetables in Kamiyama—is presented with a home-made dressing that locals would not think of using. The meatloaf reminds me more of American fare, just as the interior design of the restaurant space itself seems urbanite. Most of the plates and glasses used in the restaurant are "recycled" leftovers from local households. These elements all come together as a cosmopolitan experience in a town where eating out has previously not been a big thing in locals' everyday lives. Throughout the interview, Motoki often refers to his experiences in the United States as well as friends and partners on the West Coast that he is planning to collaborate with in the future. Once a year, he goes to see his friends in California. Motoki's vision is to engage in business with like-minded peers that he is also friends with. He touches on his ambition to live abroad with his family for some time, mentioning the United States, Thailand, and other places as possible options. The name of the restaurant, "food hub," draws on the ideology of the same name by the United States Department of Agriculture (USDA), defining it as "a business or organization that actively manages the aggregation, distribution, and marketing of source-identified food products primarily from local and regional producers to strengthen their ability to satisfy wholesale, retail, and institutional demand" (http://foodhub.co.jp/daybook/571/, accessed on 22 April 2017).

Listening to Motoki's narrative, it is evident that his extensive experience as a corporate employee in the fast-paced advertising industry in the Japanese capital has deeply shaped him: After all, he understands work as his main source of purpose in life. He concedes that he has sacrificed his family considerably for the sake of his work. Furthermore, he does not seem to have any leisure pursuits worth mentioning as his lifestyle, based between Kamiyama Town and Tokyo, is time-consuming and he finds himself in the phase of starting up a new project. When I ask him about his leisure, he smiles, pointing to the restaurant space.

Motoki's narrative illustrates the harsh reality lifestyle migrants face in their everyday lives after relocation: being even busier than in their previous lives, with less stability but energy that comes from their hope that someday, life will be better. Motoki's trajectory serves as intriguing evidence of the extent to which mid-career professionals who, though they depart from postwar salarymen in their activities, are actually still influenced by bubble-era thinking, when perseverance, sacrificing everything for work, and testing one's limits as proof of professional dedication were the key tenets of male lives. When I ask him about his work-life balance, he concedes that it is totally out of order (*kanzen ni kuzureteimasu*), with almost no time for leisure at all. For him, the ideal is to have a combination of work and leisure, but eventually he points out that personally he does not really have a sense of "leisure." While Motoki is busier than ever, he indicates that he derives great satisfaction from engaging in the food revitalization project, because in his advertising work he had to occasionally sell products he did not believe in 100 percent, while now he only offers products and services that make total sense to him. He indicates his great satisfaction at having found "new family" by working closely with local residents in his food project and the fact that this close cooperation considerably increases his happiness about living in Kamiyama town. So rather than enjoying life in the countryside for its own sake, Motoki's narrative clearly illustrates that rural life is incidentally the place where he can implement projects that he finds stimulating and the continued relation with urban partners in Japan and abroad through his (net)work is of essential importance to him personally.

Outlook

The diverse cases of individuals and networks from Miyagi and Tokushima prefectures introduced in this chapter illustrate the ongoing shift in contemporary Japan with regard to the implementation of socially oriented projects in rural areas by relatively young entrepreneurs with limited financial means. Regular exchange with the local community seems a given in most projects, the majority of which entail collaborations with local partners or members. A common feature in all projects is the strong reliance of like-minded peers either as business partners or collaborators; the idea of "starting up business with friends" seems to be gaining ground. Hand in hand with this emerging style of small-scale entrepreneurship that aims to make a difference at the local and global level and aspires to a greater work-life balance, however, we also witness a number of characteristics that seem remainders from Japan's economic bubble period: total dedication to your job in the form of an inherent "work until you drop" mentality, the melding of work and leisure, and sacrificing time with and the needs of one's family for work.

Last but not least, most entrepreneurs have spent decisive periods of their lives in other areas or countries and keep referring to these places throughout their narratives as points of relevance for their professional and private activities. The fragmented realities and experiences of these lifestyle migrants suggest that the nascent dissolution of class and gender regimes mentioned by Slater and Galbraith has in fact given rise to the emergence of "a wider range of non-corporate masculinities to claim a more legitimate place within Japan" (2011), on the one hand. However, on the other hand, narratives introduced in this chapter also reveal the persistent middle-class notions of continued dedication to work while neglecting the family and the pursuit of self-exploitative working practices in lifestyle migrants hoping to break out of corporate careers. This is ironic given the fact that many representatives of the budding Japanese social entrepreneur scene refer to a lifestyle called "work-life-social balance," that is, adding the social element to work and life and hence making both more enjoyable (Oshima 2009: 162).

Summing up, nascent social entrepreneurship in Japan embodies the inherent paradoxes of post-growth Japan in the sense that contemporary youth do not identify with materialist values yet emphasize the importance of materialist safety as they have been socialized by a generation that lived affluent materialism. For many, the priority is to do what they want and to have control of their time (Gevurtz Arai 2016: 147); yet few succeed to realize their ambitions, finding themselves entrapped in temporary employment with no long-term prospects. Many seem to get increasingly entangled in self-exploitative labor in the course of their aspirational move toward self-actualization. As Arvidsson, Malossi, and Naro cogently argue, "Passion it appears, has become a means of production, systematically promoted and put to work as part of the institution and framework within which brand values are produced" (2010: 308). Social entrepreneur Yamamoto Shigeru's statement illustrates this living paradox of balancing freedom to do what one wants, neoliberal values and constraints, and the void of material affluence: "I am quite satisfied with my present state of work and life, but at the same time I am aware that I will have to show through success whether the decision to opt for social entrepreneurship was the right one. After all, being in the social entrepreneurship scene is all about showing results and to what extent one can persevere is all up to oneself" (Oshima 2009: 120–121). Similarly, Tetsuya, the owner of the textile design shop from Tokyo introduced earlier, observes that for him Ishinomaki is the place where he tackles challenges, going so far as to describe it as "the place of fighting" (*senjō*), which shows the sense of tension and pressure that comes with engaging in entrepreneurial projects.

Budding entrepreneurs often indicate that they feel the intense pressure to succeed; however, this sense of tension seems to outweigh the positive inspiration they derive from the challenge of carving out their own path in their rural environment of choice. Many do posit that they face numerous problems but feel no regrets about the path they have chosen as they have a greater sense of self-determination and control of their everyday lives. Yet, many also observe that they hardly have leisure time or that work and leisure are so intricately intertwined that they have few opportunities for time off and for reflection about their lives. Somewhat paradoxically, they also tend to remark that they feel that their present lives make sense. This brings us back to the Foucauldian *dispositif* mentioned at the start of this chapter: a powerful norm of make-believe that one is happy, has found one's place of belonging (*ibasho*) and means of self-realization that settlers keep referring to has replaced the discourse of corporate *gambarism*. The reality is that many interviewees aspire to better work-life balance, but in their efforts to realize it, it seems to be out of reach. Interviewees frequently refer to personal well-being, spending more time with the family (if they have one), making time to enjoy leisure; however, few actually put their aspirations into practice.

Last but not least, all entrepreneurial projects introduced in this chapter indicate the outstanding importance of networks. Some draw on connections with (former) disaster volunteers, others rely on professional connections from their previous jobs. But what all these projects have in common is the relative lack of funding, the relative low age of entrepreneurs, and the strong reliance on the power of networks.

Conclusion

Deconstructing Japan's Rural-Urban Divide

The chapters of this book elucidate the significant but often inconspicuous paradigm shifts at play in contemporary Japan both at institutional and individual levels. Until now, "countryside" evoked images of quaint villages nestled in remote mountain valleys with abandoned shops and buildings occupied only by aging populations. Ethnographic data presented in this volume document the influx of relatively young settlers into rural areas across Japan for noneconomic reasons. According to a 2014 government survey, about 40 percent of Japanese are interested in moving to rural areas from Tokyo. Media in Japan are replete with reports about young lifestyle migrants who opted out of corporate careers to pursue lives that provide greater emotional and mental well-being and personal satisfaction. Terms such as "creative depopulation," "happy depopulated areas," "communities of hope," "miracle villages at the limits," and "just the right amount of depopulation" all point to this ongoing shift of ascribing positive meaning to what were previously labeled stagnant backwaters of civilization, as outlined in chapter 2.

Programs such as the regional revitalization community volunteer initiative by the Ministry of Internal Affairs and Communication were started in 2009 with the aim of attracting young individuals to rural areas; thousands of regional revitalization community volunteers have been dispatched across rural Japan over the past decade, with many choosing to remain after the expiration of their contracts. Some may argue that a few thousand idealistic migrants are not going to make a difference to the underlying demographic problems facing rural Japan. However, rather than focusing on mere numbers, I argue that such institutional incentives have contributed to a change in perception of what the countryside stands for. Rural areas have increasingly been viewed as experimental grounds for aspiring and visionary individuals with limited financial capital. Low living costs, social capital, and an abundance of vacant property mean vast opportunities for emerging entrepreneurs. Recently, individuals who consider themselves at the vanguard—often with degrees from top universities and experience living abroad—tend to opt for neorural lives across Japan.

The recent increase of funding schemes by the central government in the framework of *chihō sōsei* (rural revitalization) has clearly enhanced the attractiveness of rural areas. As a result, satellite offices, deli takeout shops, and share houses—all features that usually form part of urban infrastructure—have emerged in rural towns across Japan. These developments may seem negligible given the serious overall depopulation and aging in rural areas. I contend, however, that the empirical data presented throughout the chapters of this book elucidate the fact that the starting point of diversification of Japanese post-growth society originates from urbanites living and working in the countryside and beyond: young male migrants with infant children dreaming about working side by side with their children, individuals aspiring to a lifestyle divided between Japan and overseas, aspiring entrepreneurs in their thirties. These narratives indicate that comprehensive change may not be imminent but is bound to occur in the interim.

Being on the Cusp of the Good Life: Post-Growth Ontologies between Hope and Precariousness

As the empirical data discussed in various chapters have amply demonstrated, the theme of this book is not confined to rural areas and their future. More importantly, the key concerns touch on the limits of postwar societal norms and modes of living and working. First of all, many interviewees who decide to relocate refer to their priority of "feeling just right," appreciating inspiration, valuing experiences, and pursuing curiosity and innovation rather than treading stable paths of tedious repetitive employment. In other words, younger generations prefer challenges to lifelong employment and predictability. Having grown up in middle-class households with housewife mothers and breadwinning fathers mostly in corporate jobs who were largely absent from their daily lives, most interviewees find the prospect of pursuing their parents' life courses uninspiring. Their statements suggest that for many, ultimately, having a sense of vibrant dynamism and feeling alive (*waku waku*) is more important than having a stable income. Interviewees often elaborate on the importance of family and money, yet their practices tend to indicate that the purpose of life of many among them may not ultimately lie in stable adult roles with the three pillars of family, marriage, and work (Suzuki 2015: 236).

The irony is that the majority of lifestyle migrants are so busy turning their projects into a success that they hardly have time to feel alive, reflect on their lives, or experience *waku waku*. Self-exploitative work practices are juxtaposed with visions of the good life that seems just one step ahead, yet unreachable. Harvey's "romanticism of endlessly open projects," Berlant's "cruel optimism," and Bloch's "ontology of not yet being" come to mind. The past is brushed away as if it were an undesirable leftover, the present is all that matters, the majority of respondents have no medium- or long-term plans. They live lives that focus on the present in a state that Berlant describes compellingly as "narcissism of the now." Settlers in rural areas postpone concerns about their physical and mental well-being for some vague hope that someday everything will be better. Male migrants accept lack of time with their families for the sake of focusing on their work and making their dreams come true for themselves and their families. Ultimately, these rising entrepreneurs are taking a huge gamble in making their fantasies happen, but they do not live a life too different from corporate employees if one looks at the length of time spent on work. Seamless modes of work and purpose in life being equivalent with professional activities facilitate self-exploitative practices.

The biggest factor, however, behind migrants' total dedication to work is the enormous pressure to succeed that has shaped young generations in the neoliberal market. Self-responsibility has been delegated to individuals who have grown up in a generally risk-averse society that advocated collectivist *gambarism*, self-exploitation for larger entities and patient subjection to rules and regulations rather than emphasizing self-branding, taking challenges, and pursuing innovation. Experiences and narratives of settlers hence uneasily straddle emerging entrepreneurism, postwar salaryman–style self-exploitation, and elements of moratorium migration, that is, mobility as a way of hedging one's bets, playing for time, gaining experience.

Resistance to conventional societal norms coalesces with appropriation of traditional values, resignation with aspiration, networking with social withdrawal, viability with life at the limits. The majority of narratives in this book are characterized by inherent paradox in one and the same individual experience. We find signs of fraying fantasies side by side with grand ambitions and dreams about a better future. Settlers refer to mobility as a mechanism for them to escape societal pressures of behaving in certain ways; others describe new pressures of competition with other migrants. I argue that this inherent co-optation of mainstream and alternative values, structure and unstructure, dislocation and engagement that is salient in numerous narratives discussed in the chapters of this book show the period of transience and upheaval Japan finds itself in: these inherently contradictory traits making up individual narratives testify to the ongoing uphill struggle that individuals are facing in their quest for alternative lifestyles; settlers find themselves in a society that takes self-exploitation at the workplace for granted and has only recently started questioning the widespread assumption that resulting human loss is a necessary side effect—a society that perpetuates gender inequality in nonchalant ways and seems to fetishize the status quo rather than opting for productive change. As Guarné and Hansen put it, "Alternative realities aside, hegemonic Japan remains stanchly conservative" (2018: 5). Narratives introduced in this book indicate that even alternative realities seem to reflect pervasive ideologies of mainstream society, such as ingrained gender roles, normative life course planning, pressures of collectivist *gambarism*, and the persistent low prioritization of leisure and family. Highly reflective migrants who consciously opt out of social media testify to these very real pressures of virtually disseminating the appearance of "being successful" in migrant communities, regardless of how remote the village is that they have relocated to. Given the high rate of talented and highly skilled newcomers, other settlers talk of the pressure to come up with a business idea in order to create a livelihood for themselves in rural areas where jobs are limited. These episodes and in fact many experiences depicted in this book suggest that alternative and mainstream realities may be more intricately entangled than we like to assume.

Between Communities of Hope and Never-Starting Futures

Empirical data presented throughout this book highlight the great diversity of individuals who decide to relocate to rural areas. The only common trait that characterizes lifestyle migrants is their aspiration to the "good life," even if individual definitions vary. For many male migrants, good-life fantasies are closely related with work rather than with family. Examples of driven entrepreneurs in their late thirties and early forties provide us with ethnographic evidence how long-lasting the impact of socialization in bubble-era corporate culture is. Even after relinquishing their high-level careers in well-paying elite companies, male migrants choose to perpetuate self-exploitative practices for the prospect of achieving success as individual entrepreneurs. They elaborate in great depth on their visions of traveling abroad with their families in some distant future; their present reality, however, is that they have no time to spare for their families or anything besides work. No matter whether it is the former corporate employee from Nagoya turned self-employed regional revitalization consultant, the former corporate employee from Tokyo who leads a lifestyle based in two locations and is in the process of starting his own restaurant and bakery, or the former development worker who used to live in Ghana and has now turned to agriculture on a remote island, everyone is totally immersed in their professional activities and seems to perceive sacrificing their private life as inevitable. Female settlers seem more focused on creating work that is compatible with their families, if they have one. This gendered difference in perception per se shows how ingrained traditional gender roles are in Japanese society.

Given the vast spread of societal disparity (*kakusa shakai*) in post-growth Japan (Chiavacci and Hommerich 2017), rural areas with their images of tight-knit communities and cheap living expenses may strike us as egalitarian at first. However, as one former disaster volunteer in Miyagi Prefecture poignantly put it, "The only people who are left now six years after the disaster are the ones who either have money or those who can make money go around" (interview on 2 August 2017). This indicates the outstanding importance of class in lifestyle migration and leads to the sobering insight that, after all, financial and social capital combined with education may be the decisive factor in whether individuals manage to create a niche livelihood in the challenging circumstances of stagnating rural economies. Last but not least, only 19 of my 118 interviewees during this project did not graduate from university, which suggests that lifestyle migration may be a phenomenon prevalent in individuals from relatively affluent families.

As outlined in other chapters, mobility and the life of migrants tend to be represented in overly positive terms in recent newspaper features, magazines, and on TV in an era that often dismisses settlement as stagnation and permanent movement is inherently considered as part of the contemporary global condition (Featherstone 1995: 126). Yet many migrant narratives contain elements that indicate feelings of marginality, liminality, and difficulties of integrating into the local community. I understand marginality as "the detachment from the institutions of mainstream society" (Gill 2001: 147). The decision to move often engenders disbelief, lack of understanding, and outright opposition from migrants' families, parents, and friends. For example, one female migrant in her early thirties originally from Tokushima City narrated that her parents were less than positive about her decision to spend three years in a small town some thirty minutes from Tokushima City as a regional revitalization officer, asking her whether her career in Tokyo had not gone well. Other migrants indicated that they had been perceived as *kawarimono* (oddballs) from early childhood by their families, and their parents were not surprised about their relocation to a rural area and change in job. A lifestyle migrant in his late thirties conceded that from the point of his decision to drop out of his temp work in a pachinko parlor in Tokyo and work as a JICA overseas development cooperation officer in Africa, his family treated him as someone who could not be counted on. So when he decided to relocate to a remote island in Shimane Prefecture after his return to Japan from Africa, his family's reaction was, "Well, it's something weird again that he has got involved in for sure . . ."

Generally, migrants who had spent time abroad in developing countries mentioned their sense of isolation after their return to their home country but indicated that, for them, living in rural areas made more sense with regard to the fact that the close communal life with the culture of sharing resembled life abroad in many ways and they felt more at home in rural areas.

Whereas difficulties of integration into the local community are salient in some cases (as outlined in chapter 6), numerous migrants do mention a sense of belonging (*ibasho*) in a community of like-minded peers that make them feel "at home" in their new place of residence. An energetic female migrant from Osaka in her mid-thirties with an infant son mentioned the community of like-minded nature-oriented mothers as a big plus. Some neorurals conceded that despite years of living in a given place and making intense efforts in their initial years of relating to the local community, they eventually realize that they feel most at ease when communicating with other nonlocals with similar migratory backgrounds.

Numerous individuals mentioned their aversion to being called *ijū-sha* (migrant, literally, someone who has come to live here from some other place), and some went as far as to remark that there was no point of overcoming this wall—one would always be referred to as a migrant, especially in tight-knit communities. However, others depicted their struggles of being accepted for several years and the point of "breaking through" that wall by achieving recognition. Still others find the gap in values between locals of the same age difficult to surmount: A restaurant owner in his mid-thirties from Osaka shares his complex feelings about the pressure to take part regularly in heavy drinking sessions with locals in order to be accepted in the local community, although he cannot drink much. Furthermore, he feels that he does not share too much in terms of values with locals of his generation as they always dream about urban entertainment and material consumption, whereas he himself has abandoned exactly all of this to pursue a more fulfilling lifestyle in a rural area. Settlers who have only recently relocated tend to perceive the lack of intellectual input as a downside of living in the countryside, while interestingly, migrants who have longer experiences of rural life tend to understand the lack of entertainment and convenience as a merit in the sense that they have to think about creative ways of providing what they seek by themselves.

Relating to locals can be fraught with difficulties especially for individuals who pursue explicitly alternative lifestyles: One migrant in his mid-forties who had started a collective housing project in a small remote hamlet indicated that he used to explain to locals that he sublets his house to others, like a dormitory, in order to avoid conflict since most locals were not familiar with the notion of shared living. Yasuko, a female lifestyle migrant in her mid-forties from Osaka who runs a restaurant in a small rural town observes that in the beginning her practice of opening the restaurant for only four days a week encountered suspicion among locals; now, some locals have followed suit by closing their shops for more days and purchasing wine at her restaurant. Similarly, the same female restaurant owner mentioned that her personal habit of getting up relatively late for local standards as she works late hours in the evening was ignored in the beginning by locals; that is, residents dropped by in the early morning to bring vegetables and have a chat. However, after a while, the local community has accepted her different lifestyle and hours of getting up (and going to sleep), implying that it takes time but different lifestyles can be pursued in small rural towns.

Other lifestyle migrants observe that they have little contact with local peers of their age as there is a lack of this age cohort in the first place. A female migrant in her early thirties who has lived for nine months in the small rural town observes with regret that she knows most locals only by face but has hardly talked to them as she is busy with work and mostly spends her little free time with her (nonlocal) work peers. Especially in places with a sizeable community of urban migrants, nonlocals tend to cluster in small groups, which may limit their social relations with the local community. Here, offspring seems to make a great difference to integration: migrants with children who go to school tend to have more contact with local parents through PTA activities (another source of stress for nonlocals); single migrants have less exposure to these structural activities and hence seek more social relations with other new settlers without families.

Ultimately, it seems to depend essentially on the hamlet where one has relocated as some hamlets seem to place high demands on new settlers with regard to community work, while others seem more generous by mostly leaving new settlers alone. One lifestyle migrant in his early fifties mentioned not having to do any community work at all as he spends one third of his time in his place of origin Tokyo, the rest in his new settlement, and is hence busy with work when he is there (interview on 14 March 2017).

Transnational, Translocal Hybridity: Urban-Rural Continuum

Opting out from societal expectations has predominantly been associated with transnational mobility, as recent research compellingly shows (Aoyama 2015a; Suzuki 2015; Kato 2015; Ono 2015). Many of the narratives of individuals who moved overseas in their quest for the good life resemble those depicted in this book. Quite a number of my interviewees have experience living abroad, either as students or employees. The aspect of temporary exemption from the various obligations and responsibilities inherent in adult roles in Japanese society, especially male ones (Suzuki 2015: 243), seems a particularly common trait in transnationally and translocally mobile subjects. Narratives introduced in this monograph can be considered as ethnographic evidence of Urry's "societies of de-territorialisation" (2000: 27), with notions of place-bound identity having lost importance. Mobility is adopted as a strategic means of pursuing "malleable selves" and "portable personhood" (Elliott and Urry 2010); "home is the moment" (Gundersen 2008: 28). "I will stay here for the time being, I don't have plans to move anywhere else"—this statement by Tokyoite Hisa portrayed in chapter 6 contains a deeply paradoxical co-optation of ingrained nomadism and commitment.

This ontological aspect of mobility illustrates the strong process orientation of individual moves. The concept of "doing identity" (Widdicombe 1998) mentioned in chapter 1 naturally involves engagement with others inhabiting the new place of residence, both locals and nonlocals. The hybridity of lifestyles introduced throughout this study questions the boundedness of "rurality" as a theoretical concept. The diverse narratives of moratorium migrants confirm Gkartzios's paradigm of the "urban-rural continuum" (2013: 160). In other words, the empirical data outlined in the chapters indicate that rurality is more a means rather than an end in itself, constantly evolving and subject to metamorphosis. Settlers' experiences clearly show the multiplicity of meanings imbued in the rural; narratives also indicate the continuing pertinence of Massey's relational understanding of places (2005). Especially chapter 2 with its focus on the perspectives of female lifestyle migrants, but also other chapters, elucidate both positive and negative implications of rural life. Individual life courses highlight that mobility constitutes an opportunity for migrants to take control of their lives and work, but that it also reproduces systemic constraints, and for some life in the countryside seems a dead end. Ironically, some find themselves in stable but uninspiring office jobs despite their aspirations to live the free life in rural Japan.

Undoing Japan?

Images of Japan as a "socially homogenous, uniform society" continue to shape the associations of Japan held by the general public and many academics (Guarné and Hansen 2018). Narratives presented in this book show that despite all interviewees being Japanese citizens, several have been born abroad and close to 20 out of the entire 118 interviewees spent prolonged periods of time living and working overseas. Needless to say, these returnee Japanese tend to take different views on modes of working, family, and gender from collaborators who have spent their entire lives in Japan. Numerous settlers presented their time in the countryside as a preparatory period for eventually going abroad, although in many cases it was not clear when this move would happen. Others aspired to a life that was seasonally divided between their present place of residence and an overseas destination. Interviewees mentioned their friends abroad just as they were talking about their previous places of residence within Japan; there was little distinction between activities in and out of Japan—they all formed parts of their unique experiences. This is why I would like to contend that rather than seeing these migrants as "Japanese" representing some bounded entity, I consider them of interest as members of post-growth societies in translocal and transnational settings.

Nevertheless, what do the findings of this book imply for contemporary Japanese society? Empirical data suggest that settlers find themselves drawn between inherently contradictory forces: they aspire to more diverse and innovative lifestyles and modes of working, on the one hand, but perpetuate lingering values and ingrained societal behavioral patterns of postwar Japan on the other. This is where the concept of moratorium migration comes in, mobility that serves as a strategic mechanism that individuals resort to in order to hedge their bets, gain time, and seek assurance, inspiration, and courage to do (or further postpone doing) what ultimately makes sense to them. One could argue that moratorium migration serves as an instrument to enforce individual agency, that is, efforts toward greater self-determination, in circumstances where individuals find themselves exposed to a multitude of pressures and constraints.

In other words, moratorium migration straddles the uneasy gray zone between personal fantasies of the "good life" (that often derive from externally imposed discourses about the need to feel "happy") and the harsh neoliberal reality of individual responsibilization as "enterprising subjects" (Rose 1992: 142) and precarious flexible labor conditions. Not surprisingly, the lifestyle migrants depicted in this study tend to engage in self-exploitative practices. Many are on the cusp of finding the good life and have yet to realize it.

As unsettling as many of these narratives may be, they provide us with valuable insights into the gradual, if slow diversification of Japanese society that, I predict, will result in formative changes in lifestyle and work modes in Japan soon and in the future. For the time being, however, mobile subjects struggle to negotiate their lives between resistance to and appropriation of mainstream societal values, aspiration and subjection, societal engagement and withdrawal, regeneration and stagnation. I contend that the sustained and permanent liminality resulting from this condition is ontologically highly productive, the key feature of moratorium migrants, and the essence of post-growth Japan.

References

Adey, Peter. 2010. *Mobility: Key Ideas in Geography*. Abingdon: Routledge.

Allison, Anne. 2013. *Precarious Japan*. Durham: Duke University Press.

Ambros, Barbara. 2015. *Women in Japanese Religions*. New York: New York University Press.

Aoyama, Reijiro. 2015a. "Japanese Men and Their Quest for Well-Being Outside Japan." *Asian Anthropology* 14, no. 3: 215–219.

Aoyama, Reijiro. 2015b. "Nostalgic Migration: Factors Behind Recent Japanese Migration to Shanghai." In *Japan's Demographic Revival: Rethinking Migration, Identity and Sociocultural Norms*, edited by Stephen Nagy, 1–26. Singapore: World Scientific.

Appadurai, Arjun. 2013. *The Future as Cultural Fact: Essays on the Global Condition*. London: Verso.

Arvidsson, Adam, Giannino Malossi, and Serpica Naro. 2010. "Passionate Work? Labour Conditions in the Milan Fashion Industry." *Journal for Cultural Research* 14, no. 3 (July): 295–309.

Baker, Beth. 2016. "Regime." In *Keywords of Mobility: Critical Engagements*, edited by Noel B. Salazar and Kiran Jayaram, 152–170. New York: Berghahn.

Bantman-Masum, Eve. 2011. "You Need to Come Here . . . to See What Living Is Really About: Staging North American Expatriation in Merida, Mexico." *Miranda* 5: 1–16.

Barth, Fredrik. 1989. "The Analysis of Culture in Complex Societies." *Ethnos* 54, no. 3–4: 120–142.

Bauman, Zygmunt. 1996. "From Pilgrim to Tourist—or a Short History of Identity." In *Questions of Cultural Identity*, edited by Stuart Hall and Paul du Gay, 18–36. London: Sage.

Bauman, Zygmunt. 2000. *Liquid Modernity*. Cambridge: Polity Press.

Bauman, Zygmunt. 2004. *Identity: Conversations with Benedetto Vecchi*. Cambridge: Polity Press.

Bauman, Zygmunt. 2007. *Liquid Times: Living in an Age of Uncertainty*. Cambridge: Polity Press.

Bauman, Zygmunt. 2011. "From Pilgrim to Tourist—or a Short History of Identity." In *Questions of Cultural Identity*, edited by Stuart Hall and Paul du Gay, 18–36. London: Sage.

Beck, Ulrich. 2003. "Living Your Own Life in a Runaway World: Individualization, Globalization and Politics." In *Globalization: Critical Concepts in Sociology, Vol. IV: Culture and Identity*, edited by Roland Robertson and Kathleen E. White, 164–174. London: Routledge.

Beck, Ulrich, and Elisabeth Beck-Gernsheim. 2001. *Individualization: Institutionalized Individualism and Its Social and Political Consequences*. London: Sage.

Beck, Ulrich, and Elisabeth Beck-Gernsheim. 2002. *Individualization*. London: Sage.

Bell, Michael M. 2007. "The Two-ness of Rural Life and the Ends of Rural Scholarship." *Journal of Rural Studies* 23, no. 4: 402–415.

Bell, Martin, and Gary Ward. 2000. "Comparing Temporary Mobility with Permanent Migration." *Tourism Geographies* 2, no. 1: 97–107.

Benson, Michaela. 2011. *The British in Rural France: Lifestyle Migration and the Ongoing Quest for a Better Quality of Life*. Manchester: Manchester University Press.

Benson, Michaela, and Karen O'Reilly. 2009a. "Migration and the Search for a Better Way of Life: A Critical Exploration of Lifestyle Migration." *The Sociological Review* 57, no. 4: 606–625.

Benson, Michaela, and Karen O'Reilly, eds. 2009b. *Lifestyle Migration: Expectations, Aspirations and Experiences*. Farnham: Ashgate.

Benson, Michaela, and Nick Osbaldiston, eds. 2014. *Understanding Lifestyle Migration: Theoretical Approaches to Migration and the Quest for a Better Way of Life*. London: Palgrave Macmillan.

Berlant, Lauren. 2011. *Cruel Optimism*. Chicago: University of Chicago Press.

Berry, Brian Joe. 1976. *Urbanization and Counterurbanization*. Beverly Hills: Sage.

Blewitt, John, and Ray Cunningham, eds. 2014. *The Post-Growth Project: How the End of Economic Growth Could Bring a Fairer and Happier Society*. Norwich: Green House.

Bloch, Ernst. 1986. *The Principle of Hope*. Cambridge: MIT Press.

Boellstorff, Tom, Bonnie Nardi, Celia Pearce, and T. L. Taylor. 2012. *Ethnography and Virtual Worlds: A Handbook of Method*. Princeton: Princeton University Press.

Bonss, Wolfgang, and Sven Kesselring. 2004. "Mobility and the cosmopolitan perspective." In *Mobility and the Cosmopolitan Perspective: Documentation of a Workshop at the Reflexive Modernization Research Centre*, edited by Wolfgang Bonss, Sven Kesselring, and Gerlinde Vogl. http://www.cosmobilities.net.

Bosworth, Gary, and Jane Atterton. 2012. "Entrepreneurial In-migration and Neoendogenous Rural Development." *Rural Sociology* 77, no. 2: 254–279.

Brinckerhoff, Peter C. 2000. *Social Entrepreneurship: The Art of Mission-Based Venture Development*. New York: John Wiley & Sons.

Butler, Gareth, and Scott Richardson. 2013. "Working to Travel and Long-Term Career Dilemmas: Experiences of Western Lifestyle Migrants in Malaysia." *Tourist Studies* 13, no. 3: 251–267.

Castells, Manuel. 2005. *The Network Society: A Cross-Cultural Perspective.* Northampton: Edward Elgar.

Chambers, Iain. 1994. *Migrancy, Culture, Identity.* London: Routledge.

Chiavacci, David, and Carola Hommerich, eds. 2017. *Social Inequality in Post-Growth Japan: Transformation during Economic and Demographic Stagnation.* London: Routledge.

Cohen, Scott A., Tara Duncan, and Maria Thulemark. 2013. "Lifestyle Mobilities: The Crossroads of Travel, Leisure and Migration." *Mobilities* 10, no. 1: 155–172.

Collings, David G., Noeleen Doherty, Madeleine Luethy et al. 2011. "Understanding and Supporting the Career Implications of International Assignments." *Journal of Vocational Behaviour* 78, no. 3: 361–371.

Cresswell, Tim. 2001. "The Production of Mobilities." *New Formations* 43: 11–25.

Cresswell, Tim. 2006. *On the Move: The Politics of Mobility in the Modern West.* London: Routledge.

Cresswell, Tim, and Peter Merriman. 2011. "Introduction: Geographies of Mobilities: Practices, Spaces, Subjects." In *Geographies of Mobilities: Practices, Spaces, Subjects*, 1–15. Farnham: Ashgate.

Croucher, Sheila. 2015. "The Future of Lifestyle Migration: Challenges and Opportunities." *Journal of Latin American Geography* 14, no. 1 (March): 161–172.

da Silva, Diogo Soares, Elisabete Figueiredo, Celeste Eusebio, and Maria Joao Carneiro. 2016. "The Countryside Is Worth a Thousand Words: Portuguese Representations on Rural Areas." *Journal of Rural Studies* 44: 77–88.

Deleuze, Gilles, and Félix Guattari. 1983. *Anti-Oedipus: Capitalism and Schizophrenia.* Minneapolis: University of Minneapolis Press.

Deleuze, Gilles, and Félix Guattari. 1987. "1227: Treatise on Nomadology." In *A Thousand Plateaus: Capitalism and Schizophrenia*, translated by Brian Massumi, 351–423. Minneapolis: University of Minnesota Press.

Dumazdier, Joffre. 1960. "Current Problems in the Sociology of Leisure." *International Social Science Journal* 12: 526.

Duncan, Tara, Scott A. Cohen, and Maria Thulemark. 2013. *Lifestyle Mobilities: Intersections of Travel, Leisure and Migration.* London: Routledge.

Edensor, Tim. 2007. "Mundane Mobilities, Performances and Spaces of Tourism." *Social & Cultural Geography* 8, no. 2: 199–215.

Elliott, Anthony, and John Urry. 2010. *Mobile Lives: Self, Excess and Nature.* Abingdon: Routledge.

Erskine, Kathryn, and Jon Anderson. 2016. "Traveller Trails: Locating the Lifestyle Traveller." In *Lifestyle Mobilities: Intersections of Travel, Leisure and Migration*, edited by Tara Duncan, Scott A. Cohen, and Maria Thulemark, 129–142. London: Routledge; paperback edition, first published by Ashgate in 2013.

Favell, Adrian. 2015. "Creative East-West Cosmopolitanism? The Changing Role of International Mobility for Young Japanese Contemporary Artists." In *Transnational Trajectories in East Asia: Nation, Citizenship, and Region*, edited by Yasemin Nuhoglu Soysal, 83–105. Abingdon: Routledge.

Featherstone, Mike. 1995. *Undoing Culture: Globalization, Postmodernism and Identity*. London: Sage.

Foucault, Michel. 1980a. *The History of Sexuality*. New York: Vintage Books.

Foucault, Michel. 1980b. *Power/Knowledge: Selected Interviews and Other Writings, 1972–1977*. Edited by Colin Gordon. Brighton: Harvester.

Fujita, Yuiko. 2009. *Cultural Migrants from Japan: Youth, Media, and Migration in New York and London*. Lanham: Lexington Books.

Funabashi, Yoichi, and Barak Kushner, eds. 2015. *Examining Japan's Lost Decades*. Abingdon: Routledge.

Furuichi, Noritoshi. 2011. *Zetsubou no kuni no koufuku na wakamonotachi* [Happy youth in a desperate country]. Tokyo: Kodansha.

Furuichi, Noritoshi. 2014 [2015, 16th edition]. *Dakara Nihon ha zureteiru* [That's why Japan is out of sync]. Tokyo: Shinchosha.

Gevurtz Arai, Andrea. 2016. *The Strange Child: Education and the Psychology of Patriotism in Recessionary Japan*. Stanford: Stanford University Press.

Giddens, Anthony. 1990. *The Consequence of Modernity*. Stanford: Stanford University Press.

Giddens, Anthony. 1991. *Modernity and Self-Identity: Self and Society in the Late Modern Age*. Cambridge: Polity Press.

Gill, Tom. 2001. *Men of Uncertainty: The Social Organization of Day Laborers in Contemporary Japan*. Albany: State University of New York Press.

Gkartzios, Menelaos. 2013. "Leaving Athens: Narratives of Counterurbanization in Times of crisis." *Journal of Rural Studies* 32: 158–167.

Glick Schiller, Nina, and Noel B. Salazar. 2013. "Regimes of Mobility Across the Globe." *Journal of Ethnic and Migration Studies* 39, no. 2: 183–200.

Glick Schiller, Nina, Linda Basch, and Cristina Blanc-Szanton, eds. 1992. *Towards a Transnational Perspective on Migration: Race, Class, Ethnicity, and Nationalism Reconsidered*. New York: New York Academy of Sciences.

Gratton, Lynda. 2011. *The Shift: The Future of Work Is Already Here*. London: HarperCollins.

Green, Eileen, Sandra Hebron, and Diana Woodward. 1990. *Women's Leisure, What Leisure?* London: Macmillan.

Guarné, Blai, and Paul Hansen, eds. 2018. *Escaping Japan: Reflections on Estrangement and Exile in the Twenty-First Century*. London: Routledge.

Gundersen, Lise. 2008. "The Palace You Left, the Latitude of Home, Music as a Home and the Coordinates of Here." In *Home Is the Place You Left*, edited by Michael Elmgreen and Ingar Dragset, 21–28. Cologne: Walther Koenig.

Haghirian, Parissa. 2016. "Entrepreneurship in Japan." In *Routledge Handbook of Japanese Business and Management*, edited by Parissa Haghirian, 125–136. Abingdon: Routledge.

Halfacree, Keith. 2007. "Trial by Space for a 'Radical Rural': Introducing Alternative Localities, Representations and Lives. *Journal of Rural Studies* 23, no. 2: 125–141.

Hansen, Paul. 2018. "Afterword." In *Escaping Japan: Reflections on Estrangement and Exile in the Twenty-First Century*, edited by Paul Hansen Paul and Blai Guarné, 219–247. London: Routledge.

Hardt, Michael, and Antonio Negri. 2000. *Empire*. Cambridge: Harvard University Press.

Harvey, David. 2000. *Space of Hope*. Berkeley: University of California Press.

Harvey, David. 2005. *A Brief History of Neoliberalism*. Oxford: Oxford University Press.

Hedberg, Charlotta, and Renato Miguel do Carmo, eds. 2012. *Translocal Ruralism: Mobility and Connectivity in European Rural Spaces*. Dordrecht: Springer.

Hertog, Ekaterina. 2009. *Tough Choices: Bearing an Illegitimate Child in Contemporary Japan*. Stanford: Stanford University Press.

Hoey, Brian. 2005. "From Pi to Pie: Moral Narratives of Noneconomic Migration and Starting Over in the Postindustrial Midwest." *Journal of Contemporary Ethnography* 34, no. 5: 586–624.

Honda, Naoyuki. 2015. *Datsutokyo: Shigoto to asobi no kakine wo nakusu, atarashii ijū* [Escaping Tokyo: A new form of relocation that does away with the wall between work and play]. Tokyo: Mainichi Shinbun Shuppan.

Hynes, Patricia. 2011. *The Dispersal and Social Exclusion of Asylum Seekers: Between Liminality and Belonging*. Chicago: University of Chicago Press.

Iizuka, Megumi. 2017. "The Slow Life in Rural Japan Is Converting More Young People." *Japan Times*, January 3.

Isa Tomomi. 2017. *Ijū joshi* [Relocation of young women (to the countryside)]. Tokyo: Shinchosha.

Kakei Yusuke, issue + design project. 2011. *Chiiki wo kaeru dezain* [Design that changes the regions]. Tokyo: Eiji Press.

Kalantaridis, Christos, and Zografia Bika. 2006. "In-migrant Entrepreneurship in Rural England: Beyond Local Embeddedness." *Entrepreneurship and Regional Development* 18: 109–131.

Kanzaki Sooudi, Olga. 2014. *Japanese New York: Migrant Artists and Self-Reinvention on the World Stage*. Honolulu: University of Hawaii Press.

Kato, Etsuko. 2009. *Jibunsagashi no imintachi* [Self-searching migrants]. Tokyo: Sairyusha.

Kato, Etsuko. 2010. "True Self, True Work: Gendered Searching for Self and Work among Japanese Migrants in Vancouver, Canada." *Japanese Review of Cultural Anthropology* 11: 47–66.

Kato, Etsuko. 2015. "When a Man Flies Overseas: Corporate Nationalism, Gendered Happiness and Young Japanese Male Migrants in Canada and Australia." *Asian Anthropology* 14, no. 3: 220–234.

Kato Norihiro. 2010. "Japan and the Ancient Art of Shrugging." *New York Times*, August 21. Accessed online.

Kelly, A. 2008. "Living Loss: An Exploration into the Internal Space of Liminality." *Mortality* 13, no. 4: 335–350.

Kim, Jongyoung. 2011. "Aspiration for Global Cultural Capital in the Stratified Realm of Higher Education: Why Do Korean Students Go to US Graduate Schools?" *British Journal of Sociology of Education* 32, no. 1): 109–126.

Klien, Susanne. 2016. "Young Urban Migrants in the Japanese Countryside between Self-Realization and Slow Life? The Quest for Subjective Well-Being and Post-Materialism." In *Sustainability in Contemporary Rural Japan: Challenges and Opportunities*, edited by Stephanie Assmann, 95–107. London: Routledge.

Klien, Susanne. 2016. "Reinventing Ishinomaki, Reinventing Japan? Evolving Creative Networks, Alternative Lifestyles and the Search for Quality in Life in Post-Growth Japan." *Japanese Studies* 36, no. 1: 39–60.

Klien, Susanne. 2017. "Living and Working for the Moment: Motivations, Aspirations and Experiences of Disaster Volunteers in Tohoku." In *Happiness and the Good Life in Japan*, edited by Wolfram Manzenreiter and Barbara Holthus, 164–182. London: Routledge.

Klien, Susanne. 2019a. "Entrepreneurial Selves, Governmentality and Lifestyle Migrants in Rural Japan. *Asian Anthropology* 18, no. 2: 75–90/

Klien, Susanne. 2019b. "Young Urban Migrants in the Japanese Countryside between Self-Realization and Slow Life? The Quest for 'Small-Scale Happiness and Alternative Lifestyles in Post-Growth Japan." In *The Routledge Handbook of Contemporary Japan*, edited by Mark Williams and Hiroko Takeda, 000–000. London: Routledge.

Knight, John. 2003. "Organic Farming Settlers in Kumano." In *Farmers and Village Life in Twentieth-Century Japan*, edited by Ann Waswo and Nishida Yoshiaki, 267–284. London: Routledge.

Koehn, Steffen. 2016. *Mediating Mobility: Visual Anthropology in the Age of Migration*. London: Wallflower Press.

Korpela, Mari. 2014. "Lifestyle or Freedom? Individualism and Lifestyle Migration." In *Understanding Lifestyle Migration: Theoretical Approaches to Migration and the Quest for a Better Way of Life*, edited by Michaela Benson and Nick Osbaldiston, 27–46. Houndmills: Palgrave Macmillan.

Kuhmonen, Tuomas, Irene Kuhmonen, and Liisa Luoto. 2016. How Do Rural Areas Profile in the Futures Dreams by the Finnish Youth? *Journal of Rural Studies* 44: 89–100.

Kurosaki, Teruo, ed. 2016. *We Work Here: Tokyo no atarashii hatarakikata 100* [We work here: 100 new forms of working in Tokyo]. Tokyo: Mirai Institute.

Latour, Bruno. 2005. *Reassembling the Social: An Introduction to Actor-Network-Theory*. Oxford: Oxford University Press.

Lips, Hilary M. 2014. *Gender: The Basics*. London: Routledge.

Love, Bridget. 2013. "Treasure Hunts in Rural Japan: Place Making at the Limits of Sustainability." *American Anthropologist* 115, no. 1: 112–124.

Lunsing, Wim. 2006. "Quitting Companies: Individual Responses to Changing Employment Patterns in Early 2000s Japan." In *Perspectives on Work, Employment and Society in Japan*, edited by Peter Matanle and Wim Lunsing, 168–186. Houndmills: Palgrave Macmillan.

Maemura, Naoka, Kato Junzo, and Fujihara Takehiro. 2015. "Idou wo kikuyu suru shinri: raifusutairu imin ni tsuite no shakaishinrigakuteki kousatsu" [Social psychological considerations of lifestyle migration]. *Shakaigakubu Kiyou* [In-house magazine of the social faculty], no. 120 (March): 133–146.

Malkki, Liisa. 1992. "National Geographic: The Rooting of Peoples and the Territorialization of National Identity among Scholars and Refugees." *Cultural Anthropology* 7, no. 1 (February): 24–44.

Marsden, Terry. 1999. "Rural Futures: The Consumption Countryside and Its Regulation." *Sociologia Ruralis* 39, no. 4: 501–520.

Massey, Doreen. 1999. "Philosophy and Politics of Spatiality: Some Considerations." *Geographische Zeitschrift* 87. Jg., Heft 1: 1–12.

Massey, Doreen. 2004. "Geographies of Responsibility." *Geografiska Annaler B* 86: 5–18.

Massey, Doreen. 2005. *For Space*. London: Sage.

Matanle, Peter. 2014. "Ageing and Depopulation in Japan Understanding the Consequences for East and Southeast Asia in the 21st Century." In *East Asia in 2013: A Region in Transition. White Rose East Asia Centre and Foreign and Commonwealth Office Briefing Papers*, edited by Hugo Dobson, 30–35. Sheffield: WREAC.

Mathews, Gordon. 1998. "Selves in the Cultural Supermarket Towards a Phenomenological Theory of Cultural Identity." Working Paper, Department of Anthropology. Hong Kong: The Chinese University of Hong Kong.

Mathews, Gordon. 2017. "Happiness in Neoliberal Japan." In *Happiness and the Good Life in Japan*, edited by Wolfram Manzenreiter and Barbara Holthus, 227–242. London: Routledge.

Mathews, Gordon, and Bruce White, eds. 2004. *Japan's Changing Generations: Are Young People Creating a New Society?* London: Routledge.

Matsunaga, Keiko. 2015. *Rōkaru shikō no jidai: Hatarakikata, sangyō, keizai wo kangaeru hinto* [The age of localism: Hints for thinking about modes of working, industry and economy]. Tokyo: Kōbunsha Shinsho.

McIntyre, Norman. 2009. "Re-Thinking Amenity Migration: Integrating Mobility, Lifestyle and Social-Ecological Systems. *Erde* 140, no. 3: 229–250.

McNay, Lois. 2005. "Agency and Experience: Gender as a Lived Relation." In *Feminism after Bourdieu*, edited by Lisa Adkins and Beverly Skeggs, 175–190. Oxford: Blackwell.

McRobbie, Angela. 2016. *Be Creative: Making a Living in the New Culture Industries*. Cambridge: Polity Press.

Mitchell, Clare J. 2004. "Making Sense of Counterurbanization." *Journal of Rural Studies* 20: 15–34.

Morley, David. 2000. *Home Territories: Media, Mobility and Identity*. London: Routledge.

Mori, Ken. 2011. *Tsutomenai to iu ikikata* [A lifestyle that does not opt for employment]. Tokyo: Media Factory.

Mormont, Marc. 1990. "Who Is Rural? Or, How to Be Rural: Towards a Sociology of the Rural." In *Rural Restructuring: Global Processes and Their Responses*, edited by Terry Marsden, Sarah Whatmore, and Philip Lowe, 21–44. London: David Fulton.

Mouri, Yoshitaka. 2010. "New Art and Culture in the Age of 'Freeter' in Japan: On the Young Part Time Workers and the Ideology of Creativity." *Kontur*, no. 20: 48–53. Available online at http://kontur.au.dk/fileadmin/www.kontur.au.dk/Kontur_20/Microsoft_Word_-_VAM-MORI_MOD2.pdf.

Murdoch, Jonathan. 2003. "Co-Constructing the Countryside: Hybrid Networks and the Extensive Self." In *Country visions*, edited by Paul Cloke, 263–280. Harlow: Pearson.

Nagatomo, Jun. 2007a. "90nendai nihon shakai ni okeru shakai hendou to osutoraria he no nihonjin imin: raifusutairu kachikan no henka to ijuu no tsunagari" [Societal changes in Japanese society in the 90s and Japanese migration to Australia: Changes in lifestyle values and the relation to migration]. *Osutoraria kenkyuu kiyou* [In-house journal on research about Australia] (Otemon Gakuin Daigaku), 33: 177–200.

Nagatomo, Jun. 2007b. "Japanese Lifestyle Migration to Australia: New Migrants in the Era of Transnationalism." *The Bulletin of Kyushu Anthropological Association* 34: 1–22.

Nagatomo, Jun. 2015. *Migration as Transnational Leisure: The Japanese Lifestyle Migrants in Australia*. Leiden: Brill.

Nagatomo, Jun. 2016. "Cultural Practices of Traditional Performing Arts by Lifestyle Migrants in Ama-cho, Oki Islands, Japan: Identity Politics and Cultural Practices of I-Turn Migrants as 'Middlemen.'" *Journal of International Studies* 5, no. 1 (March): 5–17.

Neko Mook. 2016. *Shiawase na hatarakikata* [Work style book: Working in a happy manner] 2475 (29 July).

Nilsson, Bo, and Anna Sofia Lundgren. 2015. "Logics of Rurality: Political Rhetoric about the Swedish North." *Journal of Rural Studies* 37 (February): 85–95.

Nishimura, Yoshiaki. 2009. *Jibun wo ikashite ikiru* [Living in a manner that involves living for oneself]. Tokyo: Basilico.

Noda, Kunihiro. 2014. "Sōzō jinzai no yuchi ni yoru kaso he no chosen." In *Sōzō nōson: Kaso wo kuriētibu ni ikiru senryaku* [Creative farming villages: Strategies to live depopulation creatively], edited by Masayuki Sasaki, Sachiko Kawaida, and Hagihara Masaya, 188–203. Kyoto: Gakugei Shuppansha.

Ntaousani, Elia. 2016. "From Citizens to Wanderers of the World: The Noguchi Case as a Timely Study on Cosmopolitanism." In *Lifestyle Mobilities: Intersections of Travel, Leisure and Migration*, edited by Tara Duncan, Scott A. Cohen, and Maria Thulemark, 177–190. London: Routledge; paperback edition, first published by Ashgate in 2013.

Okada, Yutaka. 2016. "Japan's Population Has Started to Shrink and Polarize Geographically." *Mizuho Economic Outlook & Analysis* (April 5): https://www.mizuho-ri.co.jp/publication/research/pdf/eo/MEA160530.pdf. Accessed 24 February 2017.

Okamoto Toshihiro. 2012. *Kawaru hitobito: 3.11 no sōsharu akushon* [Changing people: Social action after 3.11]. Tokyo: Film Art.

Okonogi, Keigo. 1978. *Moratorium ningen no jidai* [The time of moratorium beings]. Tokyo: Chuo Koron.

Ōno, Akira. 2008. *Genkai shūraku to chiiki saisei* [Marginal hamlets and regional revitalization]. Sendai: Kahoku Shinpō shuppan sentā.

Ono, Mayumi. 2009. "Japanese Lifestyle Migration/Tourism in Southeast Asia." *Japanese Review of Cultural Anthropology* 10: 43–52.

Ono, Mayumi. 2014. "Commoditization of Lifestyle Migration: Japanese Retirees in Malaysia." *Mobilities* 10, no. 4: 609–627.

Ono, Mayumi. 2015. "Descending from Japan: Lifestyle Mobility of Japanese Male Youth to Thailand." *Asian Anthropology* 14, no. 3: 249–264.

O'Regan, Michael. 2013. "Others Have the Clock but We Have Time: Alternative Lifestyle Mobilities and the Resurgence of Hitchhiking." In *Lifestyle Mobilities: Intersections of Travel, Leisure and Migration*, edited by Tara Duncan, Scott A. Cohen, and Maria Thulemark, 35–50. London: Ashgate; paperback edition, first published by Ashgate in 2013.

O'Reilly, Karen. 2014. "The Role of the Social Imaginary in Lifestyle Migration: Employing the Ontology of Practice Theory." In *Understanding Lifestyle Migration: Theoretical Approaches to Migration and the Quest for a Better Way of Life*, edited by Michaela Benson and Nick Osbaldiston, 211–234. Houndmills: Palgrave Macmillan.

Osawa, Machiko, and Jeff Kingston. 2015. "Risk and Consequences: The Changing Japanese Employment Paradigm." In *The Precarious Future*, edited by

Frank Baldwin and Anne Allison, 58–85. New York: New York University Press.

Osawa, Makoto. 2014. "New Farmers from Non-Farming Families: Five Reasons to Become a Farmer." *Japan Studies: The Frontier* 9: 73–86.

Oshima, Nanami. 2009. *How to Become a Social Entrepreneur / Shakai kigyōka ni naru hōhō*. Tokyo: Aspect.

Ota, Masako. 2000. "Nande Okinawa ni ijuu shita no?" [Why have you moved to Okinawa?]. *Ushio* 499: 152–159.

Pearce, Caroline. 2013. "On Liminality: Politics of the Jap." July 18: https://politicsofthehap.wordpress.com/2013/07/18/on-liminality/. Accessed 5 June 2017.

Pen. 2016. *Ijū shiyou: Risō no kurashi wo te ni ireta hitobito no jireishū* [Let's move house: People who made their ideal lifestyles into practical reality] 4/1, no. 402 (April).

Peters, Michael A. 2016. "Education, Neoliberalism, and Human Capital." In *The Handbook of Neoliberalism*, edited by Simon Springer, Birch Kean, and Julie MacLeavy, 297–307. New York: Routledge.

Ralph, David, and Lynn A. Staeheli. 2011. "Home and Migration: Mobilities, Belongings and Identities. *Geography Compass* 5, no. 7: 517–530.

Rapport, Nigel, and Joanna Overing. 2000. *Social and Cultural Anthropology: The Key Concepts*. London: Routledge.

Rose, Nikolas. 1992. "Governing the Enterprising Self." In *The Values of the Enterprise Culture*, edited by Paul Heelas and Paul Morris, 141–164. London: Routledge.

Rose, Nikolas. 1996. "The Death of the Social? Refiguring the Territory of Government." *Economy and Society* 25, no. 3: 327–356.

Rose, Nikolas. 1998. *Inventing Ourselves: Psychology, Power, and Personhood*. Cambridge: Cambridge University Press.

Rosenberger, Nancy. 2001. *Gambling with Virtue: Japanese Women and the Search for Self in a Changing Nation*. Honolulu: University of Hawaii Press.

Rosenberger, Nancy. 2014. " 'Making an Ant's Forehead of a Difference': Organic Agriculture as an Alternative Lifestyle in Japan." In *Capturing Contemporary Japan: Differentiation and Uncertainty*, edited by Satsuki Kawano, Glenda S. Roberts, and Susan Orpett Long, 105–134. Honolulu: University of Hawaii Press.

Rosenberger, Nancy. 2017. "Young Organic Farmers in Japan: Betting on Lifestyle, Locality, and Livelihood." *Contemporary Japan: Special Issue on Food, Agriculture and Risk in Contemporary Japan* 29, no. 1: 14–30.

Sai, Yasutaka. 1995. *The Eight Core Values of the Japanese Businessman: Toward an Understanding of Japanese Management*. New York: Routledge.

San'in Keizai Kei'ei Kenkyūjo (San'in Region Economic Research Institute), ed. 2015. *San'in no minryoku* (The civil power of San'in). Matsue: Imai Shuppan.

Sasaki, Masayuki. 2001. *Sōzō toshi he no chōsen* [Challenging creative cities]. Tokyo: Iwanami Shinsho.

Sasaki, Masayuki. 2014. "Sōzō nōson to ha nani ka, naze ima, chūmoku wo atsumeru no ka." In *Sōzō nōson: Kaso wo kuriētibu ni ikiru senryaku* [Creative farming villages: Strategies to live depopulation creatively], edited by Masayuki Sasaki, Sachiko Kawaida, and Hagihara Masaya, 1–27. Kyoto: Gakugei Shuppansha.

Sashide, Kazumasa. 2016. *Bokura ha chihō de shiawase wo mitsukeru: Sotokotoryū rōkaru saiseiron* [We will find our happiness in the countryside: Theories about reviving the local in Sotokoto style]. Tokyo: Poplar Shinsho.

Sassen, Saskia. 2007. *A Sociology of Globalization*. New York: W.W. Norton.

Sato, Machiko, 2001. *Farewell to Nippon: Japanese Lifestyle Migrants in Australia*. Melbourne: TransPacific Press.

Scharff, Christina. 2016. "Gender and Neoliberalism: Young Women as Ideal Neoliberal Subjects." In *The Handbook of Neoliberalism*, edited by Simon Springer, Birch Kean, and Julie MacLeavy, 217–225. New York: Routledge.

Schnell, Scott. 2005. "The Rural Imaginary: Landscape, Village, Tradition." In *A Companion to the Anthropology of Japan*, edited by Jennifer Robertson. Malden: Blackwell.

Schreurs, Jeanine. 2014. "Downshifting and Sustainability in Japan: A Comparative Study of Living with Less." *Electronic Journal of Contemporary Japan Studies* 14, no. 3 (December 23): http://www.japanesestudies.org.uk/ejcjs/vol14/iss3/schreurs.html. Accessed 17 April 2017.

Sheller, Mimi, and John Urry. 2006. "The New Mobilities Paradigm." *Environment and Planning A* 38: 207–226.

Shikida, Asami. 2014. "Seibutsu bunka tayōsei wo ikashita tsūrizumu." In *Sōzō nōson: Kaso wo kuriētibu ni ikiru senryaku* [Creative farming villages: Strategies to live depopulation creatively], edited by Sasaki, Masayuki, Kawaida, Sachiko, Hagihara Masaya, 70–87. Kyoto: Gakugei Shuppansha.

Shore, Bradd. 1996. *Culture in Mind: Cognition, Culture, and the Problem of Meaning*. Oxford: Oxford University Press.

Shucksmith, Mark, and David L. Brown 2016. *Routledge International Handbook of Rural Studies*. London: Routledge.

Slater, David H., and Patrick W. Galbraith. 2011. "Re-Narrating Social Class and Masculinity in Neoliberal Japan." *Electronic Journal of Contemporary Japanese Studies* (September 30): http://www.japanesestudies.org.uk/articles/2011/SlaterGlabraith.html. Accessed 26 April 2017.

Smith, Michael Peter. 2011. "Translocality: A Critical Reflection." In *Translocal Geographies: Spaces, Places, Connections*, edited by Katherine Brickell and Ayona Datta, 181–198. Farnham: Ashgate.

Smith, Stephen L. J., and Geoffrey C. Godbey. 1991. "Leisure, Recreation and Tourism." *Annals of Tourism Research* 18: 85–100.

Sotokoto. 2016. *Atarashii ijū no katachi* [Finding a new home] (February): 88–89.

Stones, Rob. 2005. *Structuration Theory*. Basingstoke: Palgrave Macmillan.

Suzuki, Ayako. 2015. "Young Japanese Men's Transnational Mobility: A Case Study in Dublin." *Asian Anthropology* 14, no. 3: 235–248.

Szakolczai, Arpad. 2000. *Reflexive Historical Sociology*. London: Routledge.

Thang, Leng Leng, Elizabeth MacLachlan, and Miho Goda. 2006. "Living in 'My Space': Japanese Working Women in Singapore." *Chiri Kagaku* 61, no. 3: 156–171.

Thomassen, Bjorn. 2015. "Thinking with Liminality: To the Boundaries of an Anthropological Concept." In *Breaking Boundaries: Varieties of Liminality*, edited by Agnes Horvath, Bjorn Thomassen, and Harald Wydra, 39–58. New York: Berghahn.

Toivonen, Tuukka, Vinai Norasukkunkit, and Yukiko Uchida. 2011. "Unable to Conform, Unwilling to Rebel? Youth, Culture, and Motivation." *Frontiers in Psychology* 2, no. 207: 1–9.

Torkington, Kate, David Ines, and Joao Sardinha, eds. 2015. *Practising the Good Life: Lifestyle Migration in Practices*. Newcastle upon Tyne: Cambridge Scholars.

Traphagan, John W., and John Knight. eds. 2003. *Demographic Change and the Family in Japan's Aging Society*. Albany: State University of New York Press.

Tumugiya, 2012. *OCICA Ishinomaki Oshika Hantō Chiisa na gyoson no monogatari* [OCICA Ishinomaki Oshika Peninsula: The story of a small fishing village]. Tokyo: Ippanshadan Hōjin Tumugiya.

Turner, Victor. 1974. *Dramas, Fields, Metaphors: Symbolic Action in Human Society*. Ithaca: Cornell University Press.

Turner, Victor. 1982. *From Ritual to Theatre: The Human Seriousness of Play*. New York: Performing Arts Journal Publications.

Turner, Victor W. 1996. "Liminality and Communitas." In *Readings in Ritual Studies*, edited by Ronald L. Grimes, 511–519. Upper Saddle River: Prentice Hall.

Turns. 2015. "Through all times people who changed Japan, first changed the countryside." Special interview with Ishiba Shigeru (Winter): 10–11.

Widdicombe, Sue. 1998. "Identity as an Analysts' and a Participants' Resource." In *Identities and Talk*, edited by Sue Widdicombe and Charles Antaki, 191–206. London: Sage.

Woods, Michael. 2011. *Rural: Key Ideas in Geography*. London: Routledge.

Urry, John. 2000. *Sociology Beyond Societies: Mobilities for the Twenty-First Century*. London: Routledge.

Wilson, Fiona. 2017. "Out of the Woods—Ishinomaki." *Monocle* 10, no. 100 (February): 104–107.

Yamada, Jun. 2016. *Chihō sōsetsu no wana* [The trap of regional revitalization]. Tokyo: East Press.

Yamada, Masahiro. 2004. *Kibō kakusa shakai* [A hope-divided society]. Tokyo: Chikuma Shobō.

Yamada, Masahiro, and Jun Kobayashi, eds. 2015. *Dēta de yomu gendai shakai: Raifusutairu to raifu kōsu* [Reading contemporary society through data: Lifestyle and life course]. Tokyo: Shinyōsha.

Yamamoto Shigeru. 2009. *Yaritai koto ga nai yatsu ha shakai kigyōka ni nare* [Everybody who is not doing what they want with their lives should become social entrepreneurs]. Tokyo: Media Factory.

Yamashita, Shinji. 2009. "Southeast Asian Tourism from a Japanese Perspective." In *Tourism in Southeast Asia: Challenges and New Directions*, edited by Michael Hitchcock, Victor T. King, and Michael Parnwell, 189–205. Copenhagen: NIAS Press.

Yoda, Tomiko, and Harry Harootunian, eds. 2006. *Japan After Japan: Social and Cultural Life from the Recessionary 1990s to the Present*. Durham: Duke University Press.

Yoneda, Tomohiko. 2017. *Ikitai basho de ikiru* [Living in the place we want to go to]. Tokyo: Discover.

Zavala, Lauro. 1997. "Towards a Dialogical Theory of Cultural Liminality: Contemporary Writing and Cultural Identity in Mexico." *Arizona Journal of Hispanic Cultural Studies* 1: 9–22.

Zunino, Hugo Marcelo, Dattwyler Rodrigo Hidalgo, and Ieva Zebryte. 2014. "Utopian Lifestyle Migrants in Pucon, Chile: Innovating Social Life and Challenging Capitalism." In *Contested Spatialities, Lifestyle Migration and Residential Tourism*, edited by Michael Janoschka and Heiko Haas, 96–107. London: Routledge.

Index

www.ingramcontent.com/pod-product-compliance
Lightning Source LLC
Chambersburg PA
CBHW020350270326
41926CB00007B/369